A Dream
Is a Wish
Your Heart
Makes

A DREAM
IS A WISH
YOUR HEART
MAKES

My Story

ANNETTE FUNICELLO

WITH PATRICIA ROMANOWSKI

New York

Library of Congress Cataloging-in-Publication Data

Funicello, Annette.
A dream is a wish your heart makes / by Annette Funicello
with Patricia Romanowski. — 1st ed.
p.   cm.
ISBN 0-7868-8092-9

1. Funicello, Annette.
2. Singers—United States—Biography.
I. Romanowski, Patricia.   II. Title.
ML420.F896A3   1994
782.42164'092—dc20
[B]

93-46489
CIP
MN

Photo credits, song permissions, and other acknowledgments
will be found on page 237.

First Paperback Edition

FIRST EDITION
10 9 8 7 6 5 4 3 2 1

To my children—
Gina, Jackie, and Jason
—the loves of my life

ACKNOWLEDGMENTS

Throughout the years, and more recently, in the preparation of this book, dozens of friends have given me their encouragement and support. You know who you are, and to you I say, Thank you from the bottom of my heart.

I would like to take this opportunity to thank three very special people in my life: my Mom and my Dad, and my husband, Glen. And to express my gratitude to Arlene Ludwig and Lorraine Santoli, who make sure the public part of my life always runs smoothly.

For making this book possible, thank you to my literary agent, Suzanne Gluck, my coauthor Patty Romanowski, and the team at Hyperion: Bob Miller, my editor Rick Kot, and my former editor Tom Miller.

Finally, a very fond thank you to Walt Disney, for wonderful things words cannot express.

CONTENTS

INTRODUCTION

The first time a book publisher asked if I might consider writing my autobiography, I laughed and thought to myself, *Why me?* This was several years ago, when my life was essentially consumed by carpooling, Little League games, and the other routine activities of your typical mom (including making peanut-butter sandwiches). As far as I was concerned, I'd basically retired from show business back in 1965. Lacking the requisite tormented childhood as well as tawdry Hollywood affairs and libelous anecdotes about famous people I'd worked with, I'm afraid I disappointed the gentleman from the book company. I recall thinking, *I'm Annette Funicello. What did he expect?*

I began my career at the age of twelve almost by accident. Everything that followed—*The Mickey Mouse Club,* the Disney films, the hit records, and the beach-party movies—was, I believe, the result of hard work, a lot of good luck, and the generosity of a public that embraced me very early on and hasn't forgotten me in the years since. My approach to my career was simple, based on some advice Walt Disney gave me: "Show up on time, know your lines, and leave the rest to us." And I did. Although my early fame took the Funicello household by surprise, I will always be grateful to my parents for never letting it go to my head and for helping me to keep everything in perspective.

Even with all the success, by my teens I had decided to quit show business as soon as I married. Even as early as sixteen, I was telling interviewers that I wanted to have nine children, and I meant it. Having grown up in Hollywood among so many other child performers, I knew all too well that once I left the public stage after I married I might never be welcomed back. And that was okay. I felt comfortable closing the book on that wonderful chapter in my life. It was time to move on. I never regretted my decision, and I never looked back.

I started my family and poured my heart into being a mother to my daughter, Gina, and my two sons, Jackie and Jason. Although I made the occasional television appearance, a couple of film cameos, and some popular commercials for Skippy peanut butter, I never considered myself "back in the business." That young girl in the little black mouse ears, that highly principled, buxom young lady singing and pouting over Frankie out on the beach—*that* was Annette. To my family and my closest friends, I was just Annie.

As the years passed, however, it was clear that I had not been forgotten. I consider myself fortunate to have been taken into the hearts of so many people. I guess it was the fact that the public has always been on my side that led me to keep my struggle with multiple sclerosis a secret for over five years. After all, nothing bad could ever happen to Annette.

At first it was easy enough to hide the truth because I didn't yet have any of the visible symptoms. But as my condition progressed, that gradually changed. My walk grew noticeably shaky as my sense of balance faltered. When strangers, friends—even my own father—inquired about my increasingly unsteady gait, I explained it away as "dancer's knee" or "tendinitis." Their looks of sympathy and concern made me uncomfortable, but I still couldn't tell. But when rumors surfaced that I had a drinking problem, I was forced to confront reality: I was fooling no one. The truth had to come out.

Then came one of the most agonizing decisions of my life. For so long fear had held me back from going public. *What would people think of me?* I worried that all those kind folks—from adults who'd been Mouseketeers First Class in Good Standing back in the fifties to the young kids who had attended my last concert tour with Frankie Avalon in 1989–90—would discover that Annette's life was not quite the happy Disney fairy tale they believed and feel somehow betrayed. I had known and felt their love almost all my life; I didn't want their pity now.

I told my story and held my breath. What happened then surprised everyone who knew me, and me most of all. Not only was I embraced with support and love, but no longer hiding my illness enabled me to discover a new attitude toward my multiple sclerosis and a new attitude toward life in general. No one's life is perfect and happy all the time. I wouldn't be honest if I didn't say I've had my ups and downs. Certainly there are days I can be found sitting alone in my house, crying and asking God, "Why is this happening to me?" But then, perhaps the very next day, a stranger will approach me and say, "Thank you for speaking out about MS. My mother (or sister or brother or husband or wife or friend) has MS. Bless you."

I try to see the best in people and in life. When I'm asked how it is that I can still view the world through eyes of wonder, I want to say it is because I've been so blessed. I've had a wonderful family, a great career, and support and encouragement from thousands of people I may never meet but whom I still count among my friends. To all of them I would like to say simply, Thank you.

—Annette Funicello

A DREAM
IS A WISH
YOUR HEART
MAKES

CHAPTER 1

*I*t's probably hard to imagine, but I really do not recall too many details about the day that changed my life and my family's forever. Then again, I was only twelve years old, and a career in show business was the last thing on my mind. For me, the big event of Easter week 1955 was my dance school's year-end recital, "Ballet vs. Jive." I felt excited and honored to have been chosen to dance the lead role in *Swan Lake.* I remember very clearly the delicate white dress my mother sewed for me, and the white feather headpiece nestled in my curly black hair. I also remember where the recital took place, the Burbank Starlite Bowl, not far from our home in Studio City, California, just over the hills from Hollywood. But what I remember most of all about that very special evening is that it was the night Mr. Walt Disney saw my little Swan Queen pirouetting across the stage.

The next day one of my dance teachers, Al Gilbert, phoned my mother to say that someone from the Walt Disney Studios in Burbank had called him and asked, "Who was the little dark-haired girl in *Swan Lake?*" Mr. Disney and several of his staff had been in the audience at the Burbank Starlite Bowl scouting for child performers to appear on his new children's television show called *The Mickey Mouse Club.* Very few people knew he was there. In fact, he only happened to be there because a good friend of his, Leo Damiani, was to be conducting the orchestra that evening.

When Mr. Gilbert mentioned to my mother that the children on Disney's new show were going to be called "Mouseketeers," she misunderstood; thinking he meant "Musketeers" (as in *The Three* . . .), she couldn't imagine what they wanted with a twelve-year-old girl. We didn't know much about Walt Disney or his studio, though I had loved his wonderful animated movies, such as *Snow White and the Seven Dwarfs, Cinderella, Pinocchio,* and *Bambi,* my favorite. We lived at the center of the movie industry, but Mr. Disney was not as familiar a figure to the general public as he would become a few years later, after he began hosting his weekly television program and opened Disneyland. I have to admit that the Funicello household wasn't exactly jumping at this "opportunity." As my mother would later recall often, "We didn't know what an audition was, and who knew what a Mouseketeer was? We just didn't want to be bothered with it."

But Mr. Gilbert asked her to reconsider. "Look," he said, "to have Annette audition for Mr. Disney will definitely be a feather in my cap. Why don't you just go for the audition, and I'll come with you?" Then he explained to us that I would probably be asked to do a dance routine or two. "Annette, you have so many routines, and I'll be right there to help you." I suppose Mom wanted to help Mr. Gilbert. Then she started thinking that visiting an actual movie studio lot for a few hours might be interesting. Whatever the reason, she finally said yes, I would audition, even though I'm sure no one in the Funicello household seriously thought for one second that it would lead to anything.

Unlike so many child performers' families, mine did not make the big move to California to further my career. As a matter of fact, when my parents, Joe and Virginia Funicello, left our hometown of Utica, New York, in the summer of

1946, I had no career. I was only four years old and so shy that I would hide behind my mother's skirt every time the doorbell rang—hardly a threat to Shirley Temple. I'm sure that, had anyone suggested to my parents that one day one of their children would be a famous entertainer, they would have laughed. In fact, a few years before, someone—a fortune-teller—predicted that exact thing, and they didn't believe a word of it.

No, the reason my parents came to the Golden State was very simple: the weather. My father, a master auto mechanic, had had his fill of sweating through the summers and freezing under cars all winter long. There was nothing wrong back home; both my parents came from large and very loving families that they are close to even today. I don't think it was a decision they spent a lot of time pondering, either. My father asked my mother, "Why don't we try sunny California?" As my mother says whenever she tells the story, "I was young enough and dumb enough to say, 'That sounds good. Let's try it.'"

Until then, home for me had been a two-bedroom apartment on Bleaker Street in Utica, a small city in northern New York State. My father's parents, Anthony and Concetta (short for Congettina) Funicello, were both born in Italy. She came to the United States at the age of eight. My grandfather had arrived many years earlier. They were married in 1915.

My grandfather Funicello had worked for a while in New York City as a sanitation man, picking up garbage in a horse-drawn wagon. Lured by the promise of more work and better prospects up north, he and his new wife left New York City, only to find jobs not as plentiful as they had hoped. He went to work in the textile mills, of which there were many in Utica at the time. My grandmother, of course, stayed at home to raise their five children: my father, Joe, and Alfred (Sarge), Bobby, Elsie, and Ida.

They were proud of their Italian heritage, as I am today. But those were not the easiest times back then, since not everyone looked fondly upon the new immigrants. Perhaps for this reason everyone in my father's family—except his parents—began pronouncing their last name not as Funicello, with the "ch" sound, as we say it today, but as something that sounded like "Fun-is-sell-o." In other words, they pronounced it the way that someone unfamiliar with Italian surnames might. It didn't sound bad exactly, but it lacked that soft, melodious sound it was meant to have. It would be many more years before I knew exactly how my name was supposed to sound. I can thank Mr. Disney for that, but that's another story, for later.

My father was very young when he first showed a keen aptitude for anything mechanical. It wasn't long before he and his brother Sarge opened up their own garage. Their mother immediately insisted that the rest of the family move into the adjacent house and rent out the one they lived in so that she could be sure the boys had hot meals. Now, that's a real Italian mother for you.

My father was always very quiet and shy. Nonetheless, when he saw my mother, Virginia Albano, it was love at first sight. My mother's parents, Michael and Sarafina (or Fanny) Albano, had come to the United States from the same town in Italy—Caserta, near Naples—but didn't meet until years after they'd immigrated. My grandmother's first husband died very young and left her a widow alone in New York City with three small children. Yet my grandfather fell in love with her, married her, and moved them all up to Utica, where his parents—my great-grandparents—lived.

My mother had four full sisters—Josephine (Jo), Michelena (Mickie), Antoinette, and Carmella (Car); two half-sisters—Mary and Angie; and a half-brother, Rocco, who was known as Rocky. Unfortunately, my mother's mother passed away at a fairly young age, so I never got to know her. But I was very close to her father. Grandpa Albano was a large, round man, and what I remember about him most is that he could pick up and play virtually any instrument. I know that my love of music and ability to play several different instruments came from him.

Soon after graduating from high school my mother went to work as a secretary, but found herself out of a job when her boss suddenly died. She then took a position as a secretary and hostess at Rocky's Diner, which her brother owned and operated. My father would come into the diner every Sunday morning to meet with and pay off his creditors. My mother didn't pay any particular attention to Joe Funicello until her boss came over and, gesturing toward my father, said, "That guy really likes you."

"Forget it," my mother replied with her typical directness. "I'm a Catholic girl, and I can't go out with Jewish boys." Obviously my mother had paid so little attention to my father she didn't know his last name. If she had, she'd have known for sure he was Italian.

Some time passed, and one day my father remarked to my Uncle Rocky, "See that girl with the blue-black hair?" Meaning my mother, of course. "Someday I'm going to marry her!"

"Hey!" Uncle Rocky exclaimed. "That's my sister!"

"I don't believe you," my father replied.

"Come over here, Virgie," Rocky said. "You're my sister, right?"

"Right," she replied.

"Joe here says he's going to marry you someday."

"We'll see about that," Mom replied, smiling at Joe, but certain that he had to be kidding.

But he wasn't, and despite these early indications that this might be anything but a match made in heaven, my father just would not give up. He was in love with Virginia Albano. Still, he was so shy he couldn't fathom how to approach her, or say the words that would change her mind. When my mother left work to go home, my father would try following her, but she always ducked down the alleyway to elude him. It was a long time before he even knew where she lived!

But his quiet, steady persistence paid off. "Little by little, he wore me down," is how my mother puts it, smiling. Although the Japanese attack on Pearl Harbor was months away, young people of my parents' generation feared that the world war raging in Europe might soon touch their lives. "Everyone was getting married," my mother recalls, "because all the men were going off to war. We never knew what was going to happen tomorrow. It was just the thing to do."

And so they were married, but not exactly the way either of their families might have wished. For various reasons, both my mother and father felt sure that their families, especially my father's mother and my mother's father, would not approve of their marriage. My mother says simply, "I wasn't the girl Joe's parents had picked out for him." So they approached a friend who was a priest, and he agreed to marry them secretly at Saint Mary of Mount Carmel Church on April 17, 1941.

For months they each continued to live at home, so no one had reason to suspect anything. When they finally broke the news, nearly five months later, their families were surprised, to put it mildly. My father was the first of his siblings to marry, and being Italian, of course, their families would have liked them to have a big wedding. But my parents certainly made the right decision. Over half a century later, they are still deeply in love and devoted to each other.

When I was born, on October 22, 1942, I was the first grandchild on either side of the family. It is an Italian tradition to name the first baby after the father's same-sex parent. That meant my name should have been Congettina. Today my mother jokes that she knew that name would never fit across a Mickey Mouse Club sweatshirt without wrapping around the sides, so it had to be shorter. My grandfather's name was Anthony, so taking the *An* sound, my parents came up with Annette Joanne Funicello. My mother, who'd never owned a doll when she was young, nicknamed me

Dolly, which is what my father calls me even today.

For as long as I can remember, I felt wanted and loved, and no wonder! With five aunts and five uncles (not to mention their husbands and wives), my grandparents, and Mom and Dad, to dote on me, how could I feel otherwise? I was the only girl among all my cousins, and so my early life was one of a typical spoiled brat. My mother had wanted a beautiful, fat bouncing boy—in fact, she wanted her sister-in-law's son, who was born around the same time I was. Instead she got me: skinny, whining, never eating, hardly sleeping, always crying. As my mother still reminds me on occasion today, she was ready to throw me out the window.

Even I can admit that I was very, very spoiled, but happily so. My father's mother believed that babies should do whatever they wanted, so Mom's efforts to get me on a schedule or to eat a decent meal fell by the wayside whenever Grandma Funicello was around. The relatives streamed in and out of our house all day long. If I was sleeping and one of my aunts wanted to see me, she just woke me up. It was a rare night that baby Annette was in her crib before one or two in the morning. Over and over my mother used to warn my aunts, "Don't buy candy for Annette. I don't want her to eat it!" But no one listened, and there wasn't a time that one of my aunts came to see me without bringing me a big sack of treats. My being a fussy eater seemed to give them added incentive to cater to my every whim. For example, I was just crazy about fresh oranges. Again Mom would warn my aunts, "Don't bring Annette any oranges. I want her to eat her meal." But they would arrive clutching bags of oranges, and I would just stuff my mouth, eating one after the other, the sticky juice running down my hands. It was heaven.

My family's heritage was and remains very important to us. We attended a local Catholic church regularly, and my grandparents spoke Italian around me, so I picked up quite a bit of it. The fact that my parents chose not to keep this up is something I've always regretted. But aside from not speaking the language, we did just about everything else the Italian way. I especially remember the cooking: my Aunt Jo's ravioli, my grandmother's gnocchi (little potato dumplings), meatballs, and scrambled eggs with fiery-hot peppers—the hotter the better. Even today, when someone asks if I have a beauty secret, I reply, "Olive oil."

Of all my memories, perhaps the most vivid is of being at my grandparents' or in my own house and listening to records played on the Victrola or the radio. Except for my Grandpa Albano, no one on either side of our family was particularly talented when it came to music. Until I began taking piano lessons at age ten, there were never any instruments in our house. About the only time you heard any of us sing was on somebody's birthday. So I suppose it was somewhat surprising that at age two I learned the words to every song on the Hit Parade. One special favorite of mine was "Ac-cent-tchu-ate the Positive," which I would belt out on occasion to the delight of my "audience." More than any other song, that one seemed to suit me, and the funny thing is, I think it still fits me today. Despite these impromptu performances—reserved for my parents, grandparents, uncles, aunts, and cousins—I was far too shy ever to be a little ham.

As World War II dragged on, my parents' fear that it would tear my father from us never totally disappeared. Fortunately, being married with a child, he was exempted from active combat duty. However, he did serve his country by repairing army vehicles at the nearby Rome Air Depot. Once the war ended, life returned to normal, and things were good for my parents in Utica. But they longed for a change.

In August 1946 my father and mother loaded everything they owned into an old thirty-foot-long house trailer, hooked it to the back of Daddy's black 1940 Dodge, placed me and my nine-month-old baby brother, Joey, in the backseat, and waved our goodbyes. All the relatives were heartbroken, and although they wished us the best, they also predicted our imminent return. "You'll die lousy in California," one warned, not out of meanness but concern. And probably a little bit of hurt, too. Nothing anyone said, though, could shake my mother and father's faith that we would have a better life even though nothing awaited us there—no job, no home, no friends or family. To some, this might have seemed a daring, perhaps even foolish, journey. But to my parents, the cross-country trip promised nothing less than wonderful romantic adventure. We were to travel as part of a three-car caravan with a newlywed couple and another couple that had a two-month-old baby. The three couples saw themselves almost as gypsies, and planned to go from one state to the next, stop wherever it suited them, cook outdoors, have a ball, then pack up and travel on.

My father sold his business before we left for the trip, and shortly before he stopped working in Utica one of his customers said, "Joe, I want to take you to see this woman who was born with seven veils," a fortune-teller. Some people believe that a baby born with "veils" (actually layers of tissues from the amniotic sac that babies float in before birth) will have the gift of prophecy.

Daddy didn't believe in any of this, but he was intrigued. When he told Mom—who didn't really believe in it, either, but found the idea fascinating—she replied, "Go on, honey." I suppose she was thinking, *Why not? What could be the harm?*

But Daddy returned from the fortune-teller amazed and shaken. No sooner had he sat down than the woman said, "You are going on a long trip across the whole United States in a trailer." Daddy was taken aback, because very few people even had trailers in those days. Then she continued, "You're going to have an awful lot of problems on the way. And I see a baby falling out of a high chair. Be very careful, because he's going to get hurt very badly.

"You're going to have another child in California; it's going to be a boy. This child will be beautiful, extremely beautiful. And he's going to be famous, so the whole world will know of him. I can hear this child singing and singing, and the people going crazy adoring him. All over the world, he will be loved."

My mother listened as my father recounted his visit. Even though the fortune-teller showed amazing accuracy regarding our impending trip, Mom still dismissed the predictions as pure nonsense. Yes, the fortune-teller was right about a lot of things, uncannily so. But my parents were not planning to have any more children, and the idea that one of them might be famous—and for singing, of all things—struck Mom as absurd. As for the baby falling out of the high chair, who knew? Accidents happened.

At the end of my father's visit, the psychic suddenly became very quiet and refused to say anything further. Today my mother thinks that perhaps she saw a little too far into the future, to what later happened to me. Obviously we will never know.

Over the years, an amazing number of the fortune-teller's predictions have come to pass. My parents did have another son in 1952, my brother Michael, and he certainly was a beautiful baby. Oddly enough, everything the fortune-teller predicted for him actually happened, but to me. Several prophecies came true within weeks of my father's visit. For example, my parents stopped to rest on our way to California, and little Joey did fall from his high chair, hit his head on a curb, and suffer potentially serious injuries. For a brief time, Mom was worried he might even die.

Joey's accident was just one of many incidents that quickly transformed my parents' dream adventure into what my mother now calls "the biggest nightmare of our lives until then." I developed a case of chicken pox so severe I couldn't swallow any food. When we pulled into drive-in restaurants, I had to duck behind the seat because waitresses who saw my pockmarked face would refuse to serve us. I was absolutely miserable lying in the backseat with my stuffed bear Brownie and baby Joey, who soon fell ill with the chicken pox, too. We had a little bit of car trouble and some other problems, all of which seemed to suggest that maybe this trip wasn't the greatest idea.

Several times on the three-week journey my mother longed to return home, where everything was safe and familiar, but something kept them from giving up and turning back. Sure, it would have been embarrassing to hear everyone say, "I told you so." But I think that something stronger kept Mom and Daddy going, despite all the trouble they encountered. Just as their grandparents had crossed the ocean in search of their dreams, my parents traversed the country looking for the better life.

Like so many who flooded into California right after the war, my parents found themselves someplace well short of paradise. My father arrived in his new home without a job, but, as my mother says, "We didn't worry. We were happy. We had each other and our two babies. That's all we needed." We lived for a while in a trailer park, which my parents didn't care for. We were the only Italian family, and some of the parents didn't want their children playing with Joey and me. Fortunately for my father, good mechanics were in great demand, so there was plenty of work, and before long we moved into our own small house on Fulcher Avenue in North Hollywood and then to Valley Spring Lane in Studio City. Within just a few years, my parents' faith in their dream was rewarded. Of course, everything changes, and the Los Angeles area is no exception. Back when we first arrived, it was heavenly: a vast, bright, open city. It wasn't until 1941 that the first freeway, the Pasadena, opened, so most of L.A. was still very much like a colorful suburb, where pastel-colored houses glimmered under graceful palms and richly scented eucalyptus trees. For my parents, like millions of others of their generation, California represented all that was new and exciting. For them, it was truly the promised land.

Naturally, we all missed our family back in Utica very much, and it was lonely at first. But one surprise benefit of the move was that I stopped acting like a brat. My mother swears that from the moment I got in the backseat of our car and settled in for the long drive, my whole attitude changed. No one is sure how or why, but somehow, miraculously, I stopped whining and pouting and became, in the words of my Mom, "an angel."

One thing about me that did not change, and in fact never would, was my shyness. I was still terribly, almost painfully reserved around strangers. Nothing had ever happened to make me that way, but everyone in my family tends to be shy, so I've accepted that it's just the way I am. My first day of kindergarten I was terrified of being left among strangers. I gripped my father so ferociously that I tore off some of his shirt buttons. The classroom door had a window, and I made Daddy stand outside it for quite a while so I could see him. He obliged me for several days until I felt secure enough to be left there on my own.

Of course, soon enough I got into the swing of things with the other children, but I never became what you would call an outgoing kid. Despite being too timid to raise my hand most of the time, I did enjoy and do well in school. Perhaps because of my nervousness, I was always tapping my fingers and toes, so my kindergarten teacher told my mother, "You know, your daughter has rhythm in every bone of her body. When she's dancing, even her little curls fly in time with the song. You should start her playing some kind of percussion instrument." When my mother asked me what I wanted to play, I immediately answered, "Drums!"

So there I was, skinny little Annette behind a big drum kit, banging away and loving every minute of it. I adored my music teacher, and before long I was playing drums, xylophone, a huge timpani—anything I could get my hands on. Within a short time, I could execute drum rolls as well as older kids who'd been studying for years. Mom maintains that this ability came from her side of the family, and since my youngest son, Jason, is now also a drummer, I have to agree that it must be in our genes.

Right down the street from us lived a woman named Margie Rix, who owned the local dancing school. She remarked to Mom, "Annette needs to get out with kids, and she needs dancing lessons. Let her come to my dancing class and see if she likes it."

Coincidentally, my best girlfriend from kindergarten, Jackie, was also taking lessons there. When I recall those days, it seems as if Jackie took my hand and said, "Let's do it together!" I honestly don't think that I would ever have set foot in a dance studio if it hadn't been for Jackie. But after just a single lesson, I was hooked. Every day after school we used to rush to the dance studio, where we studied tap, ballet, modern, hula—everything—and even a little singing. It was such a wonderful experience, because it gave me an opportunity to work hard at something I loved.

At first I was always convinced that the other kids in the class did everything better than I did, but with time came confidence. It wasn't long before I started performing more solos at recitals. My specialty was toe tapping. My legs and feet grew so strong from ballet that I could dance on pointe with taps on the toes of my ballet shoes. It takes a lot of coordination and can be quite painful, but whenever I performed a toe-tapping number at a recital, it brought down the house. One number I remember especially well was "Strike Up the Band." For another, I was transformed into a jungle princess, in an animal-print dress and a big "bone" in my hair. In that one, I alternated drumming and dancing.

Seeing how much I loved performing, my parents helped all they could. Mom, who had never sewn before, started making my dance costumes. After just a few lessons, there was nothing she couldn't whip up, and every outfit she created was gorgeous, complete with accessories and toe shoes to match. She made tutus; Hawaiian "grass" skirts; Scottish plaid skirts with matching sashes; colorful, full, multitiered skirts—whatever my number called for. Sometimes my father helped too. I remember the two of them spending an entire month bleaching and rebleaching an old black umbrella white, then gluing stars all over it so that I could use it for a prop when I performed "Singin' in the Rain."

When I wasn't in school or taking dance lessons, I spent my time doing what other kids did: playing, skating, biking. After winning an impromptu poolside beauty contest and being named Miss Willow Lake at age nine, I also did a little modeling. Other than that, my life was utterly normal.

My father worked very hard six days a week, so every Sunday was set aside for family day. After church, the five of us (including my baby brother Michael) would spend the rest of the day on a big outing. My father loved to drive, and so we might pack a picnic lunch for the beach, or go up into the mountains to see the snow. Every summer for the first several years we were in California we traveled back to Utica to see the family. Whatever we did, though, in my memories we were always together, enjoying one another's company. Wherever my parents took us was special, just because they were there. Normal sibling spats aside, we were happiest together. My parents taught us not only to love but to respect one another. More important, they taught us these things by example. Recalling those times and knowing how my family has stood by me through the years, I can honestly say that I have been blessed. And I am thankful for that every day.

CHAPTER 2

*T*he day I first auditioned for Mr. Disney was unusual for southern California: gray, damp, and pouring rain. Up until the very last minute I continued to protest, "But I don't want to go!"

And I didn't. I still wasn't sure what an audition entailed, and I wanted no part of it. Just the thought of dancing in front of strangers intimidated me. Mom used some gentle persuasion. She finally resorted to promising me I wouldn't have to do anything I didn't want to do. At last, I relented.

The drive from our house in Studio City to the Walt Disney Studio lot on South Buena Vista Street in Burbank went quickly enough. As we approached the guardhouse at the studio entrance, it didn't appear especially glamorous or at all the way I imagined a studio would be. The forty-one-acre studio complex resembled a bustling college campus more than anything else.

Walking across the lot, I noticed people walking briskly from building to building along wide sidewalks named Mickey Avenue and Dopey Drive. Each of the studio's main buildings was designed in the *moderne* style of the times, with smooth, clear, rounded lines and many windows. Wide expanses of lawn and large shady trees surrounded a movie theater, the commissary, the Animation Building, and other structures housing the studio's various departments. Toward the back of the complex loomed several tall, cavernous soundstages, including number one, soon to become home of *The Mickey Mouse Club.*

Mom and I, along with Mr. Gilbert, were ushered into a room where several other children and their parents were waiting. Mom and I sat silently—not to mention nervously—as they chatted with one another, referring to their agents, their contracts, other auditions; all show-biz talk. There were some there, like us, who obviously felt a bit out of their element. As my mother says, "We were so dumb!" And I guess in a way we were. We had no idea what we were doing there, or the vaguest notion of what might happen if I passed the audition.

I was called back again within a couple weeks, and the second time, like the first, I performed ballet and tap numbers. I was also interviewed. With each call back my prospects brightened, and so Mom wrote our relatives back in Utica and asked them to pray for me. Even then we were still in the dark about exactly what *The Mickey Mouse Club* would be. Nor did anyone mention that twenty-three of the twenty-four pairs of Mouseketeer ears had already been claimed. It's probably best that I wasn't aware I was competing for the last spot—then I would have been really nervous! It's funny, but I'd noticed how my anxiety and shyness always just seemed to disappear when I danced. Well, maybe not disappear completely, but dancing and singing gave me a sense of joy that eclipsed everything else.

During the course of one audition, Mom sat in back. Not knowing who my mother was, several of the Disney men scribbled notes as they discussed me: how I looked, how I moved, whether or not I would be good doing this or that. Luckily, I was blissfully unaware of people discussing me. But for my mother to find herself sitting among strangers as they offered their critiques of her daughter was a bit rattling.

Even years later hearing people talk about my appearance or my performance is something she has never grown comfortable with. Everyone who knows my mother sees her as a bright, vivacious lady. But deep inside, like everyone else in my family, she's actually reserved.

A large, balding middle-aged man sketched each child as he or she auditioned. This was how Mr. Disney and his staff would recall each of the hundreds of hopefuls. As I danced, he turned to Mom and asked, "Who is that darling black-haired girl who's dancing down there? She's exquisite."

"That's Annette Funicello," my mother replied, afraid to mention I was her daughter. Later Mom recognized him as *The Mickey Mouse Club*'s "big Mooseketeer," Roy Williams.

For all three auditions the same small group of men attended: Roy; Mr. Disney; Bill Walsh, the show's producer; and several other men I later recognized when I started work on the show. I would glance at each of them, but I always found myself attracted to one face in particular. He had a headful of thick red hair and a very gentle smile. Whenever I began to feel a little jittery, I looked at him and felt instantly at ease. Only later did I learn that the man with the gentle smile was my soon-to-be good friend Jimmie Dodd.

Finally, during the last of the three auditions, Mr. Disney said, "Okay, now, Annette, we'd like to hear you sing something."

Stunned, I barely managed to utter—politely, of course— "I'm sorry, Mr. Disney, but I don't sing."

In the calming, reassuring manner I would come to know so well, Mr. Disney smiled and replied, "Well, surely you can sing a few notes from one of your favorite songs."

"Okay," I answered before taking a deep breath and singing "That's All I Want from You," one of Jaye P. Morgan's hits that I knew from the radio. Everyone listened attentively, and when I finished, Mr. Disney said simply, "Thank you, Annette."

As before, we left the studio not knowing where I stood.

The suspense was finally broken when the Disney people phoned shortly thereafter and told my mother that they would give me a two-week tryout to see how I got along with the other kids. If everything worked out, the studio would put me under contract and make me a Mouseketeer. Within a matter of weeks I was standing inside Sound Stage One along with twenty-three other children, ranging in age from nine to fourteen, each gazing at his or her funny-looking black felt beanie topped by a pair of big round mouse "ears" and the circular Mickey Mouse Club insignia. The girls' version came with a dainty bright red satin bow attached. *What were these?* we all wondered silently.

Several of the kids offered their assessments:

"These are silly-looking!"

"Too goofy!"

"Who are they kidding? I'm not wearing this!"

Some of the boys were incensed, for the ears would hide—or worse, flatten—their painstakingly Brylcreemed pompadours. Initially they tried pushing the ears back a little bit each day so their pomps showed through, but all in vain, as it turned out. The decree came down: The mouse ears were to sit just so, and that's where they were to stay, pomp or no pomp.

The shirts were another matter. I thought, *How are we going to get away with wearing our names across these?* It seemed so silly, and yet, like so much about *The Mickey Mouse Club,* it worked. With the boys in their nondescript pants and the girls in blue pleated skirts, we looked just like typical neighborhood kids. There was nothing particularly glamorous or dazzling about any of us. Of course, most American children didn't sport little black mouse ears, so in that way we seemed unique. (That is, until the mouse ears hit the market later that year.)

In the forty years since that day I have said countless times, "I owe everything to those ears," and I mean it. Of course the first time I put them on, I had no idea that those ears were a ticket for me and for all of us to travel straight into the hearts of children everywhere around the world. To have enjoyed such an honor I am eternally grateful.

Without Mickey Mouse, there would have been no mouse ears, and without the ears, no Mouseketeers. But going back even further, without Mr. Disney, there wouldn't have been so many things we treasure today. I know that some consider it fashionable to take something good and wonderful and tear it down. And I'm saddened to see that, despite all the joy Mr. Disney has brought to generations of children, some have been misled into believing that he was something other than a kind, caring man. There is actually very little I can do about that except to speak of Mr. Disney as I knew him.

As anyone who was acquainted with Mr. Disney could attest, he was a product of midwestern America and personified its time-honored old-fashioned values in both his life and his work. Born in 1901, Walt was the fourth of Elias and Flora Disney's five children. His love of nature and his aptitude for drawing became evident very early, and at the age of fourteen he took up art at the Kansas City Art Institute. After spending a year serving in France at the end of World War I, he returned stateside and began working as a commercial artist.

Animation, then an art form in its infancy, attracted Mr. Disney, who had always enjoyed sketching the animals. One of his earliest projects was creating animated commercials, which were shown in local movie theaters. This led to his creating his first cartoons with animator Ub Iwerks, who became his first business partner in a venture he named Laugh-O-Gram. Even in these early days, Mr. Disney's work revealed his knack for doing what everyone else had done a little bit better. He was always looking for ways to incorporate a fresh idea, a new technological advance, an untried approach. Nowhere was this more evident than in his 1928 Mickey Mouse feature *Steamboat Willie,* the first animated film in history to incorporate synchronized sound.

Mickey Mouse is probably Walt Disney's most famous creation, a bright-eyed, energetic, and sympathetic little guy, so sweet, so well-meaning, so "human," you sometimes forget he is a mouse. Legend has it that Mr. Disney was heading home by train to California after a series of disappointing business meetings in New York City when he was inspired to create Mortimer Mouse. Yes, *Mortimer.* Renamed Mickey shortly thereafter, the cheerful yet mischievous fellow soon became a celebrity of international renown, counting among his millions of fans President Franklin D. Roosevelt and film star Mary Pickford.

When Mr. Disney decided to add sound to *Steamboat Willie*, he wasn't content just to have Mickey Mouse squeak, which would have been sensational enough. He wanted to do something more. He envisioned a cartoon that not only had music and a voice for Mickey (which until 1946 would be Walt Disney's), but one in which everything the mouse did, from milking a cow to blowing a whistle, was synchronized to music and had its own sound effect. This historic cartoon short typified Mr. Disney's approach to everything. When he viewed the first disappointing results of the sound synchronization, he tried again, and kept trying until it was perfect, sparing no expense.

Innovation and imagination became Mr. Disney's stock in trade. As early as 1932 he began using the then-new color technology Technicolor. After the success of 1933's *Three Little Pigs,* which produced a hit song, "Who's Afraid of the Big Bad Wolf?" film distributors clamored for more cartoons starring pigs. Mr. Disney complied, but against his better judgment, and the three subsequent pig cartoons he produced were only moderately successful. He summed up the experience by saying, "You can't top pigs with pigs." From then on, he saw each great achievement as a stepping-stone to his next project, not a pattern to be copied from over and over again.

The Walt Disney Studio went on to produce live-action

films as well, but its reputation for impeccable quality and wholesomeness and its trademark style are based on the feature-length animated films. In the early thirties the very idea of an animated feature struck most people in the industry as absurd. First, it had never been done before. As I think back now, that's probably one reason why Walt Disney wanted to do it. Second, because each frame of a cartoon was then drawn by hand, and it took twenty-four frames to create one second of action on screen—well, clearly this would be a lengthy and expensive undertaking.

Undaunted, Walt Disney persevered over nearly four years on his first feature-length project, spending three times his original $500,000 budget. As the months passed, Hollywood wags began referring to the production, which would ultimately require over two million individual drawings, as "Disney's Folly." When *Snow White and the Seven Dwarfs* premiered in late 1937 it changed American animation forever, opening the door for the Disney classics that followed: *Pinocchio, Fantasia, Dumbo, Bambi, The Three Caballeros, Song of the South* (which mixed live action with animation), *Cinderella, Alice in Wonderland*, and *Peter Pan*. It was an incredible output, and what makes it even more impressive is that it represents only a fraction of the Disney releases from 1940 to 1954. There were other animated shorts and features, as well as such live-action films as *Treasure Island, The Story of Robin Hood*, and *20,000 Leagues Under the Sea*.

Although many of these Disney films are remembered for their technical innovations, at the heart of every classic Disney release was a great story. In its way, Mr. Disney's approach was highly sophisticated. And, contrary to popular belief, the world portrayed in Disney films was not always one of sweetness and light. Some of the most memorable scenes from the Disney works are also the most heartbreaking: Bambi hearing the gunshot that kills his mother; little Dumbo visiting his caged mother; the Seven Dwarfs discovering the "dead" Snow White; the young master having to shoot his rabid dog Old Yeller. Each of these reflected Mr. Disney's sentimental yet pragmatic philosophy: "With every laugh, there must be a tear somewhere."

Not surprisingly, Walt Disney found new worlds to explore, new media for his art. As the fifties dawned, Hollywood looked at television and saw the enemy. It was widely believed that television would sound the death knell for the film industry, because people would stay at home rather than go out to movie theaters. For this reason most Hollywood studios initially were adamant about not working in the new medium, and those who did were considered traitors. Few actually understood television's creative potential; one of them was Walt Disney.

His initial attempts were two popular Christmas specials, in 1950 and 1951, and by 1954 he was ready to jump in with both feet. That year he began producing and hosting a weekly hour-long series called *Disneyland.* (At that time Disneyland, the magic kingdom, existed primarily in Mr. Disney's imagination, in notes, preliminary drawings, and 160 acres of orange groves in Anaheim.) Over the years the show's title would undergo several changes, to *Walt Disney Presents, Walt Disney's Wonderful World of Color, The Wonderful World of Disney, Disney's Wonderful World,* and finally simply *Walt Disney* before it left the air in 1983. (Segments are now aired on The Disney Channel.) It remains the longest-running prime-time series in television history and is widely acknowledged for bringing movie-quality production values to the small screen.

Walt Disney was a television pioneer, giving the young medium and a fledgling network (ABC) an Emmy-winning program that featured documentaries, nature stories, cartoons, feature films, and serials (such as the phenomenally popular *Davy Crockett*). As host of the prime-time program, Walt Disney became a familiar face to the millions who tuned in each week.

But what few people knew then was that the television

projects served a dual purpose. Ever the showman, Mr. Disney relished bringing fun and happiness to children of all ages—and he believed everyone was still a child deep inside. But he also had a larger dream, one that very few other people believed in as fervently as he did; one that could be realized only with the kind of financing a television network could provide. He dreamed of building a place that would be not just the product of imagination, but a tribute to it. It would be a magical destination, the likes of which had never been seen before on earth: Disneyland. In fact, the very first episode of the *Disneyland* series, "The Disneyland Story," took viewers behind the scenes of the theme park in progress. Construction began in August 1954, only eleven months before the park's projected opening date. But long before the first orange tree was felled to make way for Sleeping Beauty Castle, Disneyland had been meticulously researched, planned, and designed down to the last detail.

Even though Walt Disney made it a point never to repeat himself, for his second television series he returned to his best-loved creation—some would say his alter ego—Mickey Mouse. The original Mickey Mouse Club, established in the thirties, was designed to attract children to movie theaters. The informal "meetings" of club members took place at Saturday matinees and included such activities as singing songs and celebrating members' birthdays. By then Mickey was perhaps the most easily recognized American in the world, so it's not surprising that at their peak the Mickey Mouse clubs boasted over one million members. Shortly thereafter most of the clubs disbanded, simply because they had grown too large. Nonetheless, the world's love of Mickey Mouse only intensified. In fact, in his earliest-written plans for an amusement park, dated 1948, Walt Disney referred to it as Mickey Mouse Park. It's no wonder that when it came time to develop a television show for children Mickey would be cast in a starring role.

Though television was still in its infancy, there was no lack of children's programming. Among the most popular elements of early children's shows were adventure (*Fury, Space Patrol, Sky King*), puppets (*Howdy Doody, Captain Kangaroo*), and audience participation (who can forget *Howdy Doody*'s famous Peanut Gallery?). Programs that took a more educational approach, such as the many kids' quiz shows, and *Mr. Wizard*, also drew viewers.

Cartoons proved popular as well, though the all-cartoon children's program would not arrive until 1955, with *The Mighty Mouse Playhouse;* animation did not become the dominant form of children's television until the sixties. The major animation studios still produced cartoon shorts to be shown before the feature films in movie theaters, but the rate of production was quickly declining. By 1955 Mr. Disney had all but stopped producing them. At the same time, leading producers held massive catalogs of older cartoons, for which children's television provided a fresh new audience.

Walt Disney understood this. At the same time he wanted to do something far more ambitious. The concept of *The Mickey Mouse Club* took form over a year. Early ideas included having a live studio audience and regular appearances by clowns, magicians, and other characters. Before long, however, the decision was made to incorporate a number of elements—cartoons, guest stars, special educational features, and music written specifically for the club—in a program that would seem not only to be produced for kids but *by* kids. Mr. Disney was adamant that the show not talk down to kids. He felt that if it was aimed at the twelve-year-olds, their younger siblings would naturally start watching anyway. In a memo from March 1955, Walt Disney wrote: "Call kids Mouseketeers—get costumes, sweaters, little hats. Audience not necessary, just kids."

Sounds simple enough, doesn't it? But back in 1955, when *The Mickey Mouse Club* was just getting off the drawing

board, this was a novel idea. Some people in the business—
and certainly a few at the studio—feared that a program that
centered around two dozen kids could become a headache,
especially given the difficulties inherent in working with
child performers. Walt Disney wisely instructed his staff to
seek out children who were not professional performers. He
dispatched scouts—including our director, Bill Walsh, and
Jimmie Dodd—to schoolyards, local talent shows, dance recitals, and just about anywhere you might discover an undis-
covered kid. Among the qualifications for being a Mouseketeer, talent was one Disney considered least crucial, at least
in the beginning. He felt that children could learn a great deal
as they went along. His biggest concern was that the cast be
able to get along well through the long days of rehearsing
and shooting.

For this reason, he avoided children whose parents might
be considered "stage parents." Once we started working,
each child had to be accompanied by a parent or guardian—
in almost all cases, the mother—who remained on the studio
lot, but was kept away from the set where we rehearsed and
filmed. Walt Disney set up the studio's movie theater so that
mothers could sit there and watch movies, chat, knit, sew, or
read, passing the time however they wanted.

Hundreds of children were invited to audition at the studio, most of us being what Mr. Disney described as "ordinary kids." A few of us, like my good friends Sharon Baird,
Lonnie Burr, and Bobby Burgess, had worked professionally
before. But for the majority, myself included, our show business "experience" consisted of school plays and dance-
school recitals. It is to Mr. Disney's great credit, I believe, that
during the entire three years *The Mickey Mouse Club* was in
production, we remained ordinary kids, despite the show's
tremendous success. He made sure that we were having fun.
There wasn't a day when he didn't drop by the set to see how
things were going, to ask us if we needed anything, to simply

say hello. He extended this same courtesy and consideration to our mothers, even purchasing sewing machines for them to use while we worked.

The two dozen hopefuls that were made Mouseketeers were divided into three separate groups: red, white, and blue. While all of the Mouseketeers were used for skits and numbers, the show's openings and closings were performed by members of the red group: Sharon Baird, Bobby Burgess, Tommy Cole, Darlene Gillespie, Doreen Tracey, me, and Cubby O'Brien and Karen Pendleton—the so-called "Meese-keteers" because they were just nine years old, and among the three youngest.

The other Mouseketeers from that first season were Nancy Abbate, Billie Jean Beanblossom, Lonnie Burr, Dennis Day, Mary Espinosa, Bonni Lou Kern, Bronson Scott (the youngest Mouseketeer), Mary Satori, Mark Sutherland, Michael Smith, Don Underhill, Johnny Crawford (later of the television series *The Rifleman,* and now a bandleader), Dickie Dodd (later of the Standells rock group), Ronnie Steiner, John Lee Johann, Judy Harriet, Paul Petersen (who later played Jeff on the long-running *Donna Reed* television series and is now an advocate for child performers), Linda Hughes, and Tim and Mickey Rooney, Jr. (the sons of actor Mickey Rooney).

We ranged in age from nine to fourteen. We came from a wide range of backgrounds and experiences, yet at heart we were all just plain kids. In Mr. Disney's eyes, this was the true—perhaps the only—qualification for being a Mouseketeer. We *were* just like the kids next door or down the street. When I say this, I don't mean to slight any of my fellow Mouseketeers, most of whom were talented in one or more areas. But I truly believe that a large part of our appeal derived from the fact that children could watch us every afternoon on television and say to themselves, *I could sing as well as Annette,* or *I bet I could dance just like her.* We were all very good at what we did, but we were not significantly better than many other children. Similarly, we looked like the kids next door—okay, except for those ears.

No doubt you've seen former child performers recount the abuse they suffered in show business. Not too many years ago I found myself on a talk-show panel where I was greeted with skepticism bordering on disbelief when I described our wonderful life on the Disney lot. Only after I began working at other studios, with other producers, directors, and crews, did I realize how unique the Disney lot was. For one thing, any form of profanity was strictly forbidden. If Walt Disney learned that anyone—even an adult—had uttered so much as a "damn," you could be sure you wouldn't see him on the set the next day. Second, everyone who worked at Disney lived according to the same high moral standards of behavior. We Mouseketeers were told to refer to everyone as "Uncle" or "Aunt"; so there was "Uncle Walt," of course, although I could never bring myself to call him that. To me he would always be Mr. Disney. We called our makeup man "Uncle Makeup" and our hairdresser "Aunt Hairdresser." Everyone treated us with kindness, patience, and courtesy, from the gardeners to Mr. Disney himself.

Respect, consideration, fairness—these were part of our everyday lives at the studio, and I think the work environment Walt Disney and his staff maintained for us was the key to why those qualities came through so clearly in the television show itself. But there is one person whose contributions to *The Mickey Mouse Club* were particularly important, and that is Jimmie Dodd.

Jimmie Dodd became a staff songwriter for Disney shortly before *The Mickey Mouse Club* began. Previous to that he had enjoyed a long, respected career as an actor, songwriter, and song-and-dance man. As singer and guitarist, he appeared with famed bandleader Louis Prima before beginning his film career in a William Holden picture, *Those Were the Days.* From 1939 through the early fifties, he appeared in over thirty feature films, many of them set during wartime (as in *The Flying Tigers,* with John Wayne) or in the old West, where

Jimmie often played a singing cowboy. During World War II, he and his wife, Ruth Carroll, entertained troops. (Some club viewers will remember that Ruth appeared with us in a number called "Cooking with Minnie Mouse.")

Although he was in his midforties when *The Mickey Mouse Club* began, Jimmie was very much one of us. He was our leader, both onstage and off. A devoutly religious, friendly, even-tempered man, Jimmie never once raised his voice in anger to anyone. His straightforward approach to giving children advice to grow on is familiar to anyone who watched the show. Jimmie's optimism and enthusiasm, his sense of fair play and cooperation are evident in the many songs he composed for the show, such as "Mickey Mouse March" ("We play fair, and we work hard, and we're in harmony," from the seldom-heard second verse), and "Beauty Is as Beauty Does." Jimmie also authored what we came to call "Doddisms," little expressions and truisms that instructed and inspired:

"A Mousekethought is a deed well done to see you through."

"An attitude of cheerfulness will help you your life through."

"Teamwork is the way of life."

At the end of each show, Jimmie looked directly into the camera and spoke to our audience from his heart. Often beginning with the words "May I have a word with you now, Mouseketeers?" he then shared his thoughts on such serious matters as the importance of having a vision or the reasons we shouldn't spread gossip. Of the latter, Jimmie advised good Mouseketeers everywhere to ask themselves, "Is it true? Will it do good to tell it? Is it kind?"—words many of us would do well to follow today, no matter how old we are.

Jimmie's cohort, our "big Mooseketeer," was Roy Williams, an animator and writer who had worked at the studio since Walt Disney hired him at age eighteen. How Roy came to be a member of the Mouseketeers I'll never know, but he had enjoyed a long working relationship with Mickey Mouse, having written his cartoon strips for several years. Although Roy never had as many speaking lines as Jimmie, he had the love and respect of all the Mouseketeers. Roy possessed a wonderful, warm personality that was irresistible, and everyone noticed his special way with children. While we all got along extremely well, the hours were long and the work could be hard. As much fun as it was most of the time, there were those days when a new routine wouldn't come as quickly or tempers would flare. Whenever our spirits started to flag, we could count on Roy to cheer us up with a kind word or a quickly sketched caricature of ourselves. He drew one of me in a ballet costume, tripping over the ribbons on my toe shoes.

Roy was famous for the swim parties he often hosted for the Mouseketeers. Few of us had pools at home, and we were all quite impressed by Roy's, which was done up in a Polynesian decor. Both Roy's wife, Ethel, and Jimmie's wife, Ruth, were also wonderful people, and I look back fondly on the good times I spent with all of them. In so many ways we became a family.

After the entire club was selected, we got to work very quickly. Whatever reservations I had about my new career, they were all pretty much forgotten after a couple of weeks on the set. I would wake up every morning ready to go. I couldn't wait to get on the lot and see my friends. I think it's safe to say that we all saw this as a wonderful time in our lives. After all, here we were getting paid to do what most kids love to do: play, dance, sing, and be with their friends.

It was not all fun and games, though. One of the first things each of us had to do was appear before the state board of health. California has very strict laws governing child actors, and we had to meet numerous conditions to remain under contract. For example, we were weighed and interviewed periodically. The board of health had to be satisfied that we were getting sufficient rest and eating well. They would ask our parents if we were biting our nails or wetting the bed, both symptoms of overwork and stress. Because I had never been a very good eater, these periodic examinations worried Mom no end, but I always passed.

Long before most people had even heard of *The Mickey Mouse Club,* my being a Mouseketeer was having a profound impact on my family. Each child's work permit was contingent on a parent or guardian's being on the lot with him or her every minute, every day, six days a week from nine in the morning until we stopped working around five o'clock. At the time, my brother Joey was nine, and my baby brother, Michael, just two. My father worked six full days a week at his garage on Ventura Boulevard in Sherman Oaks, and sometimes on Sunday. With few close friends and no family to turn to, my mother would drop off Michael to stay with his godmother. Poor Michael cried almost all day long, which broke my mother's heart. Siblings and other children weren't allowed on the lot—for insurance reasons, I understand—so she really had no choice. For my mother, who had never let anyone outside our family babysit us and who was used to being home all the time, this was quite an adjustment.

It was clear that if a mother ever got caught leaving the lot during a workday, her child's contract would be canceled immediately. Despite this, my mother and a few others soon figured out ingenious ways to sneak off the lot, even if only for an hour or two. My mother would run home to start dinner or take care of some other tasks; when my father came home he would finish the preparations, set the table, and have a lovely dinner waiting for us. The mothers covered for one another, so nobody would realize someone had left. It wasn't until many years later that my mother learned that several people we worked with, including the guard at the gate, knew full well what was going on, but kept it to themselves. I think they saw what a burden this placed on our families, and in their own secret way they tried to help.

The state was especially strict when it came to our education. Even while shooting, three hours each day were devoted to schoolwork. Usually the schedule called for four hours of work on the set, three hours for school, and an hour for lunch and breaks. Our tutor, Mrs. Jean Seaman, was a great teacher, whom I admired and still consider a very good friend. We were very fortunate that Mrs. Seaman was qualified to teach about forty subjects. It could not have been easy to oversee the education of twenty-four children of different ages and abilities. Our "classroom" was two little red mobile schoolhouses on the studio lot. Whenever we traveled, one accompanied us, and we continued our lessons, no matter where we were. While one group of Mouseketeers was rehearsing a new number or filming, the second would be in class. You had to get in your three hours of school each day however you could, sometimes in twenty-minute bursts. In addition, we all had homework to do every day. You couldn't continue working if it compromised your education or your grades dropped below a certain point. Looking back today, this all seems like quite a load for a bunch of kids, but we didn't mind.

Before long we all settled into a very comfortable routine. We ate our lunches together in the Disney commissary, which was renowned throughout Hollywood for its wonderful food. Our favorite day was Thursday, prime-rib day, and most of us Mouseketeers liked to chew on the bones. Next door was a coffee shop, where we could get cheeseburgers, hot dogs, and hot fudge sundaes.

Then, as now, the Disney studio buzzed with activity. We often saw other actors and actresses on the lot, working on different projects. You had a very strong impression of being at the center of something very exciting, and no wonder. It took a lot of time and manpower to produce *The Mickey Mouse Club*. Most people remember the Mouseketeers in their uniforms: the ears, the name sweaters, and skirts or pants. But each of us might wear several costumes in the course of one show, and some of these—like my flapper dress for Anything Can Happen Day—could be quite elaborate. One of my favorites, which is still preserved in the Walt Disney Archives, is the cowgirl outfit I wore for the Talent Roundup every Friday. At various times I was dressed as a ballerina, an exotic dancer in a circus sideshow (for Circus Day)—you name a costume, I or one of the other Mouseketeers probably wore it at some time. Multiply that by twenty-four, and you can see what a daunting job our wardrobe people had.

And that was just our costumes. There were also scenery, props, and music. One of the interesting facts about *The Mickey Mouse Club* is that virtually all the music used on it, from "Mickey Mouse March," which opened the show, to the closing "Mickey Mouse March (Alma Mater Theme)" ("Now it's time to say goodbye to all our company . . .") was written specifically for the program. In all, over fifty songwriters and composers contributed to the 360 episodes of *The Mickey Mouse Club* produced between 1955 and 1958.

Rehearsals and filming generally went very smoothly. Even though Mr. Disney did not want to work with "professional" children, we all became quite professional very quickly, but in a positive sense. We knew our lines, our steps, our songs. We showed up on time and followed directions. The few Mouseketeers who did not or would not cooperate, or whose parents felt compelled to meddle, were replaced. It sounds pretty basic, but it was the best training anyone choosing to enter this business could have had.

That is not to say that everything was perfect. I had not been a Mouseketeer very long before the object of America's children's affection—those ears—became my biggest source of worry. After the show aired, millions of inexpensive black-eared beanies would adorn little heads across the country. But the real mouse ears, the ones we wore on the show, were very costly and handmade from the finest felt, with little wires inside to form the ears. Back in 1955 they cost about $50 each, and to start we Mouseketeers were earning about $185 a week. Being kids, some of us were a bit careless with our ears, leaving them lying about or just forgetting where we put them. Later, as the show became popular, people were thrilled to "find" an authentic pair of ears, so some "disappeared" that way. In short order I managed to lose three pairs of ears, and the cost of each was deducted from my pay. It was a hard lesson, but one we all learned quickly and well. After a while, no one ever set his or her ears down, not even for a second. We either wore or carried our precious ears with us everywhere we went, and I do mean everywhere. Interestingly, for all the care we took to save them, there are just a few pairs of original mouse ears in the Walt Disney Archives today.

Before *The Mickey Mouse Club* TV program debuted in October 1955, we Mouseketeers were publicly introduced at the grand opening of Disneyland that summer. I'm sure most readers have visited either Disneyland or Walt Disney World, so you know how exciting it is. Well, just imagine being one of the first children to set foot in Disneyland. It was one of the most awe-inspiring experiences of my life. Again, as with the Mouseketeers, who until then knew what Disneyland was? But as we saw on the first day we went there, it was wonderful beyond our wildest dreams.

To really appreciate what it was like for us, you have to remember that a theme park of the type and size Mr. Disney envisioned simply did not exist. There had long been amusement parks and carnivals, with rides, games, and entertainment. Perhaps the most famous permanent amusement park in America until then was Coney Island. A mecca for fun lovers through the twenties, thirties, and forties, this New York seaside park had fallen into disrepair and disrepute. Across much of America Mr. Disney saw the same thing over and over: amusement parks that were poorly planned, inadequately maintained, and unattractive. For years before he began planning Disneyland, Mr. Disney toured and studied all sorts of public amusements, from parks to zoos, the world over. He paid careful attention to what adults and children alike were drawn to, what caught their attention, what annoyed them, what excited them. In an attempt to learn as much as he could about the business, he also spoke to other amusement-park owners and operators. As was usually the case with Mr. Disney, however, he had full faith in ideas that others more experienced in the field predicted would fail. For example, no one thought that a park could be open all year without the rides' constantly breaking down. Mr. Disney so deeply believed in his dream, though, that he borrowed money against his life-insurance policies and sold one of his homes to finance it.

In this as in almost all other endeavors, Mr. Disney trusted his instincts. In Disneyland he sought to create a clean, attractive, safe environment for children and their parents. It seemed a simple idea. But Mr. Disney's vision of how to create such an environment was anything but. Disneyland would be a self-contained sixty-two-acre universe made up of several main attractions. Visitors entered on Main Street and proceeded through an artfully scaled-down re-creation of an old-fashioned American town circa 1886 to a town square at the center of Disneyland. From there four other "lands"—Frontierland, Fantasyland, Tomorrowland, and Adventureland—beckoned, each filled with rides, amusements, and exhibits that were both educational and fun. Encircling it all was Mr. Disney's favorite attraction, the Disneyland and Santa Fe Railroad, a functioning train built to five-eighths scale, which he often drove himself. Beyond that was the parking lot, designed to accommodate twelve thousand cars. And towering above it all, the majestic Sleeping Beauty Castle.

A large part of Disneyland's appeal to Mr. Disney was that

it would be a living thing, something he could change, improve, and add to through the years. For a man like Mr. Disney, who avidly followed new developments in science and technology, Disneyland was a great playground. From beginning to end, no detail—not even the design of the garbage cans—escaped his scrutiny.

Disneyland opened to an invited audience on Sunday, July 17, 1955. A mere eleven months had elapsed since construction crews began transforming part of an orange grove into the eighth wonder of the world. Despite the feverish efforts of 2,500 workers to complete the park on time, there were a few hitches here and there—some asphalt that wasn't quite dry, for example, and people complained about a lack of adequate restroom facilities. But all in all, opening day was spectacular. Traffic around the site backed up for ten miles in all directions.

The opening ceremonies were broadcast live across America in a television special hosted by Bob Cummings, Ronald Reagan (then still an actor), and Art Linkletter. In addition to the 15,000 invited guests (among them such celebrities as Frank Sinatra, Danny Thomas, Don Defore, Sammy Davis, Jr., and their children), many thousands more gained admittance with counterfeit tickets. Under the crush of 33,000 visitors, food and beverage concessions quickly ran out, and some public facilities broke down.

In the middle of Main Street Mr. Disney opened his dream park with the following dedication: "To all who come here to this happy place, welcome. Disneyland is your land. Here age relives fond memories of the past, and here youth may savor the challenge and the promise of the future. Disneyland is dedicated to the ideals, the dreams, and the hard facts that have created America . . . with the hope that it will be a source of joy and inspiration to all the world. Thank you."

An American flag was raised, and the U.S. Marine Band played "The Star-Spangled Banner." Then the Air National Guard flew overhead as the parade down Main Street began.

When we appeared, Bob Cummings announced us as "the performing children"; neither he nor Art Linkletter seemed quite sure who or what a Mouseketeer was. After us came Fess Parker and Buddy Ebsen, who played Davy Crockett and his sidekick George Russel in the popular TV series; Snow White and the Seven Dwarfs; Cinderella; Annie Oakley; and countless other characters from history, legend, and storybooks.

As the ceremonies continued, twenty-nine television cameras took viewers from one area of the park to another, so millions of Americans witnessed the christening of the three-wheeler *Mark Twain*, and the dedications of Frontierland, Adventureland, and Tomorrowland. The latter was designed to represent what life would be like in 1986, which seemed a long way off back then, when "a trip to the moon is an everyday thing." There was a miniature version of "the superhighway of the future," Autopia, where passengers drove around in small cars at eleven miles per hour. There was a special exhibit dedicated to demonstrating one of Mr. Disney's futuristic passions, the wonders of the atom, and throughout the park a number of new and popular rides such as Mr. Toad's Wild Ride, the King Arthur Carousel, Peter Pan's Flight, and Snow White's Adventures.

Finally, in Fantasyland several children stood before the moat surrounding Sleeping Beauty Castle as a knight proclaimed, "Open the Fantasyland castle in the name of the children of the world!" As "When You Wish Upon a Star" played in the background, all the famous Disney characters came to life—Snow White, the Seven Dwarfs, Alice from Wonderland, Dumbo, Peter Pan, and so many others—and danced through the streets of Fantasyland. Then two actors in very primitive Mickey Mouse and Minnie Mouse costumes skipped in, opened the immense double doors, and out we Mouseketeers danced. In our western costumes, we performed the theme from Talent Roundup Day ("Saddle your pony, here we go down to the talent rodeo"), followed by a pretty hot swing-style number. For the first time ever America heard and saw Jimmie Dodd announce, "Mouseketeer roll call, count off now!" and we marched in line toward the camera and said our names. I was the last Mouseketeer in the roll call that day, followed only by Roy, Jimmie, and, of course, Mickey Mouse himself. During the number Bob Cummings predicted, "I guarantee that many a future star will come out of this group."

To call the events of this warm Sunday afternoon exciting was the understatement of the year. It was a child's dream come true. After we had performed our official duties as Mouseketeers, we were turned loose to explore the park, try out the rides, and see the sights. One of the Mouseketeers' favorites was the Mad Tea Party, with its spinning teacups, which the boys would turn as fast as they could in the hopes of making someone dizzy enough to throw up!

It wasn't too long before Mr. Disney had another historic success to his credit. Within just two months over one million people had come to experience Disneyland. No matter how popular it became or how many millions of people strolled down Main Street, Mr. Disney was always comfortable being there. Many times he was spotted driving the train around and around the park. He even kept an apartment over the firehouse on Main Street, so you could say there were times when he actually lived in Disneyland. I suppose that might sound funny, but when I think of Mr. Disney, his love for children, his amazing ability to bring out that sense of wonder in all of us, it doesn't sound so odd after all.

I have always thought of Walt Disney as my second father. It seems that every time I go to Disneyland a stranger will approach me and, smiling, say, "Somehow I knew I would see you here." I still feel the same way about Mr. Disney. I always expect to see him—smiling, with a twinkle in his eye—there.

*F*or the tens of millions of children who became *The Mickey Mouse Club*'s first fans, growing up was much easier than it is now. If you watched the show today, you might think of it as very much a product of a time that is generally dismissed as being too sedate, even boring. For example, the show's individual segments seem quaintly long compared to the current quick-edit style, and the innocent messages sound a little too "goody goody." But while *The Mickey Mouse Club* may appear an idealization, it was in fact an honest if exaggerated reflection of an America that, sadly, has faded into history.

Most original viewers of *The Mickey Mouse Club* didn't face the crush of family and social problems children have today. Divorce was not as widespread, and most mothers could choose to stay with their children rather than work outside the home. The violence and drug abuse that plague us were barely known. Over 60 percent of Americans attended church regularly, the highest rate in the country's history. Federal and local governments were expanding and improving public schools at an unprecedented rate.

To some, the fifties were a decade marked by the banal, the

predictable. Perhaps that's because what came next—the sixties—brought such dramatic turmoil and change that anything else seemed boring in comparison. And yet, that Eisenhower decade was a time of dizzying progress. The vaccine for polio, a crippling, sometimes fatal illness that parents dreaded for decades, was finally made available. The first advances in civil rights were being made. IBM sold its first business computer. Ann Landers published her first advice column. And, ever so slowly, rock 'n' roll came into our lives. Little Richard's "Tutti Frutti," Chuck Berry's "Maybellene," and Bill Haley's "Rock Around the Clock" provided a fresh, exciting alternative to the soothing sounds of "Yellow Rose of Texas," "Autumn Leaves," and "Love Is a Many-Splendored Thing." Kids as young as I was then thrilled to James Dean's romantic, misunderstood teen in *Rebel Without a Cause.* Even if we couldn't articulate exactly what he symbolized, we felt that he was speaking to us.

To have been a child then was to feel part of a fantastic age of promise and wonder, and to take for granted a future of optimism and security. It may be hard to imagine now, but we actually looked forward to the day when the atom would become the source of infinite clean energy. After all, we'd need it to power our futuristic monorail transit systems and those routine trips into outer space we'd be taking on our way to or from the era's most enduring monument: the local shopping mall.

The period's artifacts—sleek, sexy cars housing V-8 engines; eye-popping pastel kitchen appliances; armless sectional sofas; and those fascinating but taste-free TV dinners—today seem quaint and downright silly. For our parents, though, they were their reward for enduring the hardships of the Great Depression and World War II.

Defining and capturing that time forever was television. It showed us how to see the world and ourselves, and, through its programming, it shaped both. At the beginning of 1955 only about 60 percent of American homes had TVs, but that number would increase dramatically during the next three years.

Television delivered whole new worlds right into our living rooms and created a community of millions of little baby boomers who, without ever meeting one another, shared common memories of characters and performers they loved. To understand the phenomenon of a children's program like *The Mickey Mouse Club,* or the sentimental affection and nostalgia adults still feel for the club and other popular children's shows, such as *Captain Kangaroo* and *Howdy Doody*, it's important to understand that "watching television" in those days, for those kids, was not the same experience it is today. It's difficult to grasp the sense of anticipation, the thrill, that sitting before it inspired then. After years of listening to radio, we found the black-and-white images mesmerizing, right down to the Indian-chief test pattern. For the first time in history you could have a theater right in your home. We looked forward to our favorite shows, and we hadn't yet seen so many thousands of hours of TV that we were jaded by anything. Several years would pass before the family television descended from a magic box to just another piece of furniture you had to dust.

It was in this world now long past that *The Mickey Mouse Club* premiered on Monday, October 3, 1955. (That was nearly forty years ago. It sure doesn't seem like it!) We had taped some of the segments as early as the previous May, and throughout the series, we would tape segments out of sequence. One result is that when we worked on a particular segment, say the opening or a special number, we never knew whether it would be featured in our first show or, later, our last. I do know that the first number I ever taped, in May 1955, was "Talent Roundup," which I loved. Today I'm a big fan of western-style clothing, and I wonder if it started with my fringed skirt, vest, boots, kerchief, and cowgirl hat.

One date that really stands out for me was the first time

my father saw me on television. I think that my mother, being on the lot with me every day, felt more a part of my work life. For my father, however, this Mouseketeer business remained pretty abstract until he saw the first episode of *The Mickey Mouse Club.* A highly emotional man, he just went crazy. He was happy, proud, overwhelmed—you name it— to see his little Dolly's face beaming out of that screen. Need- less to say, the relatives back in Utica also went nuts. Of course, at that time I was still one of twenty-four children on the show. Life would continue fairly normally for us—for a while.

The premiere episode of *The Mickey Mouse Club* drew a huge audience. Because Mr. Disney's evening series, *Disney- land,* ranked among the top ten prime-time shows, viewers were familiar with the Disney style and expected a high level of quality in any Disney-produced children's program. I think that with our show they got it.

That first episode set the format most of the subsequent shows would follow: a newsreel and a Mouseketeer seg- ment, then, after a commercial break, the day's special num- ber. Since the premiere was on a Monday, it was Fun with Music Day, for which we performed "Friendly Farmers" and "Shoe Song." After another commercial break, we returned with an educational segment called "What I Want to Be," then wrapped it all up with our first "Mousecartoon," "Pueblo Pluto," and our closing theme.

Generally, this first show got exceptional reviews from critics, with one noticeable exception. In the review that ap- peared in the next day's *New York Times,* writer Jack Gould seemed especially critical of the Mouseketeers, whom he de- scribed as "a group of youngsters evidently . . . borrowed from the children's amateur hours around the country." Well, that was who we were!

In the end, however, the few objections did nothing to stop "the club that's made for you and me." In its first Nielsen ratings period, only the historic World Series, pitting the

Brooklyn Dodgers against the New York Yankees, drew more viewers than *The Mickey Mouse Club*. Within just a few weeks, ours was the top-rated children's program and would remain so throughout its four-season run. Kids all over America made sure they were positioned in front of the set every weekday afternoon after school in time to see the row of little Mickeys trumpet the fanfare and the parade of familiar beloved Disney characters as they marched, twirled, and trampolined their way through "Mickey Mouse March." Over the years I've seen thousands of people, most of them absolute strangers, sing "M-I-C-K-E-Y . . ."—I'm sure you know the rest—to me. And, you know something? I never get tired of it.

I think that for *Mickey Mouse Club* viewers, and even for us Mouseketeers, our opening theme was more than just a catchy tune. Beyond becoming one of the era's best-loved songs, the theme said a lot about the club and the relationship we Mouseketeers still share with our fans. Jiminy Cricket's friendly "Hey there, hi there, ho there! You're as welcome as can be!" could have been the club's motto. As thousands of fans have told me over the years, there was something about the show that made them feel *included*. Perhaps that feeling emanated from the sense of camaraderie we shared on the set, or the way Jimmie Dodd and the rest of us often spoke directly to the camera, as if talking to each viewer individually. Perhaps it was the comfortable routine of the week's schedule ("Today is Tuesday, you know what that means . . ."), or the easy familiarity our audience felt they had with each of us. (So obviously putting our names on our sweaters wasn't such a dumb idea, after all.) Whatever it was, it worked.

For those of you who never saw *The Mickey Mouse Club* or perhaps haven't seen it in many years, I'll try to describe what it was all about. After the rousing opening march, Mickey Mouse appeared on a stage, dressed in the appropriate costume for the day. Each day of the week was special.

On Monday we had fun with music, Tuesday we rolled out the carpet for Guest Star Day, on Wednesday anything could happen, Thursday was Circus Day, and on Friday we opened the Dry Gulch corral to the Talent Roundup. For Guest Star Day, Mickey, resplendent in tails (on his evening jacket, of course), played a grand piano; on Fridays, he entered shooting, in cowboy hat and chaps. Each day of the week had its own special opening number, always ending with Jimmie calling out, "Mouseketeer roll call, count off now" (except on Friday, when he addressed us as his "Mousekepardners").

Throughout the week we presented a number of other popular features. The first half hour usually included a newsreel featuring brief reports on events and trends everywhere in the world, from Palm Beach, Florida, to Nagasaki. As further proof that Mr. Disney never talked down to his audience, no matter how young, each newsreel was announced as "the news of today for the leaders of tomorrow" and ended with the words "Dedicated to you, the leaders of the twenty-first century."

Other educational series took viewers behind the scenes, for example, at the FBI, to learn about fingerprinting, or to a government mint, to see how money is made. Special reports included a trip to the San Diego Zoo with a professional photographer from *Look* magazine, who showed several Mouseketeers how to take interesting photographs, and an inside look at the then-booming world of quarter-scale miniature hot-rod racing. Jiminy Cricket regularly provided another "educational" part of the show as our guide through the encyclopedia. All over the country, tiny kids amazed adults with their ability to "spell" after hearing Jiminy sing "E-N-C-Y-C-L-O-P-E-D-I-A" a few times.

Every day one or several of us Mouseketeers stood before the Mickey Mouse Treasure Mine and chanted the magical words, "Meeseka, Mooseka, Mouseketeer, Mousecartoon Time now is here!" and, *voilà!*, a cartoon. All drawn from the

Disney Studio's vast cartoon archives, these animated shorts included, obviously, Mickey Mouse, Minnie Mouse, Pluto, Goofy, Donald Duck, and the gang, as well as vintage classics, such as the Academy Award–winning *Ferdinand the Bull*.

The show's second half was dedicated to the day's theme, and it was then that you could see how *The Mickey Mouse Club* really stood ears and shoulders above the competition. Our sets, costumes, musical numbers, and skits were lavish and unusual, yet done with just a touch of whimsy. The roll-call opening for Anything Can Happen Day had Jimmie dressed as an astronaut, Cubby O'Brien as a rabbit with a magician in his hat, Lonnie as a cowboy being ridden by his horse, Karen as a beautiful dancing marionette, and Roy as her puppeteer.

I loved something about every day. But I think the segments I most looked forward to were on Guest Star Day. Our guests included performers of all ages and backgrounds, ranging from Olympic champion ice skater Ronnie Robertson to cellist-comedian Morey Amsterdam, who would later costar on *The Dick Van Dyke Show* and play a beatnik club owner in several of my beach-party movies with Frankie Avalon. One time we even let our director, Sid Miller, be our special guest, which was a treat. Mr. Miller, who had been a child performer and was also a songwriter, entertained us with his imitations of such Hollywood stars as James Cagney and Edward G. Robinson singing "The Mickey Mouse Club Theme." Cliff "Ukulele Ike" Edwards (the voice of Jiminy Cricket) and Clarence Nash (who voiced Donald Duck) were also guests. Fess Parker, better known as TV's Davy Crockett, and Buddy Ebsen also appeared with us, as did comedian Jerry Colonna, actor Sterling Holloway, singer-comedienne Judy Canova, and many, many others. The Firehouse 5 Plus 2 became familiar to viewers for their raucous Dixieland music. The group, which began in 1949, consisted of Disney staffers. Ward Kimball, the trombonist and group founder, was also an animator; George Bruns was a staff songwriter (he cowrote "The Ballad of Davy Crockett").

Of all the many memorable guests we welcomed to *The Mickey Mouse Club,* my absolute favorites were the Lennon Sisters. I don't think I'm alone among girls of my generation when I say that I idolized Dianne, Peggy, Kathy, and Janet. They sang beautifully, and what made them so appealing to me was that they were around my age (ranging from about nine to sixteen), and so beautiful and glamorous. Apparently they had recorded two club songs, "Mickey Mouse Mambo" and "Hi to You" (a song we Mouseketeers sang during the opening to the Talent Roundup), on an album, and shortly thereafter they were invited to join us for a day. I remember asking them, "What color lipstick are you wearing?" Beyond that, it's all a blur.

Talent Roundup Day, when we featured amateur performers from around the country, was also a lot of fun. The Roundup guests, all between the ages of eight and fourteen, sang, danced, played instruments, juggled, did magic tricks, performed acrobatics—you name it. For most of these kids, getting discovered by the Disney people and brought to Los Angeles to tape the show was the thrill of a lifetime. In a way, seeing them was like seeing our own stories being played out over again. I knew exactly how they felt. The segment always ended with "Step right up, here's your hat . . . here's your ears . . . you're an honorary Mouseketeer!" and a rousing round of applause from us Mouseketeers, Jimmie, and Roy.

In our special costumes and ears, we Mouseketeers appeared to live in a world of our own, filled with adventure, discovery, and fun. We spoke our own "Mousekalanguage"—a guitar was a "Mousegetar," for example, and we performed the "Mousekadance," and our travelogues were "Mousekatours." (In 1990 I, along with Sharon, Bobby, Tommy Cole, Sherry Alberoni, and Don Grady, guest-starred in *The New Mickey Mouse Club*'s first anniversary show. In one segment the younger Mouseketeers performed a terrific "Mousekasendup" of our "Mouseka" prefix obsession.)

It looked like a happy little world, and it truly was. We were as comfortable and easygoing off camera as on. Now, I say this knowing that there might be some Mouseketeers out there who would disagree. Certainly, all being kids, a few among us didn't always get along, and we saw our share of spats. I remember one time on the road we girls got a real treat when our Uncle Makeup allowed us to wear a touch of mascara. Gosh, I felt so grown-up, so sophisticated! No sooner had he applied the black goop to my lashes than another girl Mouseketeer came up behind me, put her hands over my eyes, and chirping "Guess who?," proceeded to smear the mascara all around my eyes. With only seconds before the curtain rose, I looked like a big raccoon! I was so mad, but it all blew over, as those things seemed to do.

In fact, I started one of the most enduring friendships of my life with Mouseketeer Sharon Baird. Like me, Sharon was on the red team all three seasons. I always thought that she and Karen Pendleton were the two best dancers among the girls. Unlike most of us Mouseketeers, Sharon was a professional, having begun as a dancer at age three. Before joining the club, she worked with such stellar talents as singer Eddie Cantor, Donald O'Connor, and Dean Martin and Jerry Lewis. While working on the soundtrack to the Martin and Lewis film *Artists and Models,* Sharon happened to be spotted by Jimmie Dodd.

Sharon's dancing was, in a word, stunning. In both her solo and our ensemble numbers, she brought a combination of grace and show-stopping precision seen in few dancers of any age. When performed by Sharon, even the most athletic, complex tap maneuvers looked simple—until you tried them yourself.

Another of *The Mickey Mouse Club*'s outstanding dancers was my partner for the whole three years, Bobby Burgess. Bobby was the tallest of the boys, and I was the tallest girl, so our pairing seemed natural. Bobby and I also became good friends. Having appeared in a few television commercials and many amateur programs, he knew a little more about show business than I did. He'd auditioned at Disney for a part in the *Spin and Marty* serial, but after he sang and danced, he got his mouse ears. An accomplished dancer, Bobby later went on to work as a regular for many years on the popular *Lawrence Welk Show*.

Dancing with Bobby was always fun, and we made a cute couple, but my real—in fact my only—romantic interest on the set was my fellow Mouseketeer Lonnie Burr. Lonnie, who was just a little bit younger than me, was so cute. And very, very sweet. And cool. One of our mothers often drove the two of us to Disneyland on the weekends, so we two little lovebirds sat in the backseat holding hands. Lonnie gave me a friendship ring, which on several occasions I melodramatically threw at him after a quarrel. And Lonnie got my very first kiss. Sound stage number one was not exactly simmering with adolescent romance. But that didn't mean we were immune to Cupid's arrows or strangers to heartbreak.

My only other club-related crush was on Tim Considine. In my adoration of Tim, I was one of millions of teenage girls. Although he was not a Mouseketeer, Tim starred in several of the popular *Mickey Mouse Club* serials, of which the best-loved are surely the three Spin and Marty series: *The Adventures of Spin and Marty*, *The Further Adventures of Spin and Marty*, and *The New Adventures of Spin and Marty*. Tim also appeared with me in the *Annette* serial and then in my first Disney feature film, *The Shaggy Dog*. A few years after our show ended, he, along with Mouseketeer Don Agrati (who later changed his name to Don Grady), played two of Fred MacMurray's sons in the long-running hit series *My Three Sons*. In much-belated recognition of his contribution to the Mickey Mouse Club, I was honored to have made him an official, ear-wearing Mouseketeer during our twenty-fifth anniversary special in 1980.

As most Mousekeviewers recall, one of the show's most popular segments was the serials. These were really more like feature films cut into eleven- or twelve-minute episodes that were shown daily. The early serials included *The Adventures of Spin and Marty; Corky and White Shadow,* starring Darlene Gillespie; and *The Hardy Boys* serials, with Tim and Tommy Kirk, with whom I'd later work in six Disney films. A lot of us really did grow up together at the Disney Studios.

The first serial I was cast in was *Adventure in Dairyland,* which began airing in November 1956, during our second season. It was the story of two young actors, Sammy Ogg, who played Joe in *The Adventures of Spin and Marty,* and me, who travel to Wisconsin to learn how to run a dairy farm. Even though I portrayed Annette the Mouseketeer, *Dairyland* was the first time I'd actually acted, so that made it very exciting.

What also made it interesting was that the story was not only set in Wisconsin but filmed there as well. While surely Mr. Disney might have easily found a hundred dairy farms within an hour's drive of the studio, he spared no expense to transport the entire cast and crew to a real working dairy farm in Verona, Wisconsin. This presented Mom and me with our first chance to travel away from home and the rest of the family. We hated it! From then on, Mom accompanied me wherever I traveled for work, and no matter where we went, what we did, or who we saw, it never compared with being back home with Daddy, Joey, and Michael.

My joining *The Mickey Mouse Club* had turned my family's daily routine upside-down, but over the months we had found our own rhythm. My parents, God bless them, coped the best they could, and my brothers helped just by being good kids. When we found out that Mom and I would be away for an entire month, she started getting things ready. She cooked and froze jar after jar of her wonderful home-made marinara sauce. We later found out that Daddy poured it over everything he served my brothers! My parents found a woman who was supposed to come in and look after everything during the day, but sometimes she didn't show up, so my father would have to stay home from work.

More than anyone else, including me, Mom found our new life difficult to adjust to. For one thing, I was her daughter. She responded to situations first as my mother, not the mother of a child whose show-business obligations also had to be considered. Once while we were in Wisconsin, I asked Mom if I could go across the street to a malt shop, and she said okay. She could see me from where she was and figured, *What could possibly happen?* When the tutor saw me with the other kids without a supervising adult, she came in, asked me to come along with her, and then got my mother into trouble for letting me go in the first place. Another time, some people at the studio became upset with my mother because she'd cut my hair—as she had done for years—without first consulting them. Apparently, though I'd finished filming some *Spin and Marty* episodes, there were still close-ups to be shot. I was fitted with a wig so that I would look the same, but the studio people were less than thrilled.

Despite the separation and Mom and my having to learn to do things on our own, making *Adventure in Dairyland* was still a lot of fun. In the story, Sammy and I are the guests of a farm family and their three children, Jimmy (who has a crush on me from the television show), Linda (who of course has a crush on Sammy), and Moochie, played for the first time by Kevin Corcoran. Kevin would appear as Moochie in several other serials, including the *Spin and Marty*s as well as his own, and several Disney features. In all of them he played the mischievous but lovable little brother. Over the course of our adventures (most of which involved Moochie's getting into some kind of jam), Sammy and I got the chance to milk cows, feed calves, round up escaped piglets, make jelly—just like real farm kids. We even learned how to yodel. And we didn't just "act," we actually did these things. Except for missing my family, I loved the whole experience.

On the studio lot, we Mouseketeers were just doing our jobs, and were treated like kids, not stars. Outside the gates on South Buena Vista Street, however, things for us really started to change. Aside from the ratings, the first evidence of Mousemania was the great success of anything related to *The Mickey Mouse Club*. For a while brand-new mouse-eared beanies were being sold at the rate of 24,000 a day. Walt Disney Productions began publishing Walt Disney's *Mickey Mouse Club* quarterly magazine (in 1957 it went bimonthly, and the title was changed to *Walt Disney's Magazine*). Each 50-cent copy brimmed with educational and entertaining articles, including profiles of Mouseketeers and Disney stars, crossword puzzles and games, instructions on how to draw your favorite Disney cartoon characters, behind-the-scenes reports from various television and movie sets, and such thought-provoking pieces as "Is There Life on Mars?" The magazine also featured ads for mouse ears, Mouseketeer roller skates, cowboy boots, and costumes, as well as Triple R Ranch T-shirts like those worn in *Spin and Marty*.

Soon Mr. Disney, a pioneer in the field of merchandising, authorized the manufacture of over two hundred Mickey Mouse Club products, such as the famous $4 Mattel-produced Mousegetar. You could get your very own Annette lunchboxes, Annette Colorforms dolls, Annette coloring books, and comic books and mystery novels based on my fictionalized adventures. Not too long ago a fan gave me a copy of one of these novels—in French!

One day Mr. Disney stopped by the set and called me aside. "Annette," he said, "you must have an awful lot of relatives back east, because you're getting more fan mail than anyone else."

What that meant, and the full force of *The Mickey Mouse Club* phenomenon, didn't truly sink in until we started making personal appearances. At first we usually worked on the show five days a week, then spent one day and most of the summer performing at Disneyland. At the Disneyland circus we Mouseketeers performed an aerial-ballet trapeze act five times a day. It was really spectacular and, I thought, glamorous. We Mouseketeers were paired up, and a boy and a girl worked together. The boy held the bottom of a rope ladder that was suspended from high in the air, while the girl climbed up and did acrobatic tricks. It could be a little scary, because as the boys pulled the ropes, the ladders swung way out. I just loved it! My mother dreaded it, though; she feared that someone was going to get seriously hurt. In fact, she couldn't even watch it. I'm sure the Disney people took every possible precaution, and we had safety hooks on our wrists, so I never worried.

It was at Disneyland that we got our first tastes of the perks of fame. Not only did we get to ride all the rides, but we didn't have to stand in line. Most people were happy to see us, so I don't think they minded letting us go ahead.

Even in my own neighborhood, people were beginning to ask me for autographs, and for a while one of my brothers was even selling my phone number. But generally we Mouseketeers encountered only one fan here, another there. While we knew that three-quarters of all the TV sets in America were tuned to our show each day, the real meaning of those numbers didn't register. It was hard to imagine ten million people loving what you did.

The true magnitude of Mouseketeerdom came into sharp focus through the windows of our tour bus. The show became so popular that we members of the red group made a number of road trips across the country and performed live. As always, our mothers, a great staff from Disney, and our tutor, Mrs. Seaman, accompanied us. In town after town we saw hundreds, sometimes thousands, of kids and adults lined up, cheering us as we rode by. The Mouseketeers played anywhere and everywhere, it seemed: school gymnasiums, local TV and radio stations, theaters and arenas, county and state fairs. Each Mouseketeer performed his or her specialty; for me, that was ballet.

Sometimes the crowd's response was just overwhelming, especially when people chanted "Annette! Annette! We love you, Annette!" I don't know if this bothered any of my fellow Mouseketeers; if it did, no one said anything to me. But it made me feel self-conscious. I knew it wasn't my fault that I got more mail than the others; it was beyond my control. It did make me wish that audiences would scream just as loudly for all the others, and that I could melt back in as just one of twenty-four. Perhaps if I or my parents had wanted nothing more in the world than for me to be a "star," I'd have felt differently. But that was not the case and never would be.

Wherever we traveled, Mr. Disney always felt that we had an obligation to visit and perform for disadvantaged and hospitalized children. These visits are still vivid to me, from the disinfectant smell of the hospitals to the squeaky sounds our shoes made on the polished floors. And the expressions on these little kids' faces—your heart would just break. We were quite young then and totally unprepared for some of the things we saw during these visits. I have to admit that on more than one occasion I left a hospital room feeling physically ill or emotionally exhausted after seeing a badly disfigured, burned, or critically ill child. But it didn't matter. We entertained them a bit, then visited the children and gave them stuffed dolls of all the Disney characters.

Some of my fondest memories of Jimmie Dodd come from these times. Very often, after smiling his way through a song or speaking comfortingly to a little one, Jimmie turned away with tears in his eyes. I don't think he meant for any of us to see him like that, but I did, frequently, and I respected him all the more.

Sure, we had our sad moments, but for the most part, we had a ball. I'll never forget one icy day when we were coming back on the bus from a performance. For some reason Jimmie really wanted us to catch the airing of *The Mickey Mouse Club* at five o'clock that day, but the weather slowed us down, and it didn't look like we were going to make it. Jimmie then said to the bus driver, "Let's just pick a house at random—a house that has bicycles in front of it. That way we know they have kids, and if they have kids, they have to be watching the show."

We stopped at the first bicycle-strewn lawn we saw, and Jimmie ran up to the porch and rang the bell. Someone answered, and Jimmie breathlessly explained, "I have a busload of Mouseketeers here who would like to stop in and see the show. Would it be okay?"

He was unprepared for the cynical reply: "Sure, sure, you have Mouseketeers!"

Jimmie turned around and shouted, "Come on, kids!"

Those poor people! Before they knew it, a crowd of us—in full costume, ears and all—scampered across their lawn, up onto the porch, and into the house. Needless to say, the residents were flabbergasted, but they soon recovered, phoned up all their neighbors, and served us a wonderful dinner.

We had our little scares along the way, too. One time when we were making a personal appearance in a department store, the crowd swelled to such huge proportions that they shattered a massive plate glass window. Pandemonium ensued as shards of glass flew and we scurried for cover, running this way and that. In the confusion one of the boy Mouseketeers lost his pants, which we all found quite amusing, but, thank goodness, that was the worst of it. Due in large part to the exemplary Disney security staff, no one was hurt. Incidents like this made my mother ever wary about my being out on the road, and who could blame her?

The show changed very little during its original run. The format remained fairly consistent except for the fact that, in our third season, 1957–1958, the length was cut down from one hour to half an hour daily. I suppose the only thing that wasn't going to remain exactly the same was us, the Mouseketeers. We were beginning to grow up.

The trials and tribulations of growing up were frequently the serials' underlying theme. My next job in a serial was playing Spin's girlfriend (sigh!) in the second installment of the popular *Spin and Marty* serials. One day my mother was sitting on the studio-theater steps, waiting for me, when a director casually remarked, "You know, I'm doing a *Spin and Marty,* and your daughter's going to be in it."

"Oh, come on now, you're kidding me," Mom replied. "They're all boys in *Spin and Marty!*"

"No, I've got the script right here!" he assured her. And he was right. I appeared in both *The Further Adventures of Spin and Marty* and *The New Adventures of Spin and Marty,* playing Annette, a camper from the girls' camp across the lake, the Circle H Ranch. My character's relationship with Spin would bloom into sweet—but of course chaste—romance. One bit of dialogue seems to portend my many onscreen personae for years to come. As Spin and Annette sit together, he observes, "It's a funny deal, getting married."

"I think it's *nice,*" Annette retorts.

Darlene joined us as Marty's girlfriend, and Kevin Corcoran reprised his role as Moochie, the irrepressible mascot. This series was filmed on location at the ranch Mr. Disney would eventually purchase, Golden Oak Ranch, in Placerita Canyon, which I loved to visit. In fact, the only shots in existence of Mr. Disney and me together without others were taken there during a wrap party for a *Spin and Marty* episode.

The serial that I'm most closely associated with, however, is *Annette,* which began running on February 10, 1958, toward the end of our last original season. (The 1958–59 season, which was part of the first run of the show, was made up of edited reruns from the 1955–56 and 1956–57 seasons.) Its theme song, "Annette," had been written for me by Jimmie Dodd, and earlier in the year I performed a ballet solo as he sang it to me. That was really one of the greatest thrills of my life, and I consider that song the most precious gift Jimmie ever gave me. Every time I hear the lilting melody and Jimmie's sweet, heartfelt words, the memories wash over me and I feel as if I'm hearing the song again for the first time:

Who's the little lady who's as dainty
    as a dream?
Who's the one you can't forget?
I'll give you just three guesses:
Annette! Annette! Annette!

When she dances on her toes,
    She dances in your heart,
With her pretty pirouette.
Each little move expresses
Annette! Annette! Annette!

Though she's just a cute preteener,
And her father's pride and mother's joy,
There will come the day
    They'll give Annette away
To the world's luckiest boy.

Ask the birds and ask the bees,
    And ask the stars above
Who's their favorite sweet brunette;
You know, each one confesses:
Annette! Annette! Annette!

You can well understand why just hearing the title of the song brings my parents to the verge of tears.

Annette's twenty-one episodes told the story of Annette MacLeod, a teenage girl who is orphaned after the death of her father and leaves her country home in Beaver Junction, Nebraska, to live with her wealthy Uncle Archie and Aunt Lila. Until Annette knocks on their door, her relatives, long estranged from her father, have no idea they even have a niece and immediately plan to send her off to boarding school. But Annette's sweet, unassuming charm soon wins them over, and the rest of the story concerns her problems as she adjusts to teenage life at upper-class suburban Old South High.

Life wasn't easy for Annette MacLeod, and I think that was one of the reasons viewers responded so enthusiastically to the series. After "the most popular boy in town" (played by Tim Considine) shows an interest in Annette, the "in" clique's queen bee, his girlfriend Laura (played by Roberta Shore), accuses the new girl of stealing her valuable necklace. Of course, by the end of the serial we learn that the necklace simply fell inside the piano Laura set it upon. But in the course of the story Annette is often embarrassed by her country ways and finds herself torn between her natural friendship with some of the town's less wealthy kids and the "better" group—led by Laura—her aunt pushes her to be friends with.

Although this hardly sounds like the stuff of high drama, the *Annette* serial, like the other *Mickey Mouse Club* multipart features, had surprising depth. While set in an idealized fifties teendom, where the cool boys drove hot rods, the girls wore charm bracelets, and we all drowned our sorrows in double chocolate shakes at the malt shop, *Annette* raised some interesting and mature issues. I suppose because Annette MacLeod was an outsider, kids saw something of themselves in her as she struggled to be understood and accepted while doing what her heart told her was right.

One of the best parts about the *Annette* serial was that it gave me the chance to work with so many of my friends. Mouseketeers Sharon Baird, Doreen Tracey, Tommy Cole, Bonni Lynn Fields, and Cheryl Holdridge as well as Tim and "Marty," David Stollery, also appeared. Uncle Archie, Richard Deacon, would be well known as Lumpy Rutherford's father on *Leave It to Beaver* and as Dick Van Dyke's boss, Mel, in his series; and Aunt Lila, Sylvia Field, was familiar to millions as the long-suffering Mrs. Wilson of *Dennis the Menace*.

There is a special place in my heart for one cast member in particular: Shelley Fabares. We first met in 1955 when Shelley, whose aunt is comedienne Nanette Fabray, happened to be taking instruction for her confirmation at Blessed Sacrament School in Hollywood.

We were both very shy, but we became friends and soon learned that we were very much alike. Shortly after that, she was cast in the "Annette" series as Moselle, a friend of Laura's. Over the course of filming we forged a lifelong friendship. I think the fact that we were about the same age and in the same business played a big part in bringing us together. As we grew older, and Shelley became famous in her role as Mary Stone on *The Donna Reed Show*, we found that we understood each other and the problems of youthful stardom better than anyone else we knew.

Shelley came into my life at a particularly trying time. *The Mickey Mouse Club* had been on the air only a while when it started getting difficult for some of us to lead normal lives. For example, it was impossible to go out to a restaurant or go shopping without causing a commotion. Of course, we loved our fans. Personally, I have always felt a tremendous obligation to them, and this feeling began back in my Mouseketeer days. But it was not always easy to keep a smile on my face when, for example, someone tapped my shoulder in church during mass and politely demanded an autograph.

And, lest anyone think otherwise, despite all the exposure of *The Mickey Mouse Club* and the hours I spent working with all the other Mouseketeers and the crew, my shyness persisted. I have to admit that being "in public" took a bit of a toll on me. It simply wasn't my nature to be outgoing all the time, no matter where I was. Shelley had very much the same natural temperament, so we spent hours together at her home or mine, talking, playing records, watching television, and phoning up our other friends.

I felt most comfortable at home, at the studio, or among close friends. During hiatus (our time off from rehearsing and filming), the tutors also got their vacations, so it was decided that for that period I should attend my neighborhood public school. Although I'd never been there before and was a little nervous at the prospect of suddenly being thrust among hundreds of strangers, I was determined to give it a try. After all, what could possibly go wrong?

I got my answer my first day of school. As I walked across the playground dozens of kids surrounded me, and wiggling their hands over their heads like big floppy mouse ears, danced in a circle as they chanted, "M-I-C-K-E-Y, here comes Annette!" over and over. Some of the kids followed me to my classrooms, to my locker, everywhere, taunting me. At first I tried my best to make light of it, tossing off what I thought were clever comebacks, like "Gee, I'm glad you know the words to every song!" But even trying to play along with it did nothing to endear me to them or stop the relentless teasing. Every day I ran home crying. "Mom," I pleaded, sobbing on my bed, "I can't go back to school! I just can't!"

My mother understood but felt that I had to make an effort. "You have to go back," she said gently, brushing the tears from my cheek. "After all, Annette, it's only three more weeks."

I returned the next day, and the next, but nothing I did or said swayed these kids; they never let up for a minute. Looking back, I have to say that they were at that age when it's cool to be a loudmouth, and being on television five days a week probably made me a more interesting target for their teasing than most. Still, I was heartbroken beyond words. The school's principal phoned my mother to admit there wasn't much they could do to help me. "It's not fair to Annette. Why don't you take her to the Hollywood Professional School, where she'll be with other child actors?"

My mother was reluctant to do that because she had so

many responsibilities at home, and the Hollywood Professional School was quite a distance away. Fortunately, my six-week hiatus was cut short when I was called back to film some more *Spin and Marty* episodes. For the next hiatus period, I was enrolled at the Hollywood Professional School. Lonnie attended there, so it wasn't as if I were among total strangers. Even though I didn't become especially close to any of my classmates—among whom were Sal Mineo and Lorrie Collins of the rockabilly duo the Collins Kids—everyone was so easy to get along with, and we were all in the same boat. No one was going to tease me.

When *Annette* began running, the amount of fan mail addressed to me personally started pouring in at the rate of between three thousand and six thousand letters a month. No one was more surprised than I and, I learned later, some of the studio people, who in the beginning were quite certain that another of the girl Mouseketeers would be the show's star. I suppose that was another aspect of *The Mickey Mouse Club*'s appeal: fans could pick their favorite from among us. Each Mouseketeer had his or her own following, and that was another reason the show never had a real star above all the rest.

Going through adolescence isn't easy for anyone, and despite the accolades, I was as insecure as any young teenager. Though it must sound odd coming from someone whose full adult height is five feet three, as I kept growing, I secretly worried I'd get fired for being too tall. Among the other Mouseketeers, I already felt that I stood out, with my dark curly hair and Italian features. Some believe this uniqueness made me appear "exotic," but like most prepubescents, I despised being different. I, too, wanted to be like everyone else—have straight blond hair that I could wear in pigtails, freckles, blue eyes, and a surname everyone could pronounce with ease.

One day I approached Mr. Disney and announced, "I want to change my name to Annette Turner."

Mr. Disney looked at me, obviously surprised and probably a little bit amused, and replied, "Why would you want to change your name, young lady? You have a beautiful name, but you're not pronouncing it correctly. It isn't Fun-is-sell-o, it's Funicello."

"But no one can pronounce Funicello," I replied. "How will anyone remember it?"

"Young lady," Mr. Disney answered firmly, "once they learn your name, they will never forget it. I promise you."

As usual, Mr. Disney was right.

One other surprise came from the *Annette* serial: my recording career.

In several episodes I sing a sweet, waltz-tempo ballad entitled "How Will I Know My Love?" The first time, I'm in my room alone; the second time, I sing it at a party and then am humiliated when Laura remarks, "How corny can you get?" and leads the gang out of the room, leaving me standing. Later in the story I sing the whole song on a hayride. At first I was going to lip-sync to another singer's voice, but it was decided that I should try to do it myself.

No one thought much about the song, and I thought even less of my singing, the product of what I call my three-note range. I didn't especially enjoy performing it, because, as far as I was concerned, I couldn't carry a tune. Apparently a lot of people disagreed, because the day after the hayride episode aired, thousands of callers from all over the country wanted to know where they could buy my record.

My record?

Mr. Disney asked to see me.

"I'm signing you to a recording contract," he announced.

"But, Mr. Disney," I replied politely, my voice surely betraying a hint of panic, "I don't sing. You know I don't sing."

"Well, the public out there likes your voice a lot," he said, "and I want you to do more."

Of course, being under contract, I really couldn't say no, although I'm sure that if I had been deeply unhappy about it, I wouldn't have been forced. But one thing about Mr. Disney that I always appreciated was his tremendous confidence in me. I couldn't understand exactly why he felt that way; it may sound funny, but in all the years I knew him, we never discussed it. One of Mr. Disney's many talents was his gift for seeing what you could do, not just what you thought you could do. We all know him as a man of great vision and imagination, but what made him unique was that he could apply that sense to people. In my case, he believed I could sing, even if I didn't.

He introduced me to Tutti Camarata, a musician, arranger, and record producer, who was well known for his work with such great singers as Perry Como, Billie Holiday, Frank Sinatra, Ella Fitzgerald, and Bing Crosby, to name only a few. He had played in Jimmy Dorsey's band and later wrote arrangements for Benny Goodman's orchestra, among others.

Tutti, who was in his midforties when we first met, took me into the recording studio and led me step by step through the entire process. I was extremely nervous, yet he put me at ease with his gentle direction and good humor. It was a wonderful experience until I first heard the playback of my voice. It convinced me immediately that this was not where I belonged. *This is a disaster,* I thought to myself. For the flip side of "How Will I Know My Love?" we recorded the old chestnut "Ma, He's Making Eyes at Me," which I enjoyed because it was so exuberant and uptempo. Still, I didn't delude myself. A singer I was not.

Upon release in 1958—to my total shock and surprise—"How Will I Know My Love?" sold several hundred thousand copies, and my recording career began.

C H A P T E R 4

*T*hrough 1956 and 1957 *The Mickey Mouse Club* continued to gain viewers. At the same time Mr. Disney
was in the midst of expanding the studio's production of television programs and live-action feature films. For these he
often cast various Mouseketeers and the serial stars. I think it
is to Mr. Disney's credit that, unlike many producers who
worked with child actors, he didn't pigeonhole us. Instead he
tried to broaden our careers by making us known outside *The
Mickey Mouse Club.*

For example, among Mouseketeers I was not the only one
to make records. And several Mouseketeers, including Karen
Pendleton and *Spin and Marty*'s David Stollery, appeared in
the 1956 Fess Parker film *Westward Ho, the Wagons!* Kevin
Corcoran ("Moochie") costarred with Tommy Kirk in *Old
Yeller* the following year.

The Walt Disney Studio's prodigious output demanded
that numerous projects be in the works simultaneously. Mr.
Disney and his staff were constantly scouting for great stories to bring to life on film. Among the early live-action productions he considered making was *The Rainbow Road to Oz.*
He explained to columnist Louella Parsons his reason for
casting so many Mouseketeers in it: "Many film stars move

to TV shows, and I think it's about time to move some of the TV favorites into motion pictures." With that in mind, Jimmie Dodd, Doreen Tracey, Darlene Gillespie, Bobby Burgess, along with Kevin Corcoran, Tim Considine, Tommy Kirk, and I were cast in what promised to be a wonderful children's fantasy.

We were so excited. What child wouldn't be thrilled to be "working" in Oz? *The Wonderful Wizard of Oz,* upon which the 1939 Judy Garland classic was based, was just one of fourteen Oz books Frank Baum wrote before his death in 1919. Shortly after *Snow White and the Seven Dwarfs'* astounding success, Mr. Disney had expressed interest in obtaining the rights to the remaining books, but it wasn't until 1956 that he received the rights to all the Oz books except two. Initially Mr. Disney planned to present his Oz story as a two-part episode on his *Disneyland* television program. But in 1957 he announced that the Walt Disney Studio would soon have a new feature-length film entitled *The Rainbow Road to Oz* in production.

I was to play the part of Ozma, the good fairy princess of Oz, complete with a beautiful gown and glittering crown and scepter. Bobby was the Scarecrow, Doreen the Patchwork Girl, and Darlene was Dorothy. For me, however, the best part of the film was that I got to wear a long, flowing fall. I'd always dreamed of having long hair, and I so loved the feel of it against my neck that I begged our hairdresser Ruthie to please, please, please let me wear my wig home. At first she said no, citing studio rules, but I wouldn't stop begging, and so she relented. I remember sleeping in the wig that night, twirling the long strands in my fingers as I drifted off to sleep.

Of course, I loved the original *The Wizard of Oz,* and despite this famous predecessor, everyone at Disney had high hopes for our film as well. We completed two scenes, one featuring the Scarecrow and the Patchwork Girl, and another that included me and just about everyone else in the Cowardly Lion King's court. These two scenes were shown on *Disneyland*'s fourth-anniversary program in September 1957, along with a finale, in which all of us in our Oz costumes, joined by the other Mouseketeers, including Roy and Jimmie, parade up the spiraling tiers of a giant birthday cake, singing about the rainbow road to Oz. We had no idea then that this was all of *The Rainbow Road to Oz* the public would ever see.

For various reasons, about which we can only speculate, the Oz film was not completed, despite Mr. Disney's deep and enduring personal interest in the concept. (Later he even considered adding an Oz attraction to Disneyland, but it was not to be.) Of course, everyone was disappointed; I loved playing Ozma, and this would have been my feature-film debut. But I didn't dwell on it. Even then, I trusted that things would work out for the best. Besides, by the time we learned that *The Rainbow Road to Oz* had met a dead end, there was other shocking news: *The Mickey Mouse Club* was closing its doors.

To this day, I still don't know precisely why *The Mickey Mouse Club* ended when it did. A show that well loved almost certainly could have continued for many more seasons. No doubt several factors led to the cancellation. Though still the leading children's program, it had lost some viewers. And with all the original music, the hundreds of costumes, and the unusually large staff, the show had proved exceedingly expensive to produce. The ABC network felt that we needed more sponsors, but Mr. Disney disagreed. He was of the opinion that the show contained too many commercials.

People are often surprised to learn that our original run was so short. Because the show went immediately into reruns, followed by years of syndication around the world, several generations can claim to have grown up with us, and we merry Mouseketeers remained, at least through the TV screen, eternally young.

You can well imagine the shock and sadness when we were told toward the end of 1957 that we would be shooting

The Mickey Mouse Club for only three more months. I wasn't a little girl anymore—I was fifteen then—but my feelings for the other Mouseketeers, Jimmie Dodd, Roy Williams, our directors, crew, Mr. Disney, and everyone else I'd met at the studio were overwhelming. This was my family away from home. I felt that I was losing much more than a job. *The Mickey Mouse Club* had brought me so much happiness. From my years there I learned the satisfaction of doing what I love, how to feel at least somewhat comfortable around new people, and the meaning of true friendship. It seemed to me and to some of the other kids that a wonderful part of our lives was being wrenched away. And there was nothing anyone could do about it. This was without a doubt the greatest disappointment of my young life.

A heavy sadness colored the remaining days on soundstage number one as we counted down to the end. We Mouseketeers were heartbroken, asking one another, "Why are they canceling our show?"

"It's so popular!"

"I can't believe it! How can they do this?"

Maybe because we were children, no one felt compelled to give us the full story. Maybe they thought we wouldn't understand.

As the last day drew nearer, I cried myself to sleep many, many nights. All through the final Friday of shooting, I wept until I was sure there were no more tears left. But there were. Sharon Baird and I carried our autograph books from friend to friend and made sure that everyone signed them. All of us Mouseketeers cried, and so did our mothers. Making it even more difficult was that last day's work. We were filming reaction shots in which we all had to laugh and smile as if we were the happiest kids on earth. Now, that took acting.

"Now, it's time to say goodbye. . . ."

At that moment I would have given anything just to stay there forever. Turning to leave *The Mickey Mouse Club* set for the last time, I felt as if I couldn't bear it. When would I see my friends again? And Jimmie? And Roy? If I could have seen into the future, I'd have found comfort knowing that the promise of our closing theme would hold true: "Through the years, we'll all be friends, wherever we may be." Most of our friendships did continue and grow over the next four decades. Our mothers remained close, and our fans have yet to forget us. At the time, however, it was just the end. I sometimes find myself wishing I could speak with Mr. Disney again and learn what he was thinking and feeling on that day.

In the midst of the goodbyes and the teary hugs, Mom and I felt somewhat uncomfortable. Sometime before this, one of Mr. Disney's associates had called me aside and said, "Annette, we have to talk about something very important." My first reaction was total panic as I thought, *This is finally it. They're finally going to fire me for growing too tall.* Instead, in a later meeting Mom and I were told that Mr. Disney wanted me to stay under contract to the studio after *The Mickey Mouse Club* ended. They also told us that I was the only Mouseketeer who would be staying.

The twenty-three others were being let go, and for many of them *The Mickey Mouse Club*'s demise marked the end of their performing careers. For weeks the main topic of conversation among the kids and the mothers had been, "What are you going to do next?"

Now, many of us, such as Bobby Burgess, Sharon Baird, Cubby O'Brien, Tommy Cole, Lonnie Burr, Darlene Gillespie, and Doreen Tracey, continued working in show business, some for a number of years. Sadly, however, most child performers find it difficult if not impossible to grow up in the business. This proved true for even some of those Mouseketeers who had worked professionally before. For years to come, strangers would tease, "Hey, where's your ears?" Though people usually meant it in a friendly way, some former Mouseketeers took it as a painful reminder of better days. While appearing on *The Mickey Mouse Club* opened our

worlds and changed our lives, the show's phenomenal popularity and the country's familiarity with its stars didn't open
as many doors as you'd expect. If anything, the beaming in-
nocence and childlike charm of our younger selves cast a
large, cheery shadow from which some Mouseketeers did
not emerge. Some who met resistance as they pursued more
mature roles became embittered. And who can blame them?
As I, too, had occasion to learn, off the Disney lot, it can be a
tough, heartless business, even for a Mouseketeer.

It still strikes me as ironic that of the twenty-four kids on
the show, I—the shyest, arguably the least interested in a
show-business career—was chosen to continue working for
the Walt Disney Studio. I've often been asked why Mr. Disney kept only me, and I honestly do not know. In my many
years at Disney I was never privy to what went on behind
closed office doors, nor did much studio gossip blow my
way. And, despite my closeness to and love for Mr. Disney,
ours was not a relationship of peers. He was older, and he
was my boss, one I admired and respected immensely. While
I do feel that I got to know him much better in the years after
The Mickey Mouse Club, still it would never have occurred to
me to call him Uncle Walt or to ask him why he chose me.
Others have guessed at the reasons, but the truth is, no one
really knows.

Now more than ever the lot became my second home. The
Walt Disney Studio was always a friendly place, and over the
years Mom and I had come to know just about everyone by
his or her first name. Being fifteen and a half, and finally able
to have a normal adolescence, I'm pretty sure I'd have retired
then had I not been able to remain at Disney, where I felt
comfortable and secure.

In August I began work on my first feature film, and Disney's first live-action comedy, *The Shaggy Dog.* Needless to
say, at first my nerves were jumping, but although it was a
new experience, it soon seemed just like old home week.
Among the other young actors were Kevin Corcoran and

Tim Considine, whom I'd worked with on the *Spin and Marty* serials; Roberta Shore, who played Laura in *Annette;* and Tommy Kirk. The biggest thrill, of course, was meeting and working with such established Hollywood stars as Jean Hagen and Fred MacMurray. For both of them, the film represented a return to comedy, and for Mr. MacMurray, it solidified his image as the genial though sometimes bumbling father, a role he went on to play in future Disney films and the hit TV series *My Three Sons.*

I'm sorry to say I never really got to know Mr. MacMurray well, although I admired him greatly. Also a quiet person, he was friendly but mainly kept to himself. On the last day of shooting, I mustered the courage to request his autograph, and he kindly consented, writing: "I worked with Kim Novak in her first movie, and look what happened. I have no doubt the same will happen with you."

This was quite lavish praise for me, especially considering the fact that if you blinked twice during the film, you probably missed me. I played Allison D'Alessi, Buzz's (Tim's) girlfriend, who—naturally—is offended when he displays undisguised interest in the sexy little French-speaking girl, Franceska, who moves in next door. This was probably one of the first times I got to use my pout, which would come in so handy later when Merlin Jones and Frankie eyed other girls.

The charming story involves a boy genius, Wilby Daniels (Tommy Kirk), who stumbles upon an ancient ring that purportedly once belonged to the evil Borgias of medieval Italy. Unbeknown to Wilby, simply reading the Latin inscription inside the ring invokes an ancient curse, and he is transformed into a large, shaggy sheepdog. Of course, no one believes Wilby the dog is truly Wilby except for his younger brother (Kevin)—especially not his dog-hating mailman father, played by Mr. MacMurray. Further complicating the plot are Wilby and Buzz's rivalry for Franceska's affections and her father's secret plan to steal U.S. military secrets, which Wilby learns of and tries to prevent. Does it have a happy ending? Need you ask?

Interestingly, in an age gone mad for Technicolor, Mr. Disney deliberately produced *The Shaggy Dog* in black and white out of concern that in color the supernatural aspects of the story would seem too realistic and offend or frighten viewers. Despite its far-fetched premise and a lukewarm critical response, *The Shaggy Dog* became a very popular and commercially successful film, paving the way for later Fred Mac-Murray vehicles, including *The Absent-Minded Professor* and *Son of Flubber* (which also starred Tommy Kirk).

Just days after we completed filming, I was back in the red schoolhouse trailer, studying with Mrs. Seaman. Mr. Disney walked in, smiled, and handed me a script.

"Happy sweet sixteen, Annette. You're appearing in *Zorro!*"

Zorro! Surprised, grateful, stunned, thrilled to death, I was practically speechless.

"Thank you, Mr. Disney," I managed to reply as I ran my fingers over the bound white sheets. "Thank you!"

Being famous didn't in any way hamper my being a typical teenager when it came to boys, or in this case, men. I must have had a million crushes—all quite innocent, but none as all-consuming as the one I had on Guy Williams, who played the television series's title role. Those of you who know Guy Williams only from the mid-sixties science-fiction series *Lost in Space* may have trouble reconciling the image of him in his polyester stretch space suit with the handsome and, yes, sexy, Zorro.

For those too young to recall the show, *Zorro* was essentially a nineteenth-century Batman. In "real life," Zorro was Don Diego de la Vega, a handsome, wealthy aristocrat in the old Los Angeles of 1820. As Zorro, a black-masked caped avenger, whose secret identity was known only to his servant Bernardo (played by Gene Sheldon), he pursued villains astride one of his stallions, Tornado or Phantom, and then dispatched them with a lash of his whip or a thrust of his sword. Each episode opened with the mark of Zorro: the letter Z, carved in three lightning-quick sword strokes.

When the *Zorro* cast and crew set up shop on soundstage three in 1957, I was still in mouse ears but quite susceptible to Guy Williams's charms. I thought he was simply the cutest guy I'd ever seen (except perhaps Ricky Nelson, another long-lived crush from afar). Because the cast and crew were predominantly male, Mr. Disney explicitly banned women and girls from the *Zorro* set. You'll probably be surprised to learn that little goody-two-shoes Annette snuck over to see "Zorro" every chance she got. Getting caught, usually by Mrs. Seaman, proved no deterrent. Because I blushed like a beet and my knees quaked every time Guy looked my way, I believed I was in love, and I'm sure everyone on the lot knew it.

Guy was nearly twenty years my senior, married, and the father of two, so the most encouraging response I ever got from him was a friendly puppy pat on the head. Yet I carried my torch and regularly asked him to autograph the latest *Zorro* publicity shot I had wangled out of the studio's PR office. Every night I drifted off to sleep hugging his eight-by-ten framed photo to my chest. Afraid I would roll over and break the glass, Mom snuck in every night and gently pried the picture from my arms. One night—as my mother predicted—it did crack, and that was the end of my "sleeping with" Zorro, although I later named a little black spaniel after him.

In a three-episode story that first aired in early 1959, I played Anita Cabrillo, a young Spanish girl who comes to Los Angeles in search of her father. Through his letters Anita's father has misled her into believing he is a rich and powerful man, yet no one in town knows of him, and none believes her story except Don Diego, who invites her to be his guest at his father's hacienda. While attempting to find her father, Anita rouses the interest of some villains, who try to kidnap her and at one point leave her perched precariously on a narrow ledge on the face of a cliff. It was exciting stuff. In a scene that takes place in the hacienda garden, I sing Jimmie Dodd's "Lonely Guitar," accompanied by an acoustic guitar.

My weeks with Guy Williams were perfect in every way, except that no kiss was written into the script. Looking back, I'm sure that my interest in him was plainly obvious to everyone, and probably more than a little amusing to Guy, who teased me and called me "Zorina." Yet he did nothing to embarrass me or make me feel like the smitten young girl I was, and for that I will always be grateful.

Despite its massive popularity, *Zorro* was canceled after only two seasons. But the characters were resurrected in several hour-long Zorro stories presented on *Walt Disney Presents* (the new title of Mr. Disney's anthology series). In 1961 I returned to *Zorro* in an episode entitled "The Postponed Wedding." I even wielded Zorro's sword, thrusting it into the chest of my no-good fiancé and sending him plunging off the side of a ship, if you can imagine that!

One happy memory of working on the show was the surprise sweet-sixteen party Mom arranged for me on the set. She brought in all kinds of delicious Italian food, which everyone loved, and we had a marvelous time. Guy carved a Z into the frosting of my cake, then I used the sword to cut the first piece. I always appreciated the little things like that that Mom and Daddy did to make my life as "normal" as possible.

Next Mr. Disney cast me as Chiquita Bernal, another troubled señorita, in "Attorney at Law" and "The Griswold Murder," parts five and six of *The Nine Lives of Elfego Baca*. After the amazing success of the Davy Crockett episodes he'd presented on his *Disneyland* program in 1954–55, Mr. Disney brought the stories of several other historical or legendary figures from America's early days to the small screen. *The Nine Lives of Elfego Baca* is not as well remembered today as the stories of Davy Crockett, Texas John Slaughter, or the Swamp Fox (played by Leslie Nielsen), but it was quite good, and its star, Robert Loggia, went on to a very successful film career.

Elfego Baca was based on the true story of a Tombstone, Arizona, gunslinger-turned-sheriff-turned-attorney who holds tenaciously to the then-revolutionary belief that disputes should be settled through the law, not with guns. As Elfego tells a disbelieving deputy sheriff (who turns out to be corrupt), "Sooner or later a man learns that a gun never ends a problem, only a life." If only children's television could be this good today.

Within weeks of completing *Zorro* and *Elfego Baca*, I was "loaned out," or permitted to work on a non-Disney production. Since I was under exclusive contract to Disney, any producer who wished to hire me had to obtain Mr. Disney's personal permission. He also had full script approval on any outside project I was involved in.

The minute I set foot on the set of the popular series *Make Room for Daddy*, it was clear that everyone who worked for Danny Thomas, cast and crew alike, adored him. This was especially true of Rusty Hamer, who played his wisecracking son, and whom Danny treated like a son off camera as well. (Unfortunately, Rusty's later life was not as happy; in 1990, at the age of forty-two, he committed suicide.)

Although Danny worked very hard and demanded perfection, no one complained. Offstage Danny Thomas was very much like the character he played: aggressive, gruff, plainspoken, and volatile. Yet I also saw a man of great intelligence, sensitivity, and kindness. Filming those episodes was one of the happiest experiences of my career. I simply adored Danny—another crush, I suppose—and often wore a large sweater he gave me.

Unlike the television series I worked on at Disney, Danny's show was filmed before a studio audience. Except for the shows we Mouseketeers performed out on the road or at Disneyland, I'd never worked live, so it took a little getting used to. Soon I grew to love the immediate response you get from the audience, especially when they laugh in all the right places. To play Gina Minelli, an Italian exchange student who comes to live with New York nightclub singer Danny Williams and his family, I learned to speak with an Italian accent and to sing in Italian. When I told them I didn't speak Italian or do accents, they hired actress Argentina Brunetti to coach me.

Before taping each show, Danny would come out and talk to the studio audience, sort of warm them up, using material from his nightclub act. Then he introduced each cast member. I stood in the wings nervously waiting for him to call my name. When he announced, "Miss Annette Funicello!" I walked out to thunderous applause, then glanced up to see three hundred people climbing out of their bleacher seats and heading for the stage. Heading for me! Danny and everyone on his staff were stunned. It took a studio policeman several minutes to restore order.

The six episodes each had a different story line, of course, but they basically revolved around Gina's attempts to fit in with her American peers and "Uncle" Danny's well-intentioned but misguided—and invariably forgiven—interventions. Many of these involved Gina's sweet but sometimes thick-headed American football-player boyfriend, Buck. I liked Gina Minelli; she was extremely intelligent (too much so for her own good, her "Uncle" Danny thought), sensitive, and charming. The show's writers gave me some great lines, too. In one exchange, Danny tries to persuade Gina to give American teenagers a chance, but she retorts that she can't understand their slang: "Everyone 'digs' something, but no one has a shovel!" Each time I heard the audience roar with laughter, I'd be taken aback for a second with the realization that they thought I was funny. Frankly, I didn't know I had it in me.

One reason for *Make Room for Daddy*'s immense popularity, and why it holds up so well today, is that the Williams family was much more realistic than many other TV families. Danny yelled at the kids, his wife, Kathy, gently ridiculed him, little Linda and Rusty talked back. In the first episode, when Gina's homesickness shows no sign of abating after Danny's done everything he can think of to make her feel at home—including giving himself a crash course in Italian art and opera—he blows up and really lets her have it. Which, of course, makes Gina feel right at home, because, as she explains through tears of happiness, her dear papa back in Palermo yells at her, too.

My time on the Danny Thomas set at Desilu Studios was a great learning experience, and so much fun. I adored the two children on the show, Angela Cartwright and Rusty Hamer; and my friend Judy Nugent, who'd played Jet in the *Annette* serial, appeared in it as my girlfriend. The fact that the scripts were of such quality and brimming with humanity and humor put the icing on the cake. My last day on that set was also sad, because I knew that, unlike many of the actors and the crew I worked with at Disney, these weren't people I'd get to work with again. Perhaps because of my early work experience, I still can't understand how you can see a group of people day in and day out for several weeks or months, get to know them well, then part ways and never hear from them again. It always struck me as unnatural. That's the way it is in this business, I know, but it's one thing I've never gotten used to.

All three of these television series happened to first air in February and March of 1959, *The Shaggy Dog* premiered that March, and *The Mickey Mouse Club* was still in reruns. Shortly before, in January, Disneyland Records had released my first pop single—and my first Top Ten hit—"Tall Paul." "How Will I Know My Love?," my first single, had sold about 400,000 copies, impressive numbers for the time, and so I wasn't surprised when several months later Mr. Disney set my recording career into motion.

Rather than return to the sweet ballad style of "How Will I Know My Love?," he and my producer, Tutti Camarata, decided to aim my next record squarely at the rock 'n' roll market, which in just a few years had exploded beyond everyone's expectations.

"Tall Paul" and my subsequent hits were rock 'n' roll, but without the edge. These were fun records: sweet and bouncy or softly sentimental. At the time, young clean-cut performers like the Everly Brothers, Frankie Avalon, Paul Anka, and Pat Boone were flying to the top of the charts with songs that celebrated the innocent romantic yearnings of young love.

The late fifties and early sixties marked the heyday of the teen idol. Handsome, romantic, gentlemanly Frankie, Paul, and the others were boys you could dream of falling in love with *and* introducing to your parents, something that couldn't be said for, say, Little Richard. Around the same time, young film and television personalities began venturing into music. For most—like Tab Hunter, Sal Mineo, and Edd "Kookie" Byrnes—preexisting fame ensured only a hit or two. Only rarely, as in the case of Ricky Nelson, did dreamy good looks and catchy records combine to yield a spectacular lifelong career.

Given the times, my recording career probably struck those at Disney as a logical step. After all, except for Connie Francis and a couple of other girls, there were few young female rock stars. In my own way, I suppose, I was the girl version of a teen idol: wholesome, perky, *a good girl.* Of course, I'm sure this makes it all sound very calculated, but I assure you it was not. In fact, the right song came to me through pure, happy luck, but what a wonderful piece of luck it was, for everybody concerned.

One day in 1958 two songwriting brothers, Robert and Richard Sherman, decided to put a twist on an age-old pop-song convention. It seemed to them that there had been plenty of guys singing to and about their girls: Buddy Holly's "Peggy Sue," Paul Anka's "Diana," Little Richard's "Lucille," the Everly Brothers' "Claudette," and countless others. What about a song that a girl could sing about her guy? they asked. With that idea in mind, the Sherman boys, as we've always called them, worked furiously, and two hours later finished "Tall Paul."

When it was first recorded, by Judy Harriet (coincidentally, another Mouseketeer), "Tall Paul" was not a hit. But someone from Disney happened to hear it played on a New Jersey radio station and brought it to Mr. Disney's attention. Everyone agreed that "Tall Paul" fit me perfectly. The simple, heavily accentuated lyrics had the playful bounce of rhymes kids recite while jumping rope. With the Sherman boys and Tutti behind me in the studio, I was relaxed and confident. The song itself was easy to sing. What tripped me up more than a few times was learning the clapping and finger-snapping routine that came after each verse line.

By March 1959 "Tall Paul" had reached number seven on the *Billboard* chart. I've always regarded the recording side of my career as something of a departure, a surprise bend in the road. For the Shermans, whose father composed such Tin Pan Alley classics as "You've Got to Be a Football Hero" and counted among his collaborators such greats as Ira Gershwin, it was an early step in what would become a long and illustrious career.

Over the next five years, the Shermans wrote thirty-five more songs for me, but this is not what they're most famous for. Rather, it is their amazing creative output during the eight years they toiled in an office at the corner of Mickey Avenue and Dopey Drive that earned them their place among the twentieth century's great songwriters. Not long after they'd joined the Disney staff, Mr. Disney asked them to compose something for *The Horsemasters*, a film I made with Tommy Kirk in 1960. This led to their writing songs for another Disney film, *The Parent Trap*; one of the songs, "Let's

Get Together," became an American and British hit for the film's star, Hayley Mills.

The Sherman Brothers wrote for dozens of Disney films, including *The Absent-Minded Professor, In Search of the Castaways, The Misadventures of Merlin Jones, The Monkey's Uncle, Winnie the Pooh and the Honey Tree, The Happiest Millionaire,* and *Bedknobs and Broomsticks.* They're probably most fondly remembered, however, for their musical contributions to Disney's second live-action musical feature, *Mary Poppins,* the animated classic *The Jungle Book,* and "It's a Small World," for the Disneyland attraction of the same name (which remains my favorite attraction). Interestingly, the Shermans didn't totally abandon writing rock 'n' roll. Their "You're Sixteen" was a hit for Johnny Burnette in 1960, then revived by ex-Beatle Ringo Starr some fourteen years later.

In the years since we first met, I've been pleased to regard Richard and Robert as among my dearest friends. Though they've been profiled in countless magazine articles and honored with Oscars and many other awards, I've yet to read a piece about them in which they do not mention our work together and credit my early hits for the role they played in their career. How proud I am that they consider me, in Richard's words, "our lucky star."

The Shermans' contribution to my singing career did not end with writing songs. While we were recording "Tall Paul," they and Tutti came up with the idea of double-tracking my voice and adding echo. In the studio, I sang along to a playback of the instrumental tracks. Then I sang my parts again to a playback that included my first vocal take. It sounds pretty simple, but matching the two sets of vocals in tone, pitch, and intonation could be tricky. With the added echo, my little voice suddenly had a distinct presence—wide-eyed, energetic, unerringly sweet—and the so-called "Annette sound" was born.

* * *

From an unknown would-be ballerina little more than three years before, I'd become a celebrity. Fan and movie magazines portrayed me as the queen of teen, a girlfriend next door who just happened to be a famous, successful actress and recording star. Each story had a happy ending. Even in the magazines that favored a more risqué approach (as in the headline "My Hobby—Collecting Boys"), I was the notable exception among other young actresses who, at least allegedly, were conducting torrid love affairs and running away from home. I was just a happy, well-adjusted, normal teenager.

And it was all basically true! While many young actresses of the time moved away from home early and became involved in numerous love affairs, I lived contentedly with my parents, Joey, and Michael until I married. Nowadays when writers profile me for magazines, they write something to the effect that back in those days I "represented" wholesomeness. In fact, though, I *lived* it, and it wasn't an act. Even in the late fifties and early sixties Hollywood tolerated promiscuity, drinking, and wild partying, and everyone knew who did what. While I wouldn't presume to pass judgment on anyone, that kind of lifestyle didn't attract me. I came home from work each day, sat down to dinner, helped my parents with chores and taking care of my brothers, did my homework, talked on the phone or had a friend over, then fell asleep. Despite my apparent success, my family hadn't become rich from it; my father still worked five days a week at his gas station, and we still did all our own housework.

Then and for the rest of my life, the minute I stepped off a lot or a stage, I left the public Annette behind. Among my family and friends I was not a star. My parents held me to the same standards of behavior as any "normal"—that is, non-show-business—child. The fact that I happened to be on television, in the movies, and on the radio really meant nothing as far as what my parents expected of me. Family always

My parents, Virginia and Joseph Funicello,
newlyweds in the early forties.

I was the first grandchild and
the first girl on either side of the family.
No wonder I was spoiled with love!

Here I am, three and a half years old and the flower girl at my Aunt Mickie's wedding in Utica, New York, July 1946.

LEFT: *I always loved dancing, but the drums were my first talent. Here I'm performing "Strike Up the Band."*

OPPOSITE: *These are just a few of the wonderful costumes my mother learned to sew for me.*

LEFT: *After winning the title Miss Willow Lake in an impromptu poolside beauty contest at age nine, I did some modeling.*

OPPOSITE: *Some of the cast of* The Mickey Mouse Club, *September 1957. (Left to right, back row): Tim Considine and David Stollery of the* Spin and Marty *serial, Mouseketeers Roy Williams, Lynn Ready, Jimmie Dodd; (third row) Don Agrati (Grady), Linda Hughes, Cheryl Holdridge, actor Tommy Kirk, Lonnie Burr; (second row) the Meeseketeers Karen Pendleton and Cubby O'Brien, Walt Disney, Kevin "Moochie" Corcoran, Sharon Baird, Bonnie Lynn Fields; (front row) Tommy Cole, Darlene Gillespie, and me.*

*My dear friend Jimmie
Dodd was the heart and
the soul of* The
Mickey Mouse
Club.

*Three merry
Mouseketeers. Left to
right: Darlene
Gillespie, my close friend
Sharon Baird, and me—
the twenty-fourth and last
chosen Mouseketeer.*

Left to right: David Stollery, me, and Tim Considine from one of the two
Spin and Marty *episodes I appeared in.*

OPPOSITE TOP: *One of the many lavish musical numbers* The Mickey Mouse Club *was known for. This is another scene from a* Spin and Marty *episode.*

OPPOSITE BOTTOM: *As a member of the "red group," I toured the nation and performed live with other Mouseketeers. My special number was always a ballet, seen here in a high school gymnasium.*

RIGHT: *This photograph — one of only a handful of Mr. Disney and me together without others —was taken during a wrap party for* Spin and Marty *at Mr. Disney's ranch.*

OPPOSITE:
*My first solo singing
number, "How Will I
Know My Love?,"
from* The Mickey
Mouse Club *serial
"Annette" was filmed
on the Walt Disney
Studio soundstage. I
never dreamed this
would be the beginning
of a recording career.
Seated to my right is
Tim Considine.*

RIGHT:
*Without my producer,
Tutti Camarata, to
support and encourage
me in the studio, I
don't think I could
have opened my
mouth.*

BOTTOM RIGHT:
*The Sherman brothers
—Richard (left) and
Robert (right) —not
only formed one of the
Walt Disney Studio's
most prolific songwrit-
ing teams but wrote
my biggest pop hits,
including "Tall Paul"
and "Pineapple
Princess."*

With my friend Dick Clark shortly after my first hits. The weeks I spent touring as part of Dick's Caravan of Stars in 1959 were lots of fun — and lots of hard work.

OPPOSITE TOP: *After the surprising success of "Tall Paul" and "First Name Initial," I, like most teen idols, performed live across the country.*

OPPOSITE BOTTOM: *In a rare public outing with Paul Anka, whom I was then dating. Although we spent most of our time together out of the spotlight, our relationship ended partly due to the pressures of our respective careers.*

From a teen magazine date layout, one of my favorite pictures of Fabian and me clowning around.

An all-American girl and
her family at our home in
Encino, California, 1959.
Left to right: Michael, Joey,
Mom, and me.

My passion for perfume goes
way back. At various times in
my teens, my collection included more than 150 different
scents.

On my first job off the Walt Disney Studio lot, I appeared with Danny Thomas in his television series Make Room for Daddy *in early 1959.*

came first, as I still believe it should, no matter what business you are in. The only stars we socialized with were the other Mouseketeers and their families, Jimmie and Ruth Dodd, Roy and Ethel Williams, and Shelley Fabares, and they were practically family, anyway.

I suppose because I came of age in the sixties, in Hollywood, in show business, some people find my attitude surprising. But when I look at my family and how I was brought up, really, I don't see how I could feel any other way. Thanks to their guidance, I've always known which way I was headed and why. Compared to the happiness and security I knew with my family, "temptations" normal teenagers and some other young performers succumbed to held no allure for me. As for the dazzling trappings of stardom—the premieres, the limousines, the beautiful gowns—I admit they were a lot of fun. But something to center your whole life around? Even at sixteen, I knew it wasn't for me. As my mother said one day when explaining to someone how she and my father managed to keep everything "normal": "Nothing impressed us."

Perhaps being such an apparent anomaly on the Hollywood scene added to my appeal. I think fans, especially the girls, liked me because my life resembled theirs in so many ways. Here I was, in movies and on the covers of magazines, yet forbidden to wear black until I turned eighteen or to wear eye makeup except on special occasions. Dozens of magazine articles invited readers into what one piece called "The Wonderful World of Annette." Yards of type quoted me talking about my latest adventures (with boys), sharing my dreams (about boys), and giving advice (about boys). Among my youthful pearls of girlish wisdom:

"Don't accept a dancing date if you're not a good dancer."

"Flirting can get you into trouble."

"It's all right for a boy and girl to 'make out' within the bounds of good taste." I wonder what I meant by that.

To read these pieces you'd assume I was on a twenty-four-hour-a-day date seven days a week with Phil Everly, Tommy Rettig (Timmy on *Lassie*), Tim Considine, Sammy Ogg, Bobby Darin, Bobby Rydell, and Tommy Kirk. In fact, my parents didn't allow me to date until I was sixteen, and even then I observed a strict curfew.

My first real date was with the young man who umpired my brothers' Little League games, Steve. I'd go to see my brothers play, and Steve and I would flirt a little. After I turned sixteen, Steve asked my father for permission to take me to a party. Daddy agreed, but added, "Annette has to be in by eleven."

"Oh, Dad," I wailed later. "Eleven! Nobody else has to be in that early! Nobody else has the strict rules I have!"

I cried in my bed that night, and the next day appealed to my father again. "Please, Dad, eleven o'clock is so early, I'm going to be embarrassed in front of the other kids." Eventually Daddy relented, although I think it was my tears that changed his mind, not my words. I got to stay out an extra half hour, and of course, was home right on time.

My parents trusted me, but they remained vigilant about who I dated. A year or so later I met a really cool guy at Disneyland, where I was performing with a live band for Date Night, a dance for teens. He was just a dream, as we used to say, and when he asked, "Can I come to your house and take you out?" I said sure.

The night of our date, I was just stepping out of the bathroom when I heard a loud *vroom, vroom, vroom.* The doorbell rang, then I heard my father say sternly, "I'm sorry, but Annette is not home." I was absolutely crushed, and when my date called me to ask what happened, I explained that my parents wouldn't allow me to go out with him because he rode a motorcycle. The next time he came to pick me up, he drove a car. He sat and talked with Daddy, and everything was all right. Of course, I'd been embarrassed, but I understood that my parents' protectiveness grew out of love. And almost without exception, their intuition about boys proved correct.

Was I ever a bad girl? Well, it depends on what you mean. Certainly I never did anything I couldn't have told my parents about, but, yes, there was one time when my heart overruled my head with potentially serious consequences. Ever since I'd worked at Disney there was one crew man whom I felt I truly loved. This wasn't just a crush, this was, to my heart, something more. Being ten years older than me, he sort of humored me. "I'll wait for you, until you're old enough," he told me, and sent me a beautiful bouquet of red roses for my sixteenth birthday.

As I got older, I honestly believed that he cared as deeply for me, though looking back, it's clear that I was reading it all through the eyes of an infatuated girl, not a woman. He owned a motorcycle, and several times we sneaked off the lot and rode up into the hills, to Mulholland Drive and Griffith Park, to enjoy the breathtaking view of Los Angeles. It was all perfectly innocent, but one day someone saw us leave and called my mother to tell her that if we ever left the lot together again, he would be fired. I understood, and we only saw each other at work after that. A couple of years later, while I was overseas working on a film, I learned he'd gotten married. I was surprised and, for a while, heartbroken.

I was an American teenage girl living in a house with a pool, her own telephone line, a bedroom furnished with a round bed, a hi-fi, a stack of rock 'n' roll records, and a menagerie of stuffed animals. A born clotheshorse, I kept a closetful of stylish clothes, including a rainbow of capri slacks to wear under oversized sweaters, dozens of pastel organza and chiffon party dresses, and frothy mountains of petticoats.

One of my favorite photos from the time is of me sitting before a vanity table covered with perfume bottles. In one article my perfume collection was reported to be about 150 bottles, and that's probably a conservative estimate. From the time I was twelve or so, I was famous—or maybe infamous is the better word—for my love of perfume; the sweeter, the fruitier, the better. Everything about perfume appealed to me: the color, the different-shaped and textured bottles, the mood each scent created, the simple, feminine act of dabbing it here and there. Or in my case, here and there and there and there. I practically bathed in the stuff. When I accompanied my parents on visits to our family friends, a heavy cloud of Shalimar or Jungle Gardenia hung around me, enveloping everyone in my path. To my young thinking, this was the epitome of sophisticated glamour. To just about everyone I came near, I was a walking headache. Finally, after my mother tactfully passed on our friends' complaints, I took the hint and toned it down—a bit.

During those years, my parents' one extravagant gift to me was a white 1957 Thunderbird convertible—wrapped in cellophane and gigantic red ribbons—they gave me on Christmas Day, 1958. My father, a lover of cars, thought it was too plain, so he took it to George Barris, a master at customizing. George later became famous for his imaginative work on the Monkeemobile and the original Batmobile, and in my opinion what he did to my little T-Bird was just as amazing. First the car was repainted my favorite color, purple. And not just any purple, but a smooth, glossy candy purple, made all the richer looking with *forty* coats of paint. The interior was transformed with yards of purple tuck-and-roll upholstery so luxurious you almost wanted to eat it, and a three-inch-deep purple shag carpet. Talk about a dream car. Before long the purple T-Bird was as famous as I was. Just a few years ago, a man contacted me and offered to sell me back the car for about ten times what Daddy paid for it. I said no thanks.

Although I'd reached the legal driving age in California, and I owned my car, my parents would not permit me to drive more than a few blocks away from our new home in Encino, up in the hills northwest of Hollywood. Actor Clark

Gable owned a ranch literally around the corner from us, a large piece of property that has since been subdivided into what is now known as the Clark Gable Estates. Over the next several years, I met and dated many of the idols of my generation, but in my opinion, there was nobody like Clark Gable. I'd seen *Gone With the Wind* about a dozen times by then (and have probably watched it another dozen since). The very thought that one day our paths might cross, that we might even meet—that would have been a dream come true.

Whenever I went out, I sort of casually looked for him. Then one day as I was driving down a main boulevard, not paying enough attention, a car suddenly emerged from Mr. Gable's private driveway and turned in front of me. I slammed on my brakes and looked up. There I was, gazing right into Clark Gable's eyes. I believe he recognized me, and as I stared blankly (probably with my mouth open), he smiled that incredibly sexy smile and, in a gesture that recalled Rhett Butler, tipped his golf cap, and cruised away. I was in heaven!

CHAPTER 5

With the Top Ten success of "Tall Paul," a whole new world opened up to me. Sure, having hit records was exciting, but to tell you the truth, I have a special fondness for this part of my career for more personal reasons. Unlike the movies or the television work I did after *The Mickey Mouse Club,* music brought me into a world of people my own age. Some of them—like Frankie Avalon—became dear, lifelong friends. And then there was my first true, albeit puppy, love, Paul Anka. My first hit launched my career into a new orbit, one that often spun around another good friend, Dick Clark.

During the years when I made most of my records, rock 'n' roll was still a new and predominantly American phenomenon. Looking back today, it appears that Elvis Presley opened the world for rock in one quick swivel of his hips. But, in fact, in the late fifties rock 'n' roll still met a lot of resistance and had its share of sworn enemies. Thousands of concerned citizens, police chiefs, and religious leaders called rock 'n' roll garbage and blamed it for everything from rising juvenile delinquency to the then-imminent Communist takeover. When Bill Haley and the Comets' first big hit, "(We're Gonna) Rock Around the Clock," played over the opening credits of the film *Blackboard Jungle* in 1955, the connection between rock and all forms of teen misbehavior seemed set. When the record became the first rock 'n' roll song to hit Number One, the rock era began.

Rock 'n' roll was a lot more than just music, though. For those of us coming of age during its first wave, these fresh new sounds comprised the soundtrack for the life of a new demographic category, the American teenager. Never before in history had so many postadolescents come of age at once. Unlike many of our parents, we weren't forced to go to work right out of high school; many of our parents could afford to send us to college. Also for the first time, girls didn't automatically assume they would marry after graduation, nor did they rule out pursuing a career. Neither young adults nor older children, teenagers were suddenly treated as a separate group, with our own language, our own styles, our own values and dreams.

I absolutely loved rock 'n' roll. In fact, I still do. Today it's not unusual to find me humming a Black Crowes or Guns N' Roses tune. (And, no, I'm not kidding.) Back then, of course, things were a little tamer, but my radio was on constantly, and my record collection grew weekly, as I ran to the record store to scoop up all the latest hits: the Platters, the Coasters, Sal Mineo, Jackie Wilson, Bobby Darin, the Drifters, Pat Boone, Connie Francis, Tommy Sands, Duane Eddy, the Everly Brothers, Johnny Mathis, Ricky Nelson—these were my idols. A typical teenager, I was never satisfied to just play the hi-fi or listen to my car radio—I had to blast them.

"Annette, can't you just please turn it down?" Mom used to beg.

"Why does it have to be so loud?" my dad would ask in exasperation. I didn't know. It just did.

Rock 'n' roll seemed to be everywhere, but nowhere was it more evident, more alive, or more enticing than on Dick Clark's *American Bandstand*. In its way, I suppose, *American Bandstand* had the same impact on older kids and teens as *The Mickey Mouse Club* had had on their younger brothers and sisters. *American Bandstand* was much more than a nationally televised record hop or the voice of authority for the day's Top Ten. For an hour and a half every weekday afternoon, host Dick Clark transported millions of viewers from around the country into a Philadelphia TV studio, where dozens of teens danced and clapped, bopped and strolled, held hands, rated records, and screamed for the guest-star idols. *Bandstand* resembled *The Mickey Mouse Club* in another way, too: the kids we saw rocking on the screen were real kids, just like us. Of course, they didn't have scripts, skits, costumes, or rehearsals, but in their own way, and in a lot of our hearts, they became stars. And by being on *Bandstand*, they disseminated their local trends in dance, fashion, hairstyles, and slang across the nation. The show unified kids everywhere, as they studied and emulated what they heard and saw every afternoon. We all subscribed to the basic belief that if it was on *Bandstand* it was cool.

Like most American teenagers of the time, I adored *American Bandstand* and Dick Clark, still the world's youngest teenager. Most of the time, I was working, but whenever a free afternoon came my way, I spent it dancing along to *Bandstand*. My long relationship with Dick and his show isn't really surprising, especially when you consider that from the day it was first broadcast nationally in October 1957, Dick and Mickey Mouse were "neighbors," at least in the TV listings. For the next five years, *Bandstand* preceded *The Mickey Mouse Club*. In those days, Dick always signed off by saying, "The Mouse is coming, and for now, Dick Clark, so long!" and giving his trademark salute.

Today when you think of show-business capitals, Los Angeles, New York, and Nashville come to mind. But from the mid-fifties into the early sixties, the heart of rock 'n' roll beat in Philly. The City of Brotherly Love was also, probably not coincidentally, the hometown of three of that era's biggest teen idols, three guys I've since been lucky to call my friends: Frankie Avalon, Fabian Forte, and Bobby Rydell. Why Philadelphia? Why not? After all, Philly had Dick Clark, who stood quietly yet firmly behind rock 'n' roll and, most important, behind the kids who loved it. With dark, clean-cut good looks (boy, did I have a crush on Dick!), a soft-spoken, friendly manner, and a wardrobe of conservative suits and ties, Dick looked nothing like what most rock-hating adults envisioned when they thought of the nation's biggest promoter of rock 'n' roll. Rather, Dick was more like your best friend's cool but married big brother, or the most understanding high school teacher you ever had. He just seemed so nice, and he really was.

Equally important, though, the kids who danced in the *American Bandstand* studio, and especially the so-called "regulars," quietly shattered the "rock 'n' roller as juvenile delinquent" stereotypes. No skin-tight capris or scruffy leather jackets there. Everyone dressed to conform to the *Bandstand* style: the boys in shirts and sweaters or sports jackets, and, of course, ties, while the girls spun around the studio dance floor in either straight, long skirts that gently hugged the hips, or full-circle skirts that bounced on clouds of petticoats. And who could forget those ubiquitous bobby sox and saddle shoes?

Dick Clark didn't really make rock 'n' roll safe for America, as some people think. If anything, by delivering it neatly wrapped to millions of American homes, Dick played a huge role in making rock 'n' roll a stronger cultural force than it might have been otherwise. Without intending to do so, he proved to parents and doubters everywhere that good, clean-cut kids could enjoy rock 'n' roll and still be good kids.

For anyone who had a record out, all roads led to Dick Clark's show. By listening to kids and studying the sacks of fan mail his show received, Dick chose the records he would play and the guests who would appear. On the program's most popular segment, Rate-a-Record, two members of the audience gave their opinions on a couple of new records and predicted—with uncanny accuracy, too—which would hit and which would miss. When it came to the music, Dick usually kept his opinions to himself. You never had the feeling that he was pushing one artist over another, or that he favored anyone. He treated everyone equally, which also made working with him such a pleasure. And as countless recording stars will attest, just appearing once on *American Bandstand* to perform your latest record was often the only boost it needed to become a hit.

When Dick Clark invited me on the show to do "Tall Paul" I was thrilled beyond words. And nervous. I looked forward to meeting him, but I began worrying about my hands. Yes, my hands. You see, from watching *American Bandstand,* I knew that after you sang your number (lip-synced it, actually), Dick came onstage, greeted you, and shook your hand. Whenever I began feeling nervous, my hands got cold and clammy. The thought of Dick Clark approaching me and then reaching out to hold what felt like a wet fish drove me crazy. I had to do something, and I did. From the first time I appeared on his show, and for some years to come, I never went anywhere without my gloves. It may have looked a little odd at first, but this was the fifties; older women in gloves were a common sight. And, after all, I was a teenager, and who knew what kids would be wearing next anyway? Without intending to, I launched a brief fashion craze, and within a few months I had a pair of gloves dyed to match every outfit in my closet. My glove thing became such an obsession that my mother and Paul Anka eventually spent hours trying to talk me out of wearing them onstage. Sometimes I'd oblige them, but more often than not I'd slip on a pair at the last minute.

In addition to *Bandstand,* beginning in February 1958, Dick hosted *The Dick Clark Saturday Night Show,* a weekly hour-long all-rock program that featured a lineup of rock stars sans dancing kids and Rate-a-Record. It was more like a rock 'n' roll *Ed Sullivan Show,* minus the jugglers. The *Saturday Night Show* was broadcast live from New York City's Little

Theatre on Broadway at Forty-fourth Street, in the heart of the theater district. For rock performers of the time, a spot on *Bandstand* was considered a great coup and an almost guaranteed promotion bonanza, but an invitation to the *Saturday Night Show* meant that Dick really liked you. It was prime time, at night. It was New York. It was the top. And best of all, it meant a trip to New York City. The day I learned that Dick wanted me on the *Saturday Night Show,* I felt like I'd really made the grade.

Over the next several years I'd find myself in New York on a regular basis, and I loved it. The Big Apple was a different place then, still clean and safe. The "in" place was the Harwyn Club, a posh Manhattan dinner club, where on any given night I might run into Bobby Darin and Connie Francis, Joey Dee and the Starliters, Sal Mineo, Dion DiMucci of Dion and the Belmonts, and whoever else was in town.

Another reason I hold such fond memories of those days in New York is that while working on the *Saturday Night Show* I had the privilege of seeing so many truly magnificent singers perform. There was my friend Bobby Darin, whom I've always felt was never as appreciated as he deserved to be; Jackie Wilson, whose lightning-quick but graceful dance steps had women swooning in the aisles; and the incredible Connie Francis.

I have especially fond memories of Connie and Bobby, with whom I worked many times in those years. I felt a natural rapport with Connie, perhaps because our relationships with our families were so similar. Like my parents, hers were deeply involved in her career and always there to support and encourage her. I remember once going backstage to say hello before a show and seeing Connie's mother gently holding her daughter's hand. It was such a loving, tender gesture.

Connie and Bobby were at the time very deeply in love. In the late fifties and early sixties, they were both at the peak of their careers, but whenever I saw them together, it was obvious that they cared more about each other than anything else. At one of Connie's club dates in Los Angeles, I happened to glimpse Bobby in the audience. From the look on his face, he was not only in love with but so proud of Connie. Unfortunately, like too many show-business relationships, theirs eventually crumbled under the weight of their professional obligations and ties. It made me wonder sometimes if their story, as well as some others I've known, might have had a happier ending if they were people you'd never heard of.

Over the next two years I made many appearances on *American Bandstand* and the *Saturday Night Show,* and got to know not only Dick Clark but many of the *Bandstand* regulars, many of whom had followings of their own. I became especially close to Arlene Sullivan, a sweet little brunette who'd begun dancing on the show when it was still a local program. With her partner Kenny Rossi, Arlene, along with Justine Carrelli, Bob Clayton, Pat Molitierri, Carole Scaldeferri, and the others, became such a celebrity in her own right that she received thousands of fan letters and even had her own column in 16 Magazine. One of my favorite parts of going to Philly was spending the evening after the show having dinner or going out with Arlene and some of her friends.

Before long, going to Philadelphia for *American Bandstand* was really more like going to visit old friends. But with the hits, I found myself bouncing all over the country, as always with Mom and a tutor in tow. The music business was entirely different then, and rock was so new that virtually everyone in it was a pioneer of sorts. In just a few years the older, more established segments of the music business had been sent reeling at the unlikely success of artists like Elvis Presley and Jerry Lee Lewis, not to mention some of the more eccentric figures.

Today we have music video networks and an international media reporting on rock music and its stars constantly. Back in the fifties rock 'n' roll was a fiefdom ruled by powerful local disc jockeys and promoters. Except for appearing on one of Dick Clark's shows, or, if you were really fortunate, landing a guest spot on one of the network variety shows, like Ed Sullivan's or Pat Boone's, there were few ways to effectively promote a single nationally. Getting out and working your latest record usually involved traveling thousands of miles to appear at radio stations and rock 'n' roll TV shows, as well as record hops, which were dances sponsored and hosted by local disc jockeys.

One of the more popular DJ shows then was Peter Potter's *Jukebox Jury*. Like most local rock 'n' roll shows, *Jukebox Jury* was not unlike *Bandstand*. One big difference, however, was its record-rating segment, which included celebrity judges. During one of my appearances, my latest record happened to be a Sherman Brothers composition, "Jo-Jo, the Dog-Faced Boy." I liked the song, but I must admit that I wasn't so sure it would be to everyone's taste. Let's just say different.

Sometimes the performer whose new record was being judged was in the studio and sometimes not. In the case of "Jo-Jo," I waited backstage, worried to death that no one would like the record and then I would have to walk out smiling, and then what? I just couldn't relax. Fortunately, one of the celebrity jurors that day was actor Tab Hunter, and he knew I was present. While I'm pretty sure he was less than crazy about my record, he gallantly and generously gave it an incredibly high and probably undeserved rating. As a result, no doubt, the other jurors followed suit, and so when my name was announced, I emerged smiling and forever grateful to Tab.

It's funny how one thing leads to another. For example, I first met Dick Clark when I was asked to perform at a concert held in his honor at the Hollywood Bowl. Although still based in Philadelphia, Dick had come to Hollywood to work on his first motion picture, *Because They're Young*. It was Dick's first trip to Los Angeles, and the show, "A Salute to Dick Clark," was the first rock 'n' roll show ever to be held at the Hollywood Bowl, a venue usually claimed by symphony orchestras. Also on the bill that night were Frankie Avalon, Bobby Darin, Freddy Cannon, Duane Eddy, and other rock stars.

It was a wonderful evening, and one of the first times I'd performed any of my records live. Even with all the shows I'd done at Disneyland and on the road with the Mouseketeers, nothing was ever like this. To look out into the night and see over eighteen thousand screaming kids took my breath away. Experiencing all that energy is something I still find hard to describe. It goes without saying that I was petrified. Yet at the same time, there was something wonderful about it that made me wish I could enjoy it more.

The Hollywood Bowl concert holds a special place in my heart for another reason. It was right around that time that I met one of my best buddies for life, Frankie Avalon. Frankie's career had recently shifted into high gear, and as one of his biggest fans, I owned copies of all his hits: "Dede Dinah," "You Excite Me," "Ginger Bread," "What a Little Girl," "I'll Wait for You," and, naturally, the single that was just about to hit Number One when we first met, "Venus."

At this point, I also had a big crush on him, too. Soon after we met, a little romance sparked, but it was kid stuff. My parents absolutely loved Frankie and still consider him part of our family. What I loved about Frankie—his kindness, his sincerity, his terrific sense of humor—were traits that also make for great friendship, and that is what our relationship soon became and has remained. Today, we're older and wiser—or so we like to think! In fact, today Frankie is a grandfather! And not to say that Frankie's not a good-looking man today, because he certainly is, but back in early 1959, he was, in a word, a dream.

Frankie grew up in Philadelphia, with his eye on show

business from a very early age. A musical prodigy on the trumpet, he won a number of local talent shows before appearing on several national television programs. As a teen he joined a local group called Rocco and the Saints, which included another future "boy of *Bandstand*," his good friend drummer Bobby Ridarelli, better known as Bobby Rydell. In fact, Frankie, Bobby, Fabian, and the actor James Darren all grew up in the same neighborhood. Managed by Bob Marcucci, who would also manage Frankie's friend Fabian Forte, Frankie was signed to Bob's label, Chancellor Records. He released two unsuccessful singles before hitting the top ten in 1958 with his debut single, "Dede Dinah." The funny thing about the record was that Frankie didn't really like the song and so, as a joke, recorded it while pinching his nose. In 1958 it hit number seven, and his career took off.

For a while there, it was Frankiemania. Once, during a rehearsal for *The Dick Clark Saturday Night Show*, screaming girls ran down out of the audience during an afternoon rehearsal and tore poor Frankie's clothes to shreds. But Frankie never seemed to mind. In fact, he found it all pretty amusing. Unlike me, he always felt at home onstage and learned to take life on the road in stride. I learned a lot from Frankie, not only about the business, but about friendship.

Not surprisingly, the teen magazines absolutely ate our relationship up, and for the first time coined the now-immortal term: "Annette and Frankie" or "Frankie and Annette." It would be several years before our first beach-party movie together, but looking back, I can see that we must have been destined to be together, if not romantically then certainly the way we are now.

Around the same time, Frankie's friend Fabian was just entering the charts with his very suggestive "I'm a Man." Frankie himself was cute in a sort of young Frank Sinatra way; you know, clean-cut, sweet. Fabian, however, was something else: sexy. It was an image his records—like "I'm a Man," "Turn Me Loose," and "Tiger Man"—drove home with a vengeance. His wearing skin-tight pants didn't hurt, either. Sporting a long, high pompadour and stunning blue-green eyes that peered sleepily, or dreamily, Fabian had more than a passing resemblance to Ricky Nelson. In fact, he'd acted as a decoy for Ricky at one of his Atlantic City concerts in 1958, before Fabian's own singing career began. Fabian soon replaced Guy Williams as my biggest crush. And if my parents had been less than thrilled about my sleeping with Guy's picture pressed to my chest, imagine their exasperation at having to hear Fabian softly growl, "Turn me loose . . ." over and over every single night. That was how I fell asleep, with Fabian crooning in my ear—via the hi-fi, of course. It drove my folks absolutely crazy.

I finally got to meet Fabian later that year in Chicago, where we were appearing on a show with Dion and the Belmonts, Paul Anka, Lloyd Price, and the Skyliners. We said hello and chatted a little, but we really got to know each other well back in Los Angeles, where we posed for a date layout on the beach.

Now a "date layout" was really just a planned "date" that the fan and movie magazines arranged and then photographed and reported on in the next issue. By then we'd each done dozens of these, but this one was special. Fabe's hair got totally mussed, and I kiddingly shoved a wedge of watermelon into his face, then we doused each other with hoses. We got to be big kids for the day, and it was wonderful. You can see from the pictures what a great time we were having. That part of it was never staged.

And what more perfect end to a beautiful day than to have Fabian ask me out that night?

I was breathless, until, of course, I realized that my naturally curly hair—my crowning glory and at times the bane of my existence—would never be dry in time and I'd have to go out with it wet. But what girl could turn down Fabian? And so I pulled my damp locks up into a ponytail, put on one of my hooded tops (which, thank goodness, were all the rage that season), and off we went. There I was on the dream date of a lifetime with a hood over my head.

Overall, it turned out to be a fabulous night, but a big romance wasn't in the cards for Fabe and me. I'm very happy, though, to say that we have continued to work together and remain friends.

Back in the late fifties, there were really four major teen idols: Ricky Nelson, Frankie, Fabe, and Paul Anka. Ricky and I had crossed paths a couple of times, and while he was endearingly sweet, he was also extremely, almost painfully shy. One time a boy I knew happened to be with Ricky, phoned me from wherever they were, and put Ricky on. I almost died! But we didn't have much to say to each other, although through the years I always enjoyed being in his company whenever we met or worked together. Of course, I had grown up with Ricky from his family's television series, *The Adventures of Ozzie and Harriet*, and loved his records, like "Be-Bop Baby," "A Teenager's Romance," "Stood Up," "Never Be Anyone Else but You," and "Lonesome Town."

And then there was Paul. You would think that with all the traveling we both did promoting our records, Paul and I would have met somewhere on the road, but we hadn't. Paul's manager, Irvin Feld, happened to be a friend of some friends of my parents. When he asked if Paul could meet me, my parents agreed, and a dinner was arranged. During the course of our dinner Mr. Feld, who was also a big promoter, asked if I would like to join Dick Clark's upcoming Caravan of Stars tour, which I'll tell you all about later.

I liked Paul well enough, but at first I didn't sense the kind of attraction I'd felt toward Frankie or Fabian. As I would learn, however, that was because Paul was a very different kind of boy. Eventually Paul and I developed a close relationship. He was unlike any boy I'd ever met. Though handsome and charming—and, it goes without saying I suppose, the idol of millions—his attitude toward his career and life in general was more intense, more serious, than that of most young men his age. Although he got lumped in with all the other teen idols, Paul stood out, always following his own path. Not only was he just sixteen when he made his first record, but he wrote most of his own songs, a real rarity in those days. Whereas other performers might have been content to stick with the teen market, Paul, like Bobby Darin, wanted to transcend the teen genre and be taken seriously as more than a teenage crooner.

Judging from his astounding success, I think it's safe to say that Paul's dream did come true. He's composed hundreds of songs, including Buddy Holly's "It Don't Matter Anymore," the English lyrics to Frank Sinatra's "My Way," Tom Jones's "She's a Lady," the theme for *The Tonight Show*, and movie scores, as well as his own hits, running from 1957's "Diana" to his 1974 Number One hit, "(You're) Having My Baby."

Initially Paul's no-nonsense attitude didn't appeal to me. I was used to guys who wanted to have fun: maybe go out for pizza or to a show. Paul, in contrast, wanted to talk about *things,* important, serious things. In fact, we sort of fell in love over the phone, during several of the hundreds of three-hour-long late-night conversations we shared over the next few years.

One of the best things about the time I was dating Paul was the unyielding support he gave me. I suppose because he was also reserved in his own way, he understood how I felt, and he did so much—through little pep talks or just a squeeze of his hand—to make me feel more confident. I don't think I could ever thank him enough for the many wonderful things he did for me.

My romance with Paul really bloomed when we were both booked on Dick Clark's Caravan of Stars tour in the summer of 1959. By then I had released several more singles and had a couple of more modest hits, including "Jo-Jo, the Dog-Faced Boy" and a somber, all-electric version of Jimmie Dodd's "Lonely Guitar." Neither of them went Top Ten, but

I took it in stride, knowing how unpredictable the business could be. The Sherman Brothers worked very hard, constantly coming up with new songs, so I felt it was only a matter of time. And if, for some reason, the legacy of my recording career was a single hit, so be it.

Going on Dick's Caravan of Stars tour, however, forced me to look at my career in a new light. Night after night for six long weeks, we traveled across the country doing one, sometimes two, shows at each stop. Difficult, grueling, exhausting, the Caravan of Stars was an experience few performers, not even Dick himself, look back upon with unalloyed fondness. However, that tour brought me out into the world, and in a sense, out of my shell.

Through the late fifties and early sixties package tours, for which a group of acts traveled together and performed a string of one-nighters, were very popular. Rock 'n' roll wasn't the big business it is today, and very few acts could economically mount an extended tour on their own. Promoters such as Irvin Feld, Dick Clark, Alan Freed, and other disc jockeys often assembled the acts and handled the booking and the itinerary. More often than not, acts traveled by bus, all hours of the day and night. Suffice it to say, this was not the most glamorous aspect of the rock 'n' roll star's lot, nor the most lucrative. And, with all due respect to Dick's class and concern for his artists, the Caravan of Stars was no exception.

"Caravan of Stars" conjures up quite a romantic image: a long train of buses and cars, filled with happy stars, traveling merrily from town to town, perhaps even singing as they went along. Ha! The Caravan (which, by the way, was the name of one of Dick's early Philadelphia radio shows, "Dick Clark's Caravan of Music") was actually one bus that seated about thirty. And when I say "seated," I should probably add "slept," too, since on the nights when time was very tight, the performers dozed fitfully as the bus hurtled through the darkness to the next town. All the performers' equipment, their clothes, their food—everything was packed onto that one bus. Whenever time allowed, the Caravan would stop overnight so everyone could get a good night's sleep and freshen up in a motel, but in some parts of the country, where racial segregation was still the norm, the black artists wouldn't be allowed in. Dick, much to his credit, decreed that if an establishment refused to accommodate even one of his people, none would eat or sleep there.

When I was first invited to join the Caravan, it sounded intriguing yet frightening. First, I would be singing live, something I hadn't done that much of yet. Also, remember, on all my records, my vocals were double-tracked and echoed. The Annette you heard blaring from your car radio sounded a lot better than the Annette you might hear singing around the house. Or onstage. I spent a lot of time worrying about whether or not I could handle the rigors of touring and facing a live crowd every night, without the sonic accoutrements of my "Annette sound."

My second concern was the travel. As I've said, Mom and I had been taking trips here and there, making appearances, but usually it meant a few days or a week away from home at a clip. We weren't happy about it, but we made friends wherever we went and always managed to have a good time. But six weeks away from Daddy, Michael, and Joey? That part was going to be difficult.

On the brighter side, though, I was almost seventeen and felt up for new challenges. In the past several months, I'd found myself in a whole new world, what with making new friends in Philly and in New York. The whole rock 'n' roll scene—everything about it, everyone in it—was colorful and exciting. So, my misgivings aside, I began looking forward to the tour. It seemed like a great opportunity to see the country and to feel like part of a group again. You know, just one of the guys.

The star-studded roster for Dick's first Caravan of Stars

was a Who's Who of rock: the great R&B singer LaVern Baker, the Drifters, Bobby Rydell, Duane Eddy, Paul Anka, Jimmy Clanton, the Coasters, the Jordan Brothers, Phil Phillips, Lloyd Price, the Skyliners, and others. The Caravan of Stars, and large package tours like it, were important not only because they brought rock 'n' roll performers to high school auditoriums, state fairs, civic centers, and other venues all over the nation, but in some places, they presented the first racially integrated bill those folks had ever seen.

Large package tours also brought together a wide variety of acts, so there was something for everybody. LaVern Baker, for example, had long been a favorite R&B artist, with such hits as 1953's "Tweedle Dee" and "Bop-Ting-a-Ling," followed a few years later by "Jim Dandy," and finally in early 1959, her first and only pop Top Ten hit, "I Cried a Tear." At the other end of the pop spectrum was Freddy Cannon, a young white man from Massachusetts whose big hit that summer was the rollicking "Tallahassee Lassie." His later hits would include "Palisades Park," "Way Down Yonder in New Orleans," and the theme song for Dick's midsixties afternoon rock show *Where the Action Is.*

Being such a rock 'n' roll fan myself, I thought one of the best parts of the tour was getting to see these great performers work close up. I especially enjoyed watching Lloyd Price, another longtime R&B star who found favor with rock audiences during that wonderfully open-minded time. A native of New Orleans, Lloyd wrote a number of his biggest hits, including "Personality," and also in early 1959 had topped both the pop and the R&B charts with "Stagger Lee." The highlight of his segment was the end of his closing number, "Stagger Lee," when Lloyd, resplendent in a gorgeous white suit, and several of his background singers crouched down at the edge of the stage like they were shooting dice and sang, "Oh, Stagger Lee, oh, Stagger Lee." The audience always went wild for that. It was really something to see, and no matter what else I was supposed to be doing backstage—like studying!—I always found my way to the wings to catch the last bit of Lloyd's act.

Having the beginnings of a crush on Paul Anka didn't stop me from paying close attention to the very handsome and very kind Duane Eddy, who was only a few years older than me. One of the first male rock stars who didn't sing, Duane was famous for his "twangy" guitar sound, captured in a series of hits, including "Rebel Rouser," "Ramrod," and "Forty Miles of Bad Road." Duane had the most sensuous eyes, and I admit that on a couple of occasions, while Mom and my tutor napped in the back of the bus, we stole a few kisses.

Another young man on the tour I really liked, but only as a friend, was Phil Phillips, whose sole hit was the original version of the ballad "Sea of Love." He was a soft-spoken, well-mannered guy, and he sang so beautifully. I was surprised that his career didn't continue.

Also on the tour were the Drifters, one of the era's premier vocal groups. Like many vocal groups of the time, the Drifters endured through many, many changes in personnel. The version on this tour, however, included the great Ben E. King, and their signature number then was the classic "There Goes My Baby," a song I never tired of hearing. This basic lineup would later chart such romantic hits as "This Magic Moment," "Dance with Me," and "Save the Last Dance for Me." At the other end of the spectrum were the Coasters, five black singers who tore up the stage with their raucous comic vocals, stunning choreography, and unforgettable hits: "Yakety Yak," "Charlie Brown," "Searchin'," "Along Came Jones," and "Young Blood," to name only a few.

All this and more for just $1.50 a ticket! How could you go wrong? Not surprisingly, the Caravan of Stars drew fans from hundreds of miles around wherever we played. For lots of those kids, it was the first rock 'n' roll show they'd ever seen, and that made it even more exciting for us as performers. Sometimes the kids got a little too carried away. In the wake of the riot that broke out during an Alan Freed show in Boston the year before, all of us performers were acutely aware of how easily a crowd of rambunctious kids could get out of control. Dick, ever mindful of maintaining his good reputation with local civic leaders and promoters, instructed us to stop singing if the crowd started to get wild. Thankfully, that rarely happened, and the kids' excitement was inspiring and contagious. After all, I was still just a kid, too, and as much a fan of my costars as anyone out in the stands.

I embarked on the Caravan of Stars tour naïvely hoping that among my peers I might get to be just one of the gang. But not long after we boarded the bus, I realized that I could never be. At least not there. For one thing, I was at least a couple of years younger than some of the other performers, and in the case of LaVern Baker and the Drifters, younger by ten or fifteen years. Even some of the people around my age were in many ways older, matured and hardened by years on the road that made my career look like a recital in a nursery school in comparison. I'd come to know Dick as a pretty straight, level-headed guy, and so I assumed that the tour would be run as strictly as the *Bandstand* dress code. Boy, was I in for a surprise.

Dick ran a tight ship, as far as the show went. But when it came to the personal lives and offstage behavior of the performers, his approach was strictly hands off, which is as it should be. The problem, then, wasn't the other performers—who welcomed me warmly—but me. As I learned later from Paul, when they heard that I was coming on the tour, they were informed to clean up their acts offstage: no cursing, no drinking, no messing around in front of Annette. Needless to say, and perhaps understandably, people—adults—who toured as hard as this for a living weren't too happy to have to change their behavior simply because little Annette would be joining them. From time to time I sensed a tinge of resentment, but I didn't really understand why, and I was too shy to ask outright.

Still, Mom, my tutor, and I soldiered on, full of optimism. After all, how bad could it get? We soon found out. Thinking back to this time, I always recall an image of my mother practically staggering under a pile of my dresses and petticoats, struggling to hold on to all that and the little "portable" (and you know what that word meant in those days: small and heavy) typewriter I needed to complete my schoolwork. Mom also carried with her a portable iron, so she could press my stage clothes backstage before I went on. What a sight that was! Mom bending over a makeshift ironing board, sometimes by the glow of a single lightbulb, while my tutor and I pored over my lessons. Invariably, the show began and the music washed over us, drowning out our words and sometimes even our thoughts. I reveled in it. Lots of kids did their homework to music, but how many got to compose book reports with the Drifters singing just twenty feet away? I almost drove my tutor crazy with my incessant finger-snapping or toe-tapping. What could I say? I was born with rhythm. I just couldn't help it.

My tutor, who never learned to appreciate the rock 'n' roll lifestyle, seemed to dread almost every minute. And I wasn't much happier. At the time, California had the strictest regulations regarding a young performer's education on the road. There were so many times when I just wanted to take a catnap or watch the show, but my tutor would remind me, "You finished only two hours of work today. You've got another hour to go," and then it was back to the books. Of course, Paul's putting a realistic-looking rubber snake in another tutor's bed one night didn't exactly help matters either.

For my first tutor on the tour and my mother, the adventure ended almost as quickly as it had begun. We opened in a New York City suburb. Until then I don't think I ever saw a place so jam-packed or a mob of kids so wildly happy. Before each show we were instructed on the strategy for leaving the auditorium. These instructions were as elaborate as battle plans, and that's no exaggeration. The kids in the crowds sometimes got themselves worked into such a frenzy that stepping outside the stage door you felt as if you were entering a war zone. The big flashbulbs exploded just inches from your face, while scissors cut through the air—and your hair and clothes—as fans helped themselves to personal souvenirs. From the moment I got the signal to run for the bus or the car, my adrenaline was pumping.

This particular evening, it was decided that Paul Anka and I would leave in a limousine, which would be parked out back, waiting to whisk us away. The other performers would make a run for the Caravan of Stars bus. It seemed like an easy enough plan. The problem was that no one had thought to inform Mom and my tutor. The show ended, and the kids surged toward the stage door, blocking our way. Paul and I sprinted through the crowd as quickly as we could, while the others scrambled for the bus. Somehow signals got crossed, and the bus driver, certain that Mom and my tutor were in the limousine with Paul and me, and the limo driver, content that they were safely on board the bus, took off.

Somewhere in the middle of this screaming throng stood Mom and the tutor. The kids knocked the tutor to the ground, and she got up crying, "That's it! I'm leaving the tour!" They were alone, with no money and no idea where they were—with nothing really, except a big pile of my dresses and books, and that darn typewriter. Mom managed to flag down a couple of taxicabs, but none would take her to New York City, where we were all staying, without getting their money first. It was a nightmare. Finally, we were reunited, but it was a tough night for everyone. And the tutor, terrified of confronting another mob, left for home the next morning.

For Mom, life on the road was especially hard. Not only did she miss Daddy and her two boys desperately, but she never has become fully comfortable in the spotlight. Even after all these years, the sight of a microphone makes Mom freeze in her tracks. We still laugh about the time Dick Clark interviewed her and casually asked, "Mrs. Funicello, how many children do you have?" Mom just stared at him. She honestly could not remember!

Making things doubly difficult for us was the fact that I had to keep up my schoolwork. That meant there was no time left in the day for just an hour of relaxing or even sleeping late. We were constantly on the go. We weren't out on the road too many nights before Paul noticed the toll the crazy schedule and hard travel were taking on us, and he very generously offered to pay for us to travel between stops via plane or train. This special kindness is one my mother and I will never, ever forget. And as much as I wanted so badly to be "part of the gang" with the other performers, I guess it just was not to be. Now that I'm older, I understand why. Then I was a little bit hurt, but I was beginning to realize that the world outside was not *The Mickey Mouse Club.*

In the meantime, even traveling in these comparatively luxurious modes, Mom and I still found life on the road less than appealing, but we tried to make it work. Thank goodness, Mom had my tutor to talk to, and I made friends with a young woman named Janet Vogel, the only female in the singing quintet the Skyliners. Then at the height of their chart success with "Since I Don't Have You," the Skyliners were famous for their mellow sound. I don't think most people hearing it today would call it rock 'n' roll, but it was quite popular then. Janet and I hit it off right away. Being the same age, we were the youngest singers on the tour, and we found we had a lot in common. I was very saddened to learn from Frankie that she died in 1980.

Our tour did have its bright moments, though. We were joined at the Michigan State Fair by Frankie Avalon and Jan and Dean, among others, for a four-day run that drew a record-breaking fifteen thousand fans. Later, while we were in

Texas, I celebrated my birthday, somewhat glumly, I admit, because I missed Daddy and my brothers so. At one point during my segment Bobby Rydell came out on stage and started singing "Seventeen candles . . ." to the tune of the Crests' big hit "16 Candles." Someone brought out a huge birthday cake, and then came the best surprise of all: Daddy and the boys! We were hugging and kissing and crying. Of course, everyone called for Mom to join us onstage, but she refused and had to be dragged out. It was a great seventeenth-birthday present.

The next day, Sunday, Dad and my brothers flew back to Los Angeles, because the boys had school on Monday. Around the time they were supposed to be home, Mom and I phoned to be sure they'd gotten back safely. No answer. We dialed the number over and over again; we asked the operator to check the line; we did everything we could think of, but still the phone rang and rang.

Mom and I were both becoming overwrought with worry. This just wasn't like Dad, and after a couple of hours, we were expecting to hear the worst. When Paul found out what was going on, he came to our room and spent the next few hours calling the airlines, asking questions, and tracking down information until he finally discovered that an engine on their plane had caught fire, forcing an emergency landing. They'd landed safely and were put on another plane to complete their journey.

Mom and I were so grateful to Paul for taking charge and comforting us. The next day Paul gave me a beautiful, precious gift, a heart necklace with a single pearl nestled in the heart. Even years after our romance cooled, I still wore that necklace, because it symbolized a deep caring that can be more enduring than even love.

As I said before, it was on this tour that Paul and I realized we were falling for each other, and we fell hard. At least I know I did. Along with Mr. Disney, Tutti Camarata, and a few others, Paul was one of my biggest boosters. At the time of the tour, I had only two hits, "Tall Paul" and "Jo-Jo, the Dog-Faced Boy" (which I did not sing live then), and I sang "Ma, He's Making Eyes at Me." Usually I finished with "Tall Paul," and I would sing the last line, quickly mutter "Thank you" into the microphone, and absolutely flee from the stage.

One night Paul was standing in the wings as I came off, and he gently grabbed my arm and said, "Annette, my God! You can't just run off the stage like that! You have to have some stage presence.

"First, after you finish your song, you have to wait for the applause to die down. Then you bow, and calmly and slowly say, 'Thank you very much, ladies and gentlemen,' and walk off leisurely. You look like you can't wait to get off that stage."

"But, Paul," I admitted, "I can't!"

"Oh, yes, you can, Annette. I know you can. You just have to try."

I promised I would try, and slowly but surely I got the hang of actually standing there and calmly smiling at the cheering crowd without bolting. But there were some aspects of my "stage presence," if that's what you want to call it, that took some work. This sounds absolutely crazy today, and looking back it's funny even to me. But at the time I was positively mortified every time something embarrassing happened onstage. For example, when you first came out, the big, old-fashioned silver microphone was in its stand, and the first thing you did was walk over and casually remove it from the stand and start your number. I can't tell you how many times, in my attempts to appear calm and professional, I jerked the microphone out of the stand and hit myself on the head with it. Or the times I tripped over the microphone wires as I tried to stroll casually across the stage while I sang. I was just a fish out of water, and as much as Paul and others tried to help and as much as I improved as the tour wore on, it would be many years before I could comfortably sing live.

Through it all, though, Paul really believed in me. One of

the enduring results of that faith was my third album, *Annette Sings Anka.* It was while we were appearing at the Carter Barron Amphitheatre in Washington, D.C., that Paul approached Tutti Camarata and told him that he'd written a song for me. When Paul and Tutti met in New York City the next day, Tutti was so impressed that he encouraged Paul to go ahead and write a whole album for me. Recorded later that year and released in 1960, *Annette Sings Anka* remains my personal favorite and was my highest-charting album.

Paul spent a lot of time with me and my family, and he and I passed many happy hours sitting on the piano bench while he worked on songs or helped me with my singing. Sometimes we tried to come up with songs together, which is how "Teddy" came about. "Puppy Love" was one of many songs Paul wrote in my parents' living room.

One day I was sitting next to Paul, feeling comfortable and in love. I moved closer and rested my head on his shoulder, as Paul started picking out a melody on the keys. Then he sang so softly, "Put your head on my shoulder, hold me in your arms . . ." Well, you know the rest.

CHAPTER 6

*M*y relationship with Paul continued on and off over the next couple of years. Of course, when you're in your teens you don't always know what real love is. Are you truly in love or just infatuated? But does it matter? As Paul wrote in his hit song about us, just because we were seventeen didn't mean that, for us, our love wasn't real.

A lot of the problems Paul and I faced could be traced directly to the fact that both of us were in the grips of our respective careers. And if I hadn't been inclined before not to marry into the business, my time with Paul steeled my resolve. This is in no way meant as a criticism of Paul, but of the business itself and the personal sacrifices it often demands. In the time we dated, Paul had one hit record after another: "Put Your Head on My Shoulder," "Lonely Boy," "It's Time to Cry," "My Home Town." In addition, he, like most of the other young singing stars of the time, embarked on a film career, appearing in several movies, including the 1962 World War II epic *The Longest Day*, for which he also composed the score.

Paul wanted to build a career that would weather any changes in music trends, and to that end he was among the first so-called teen idols to perform in nightclubs, in Las Vegas, and in Europe. It was his dream to become an internationally known singer, songwriter, and performer, and he had to follow it. I understood that.

After a while it became clear that Paul was much more worldly and mature than I was. At times impatient and moody, Paul often seemed the polar opposite of me, with my usually happy-go-lucky outlook. Another problem was that in my teenage heart of hearts, I longed for the everyday relationships other girls my age had, with a boy who lived in the neighborhood, whom I could see after school and go out on dates with. Ironically, thousands of girls would have traded all that for one date with Paul. I did see boys from my neighborhood from time to time. But these simple things were impossible with Paul. We rarely ventured out together on a date, for fear of being recognized and sometimes mobbed.

Even the precious private moments we did share came only after a lot of strategic planning. Perhaps because I didn't really have anything to compare my life to, the situation didn't bother me as much as it might have. Mom, on the other hand, really felt sorry for me. She still talks about how it broke her heart to see me miss so much of the typical teen life other kids take for granted. It wasn't until my own daughter, Gina, reached her teens that I began to understand how my mother felt and to see what I had missed. Mom and Daddy simply wanted me to be happy, and to that end, Mom made all kinds of accommodations for me and Paul.

Usually when Mom and I traveled we shared one room and bath; there were no suites, no extra sitting-room areas. When she felt that Paul and I should be alone, Mom generously volunteered to sit in the bathroom on its most comfortable piece of "furniture"—an empty tub—and read so that Paul and I could visit and listen to records on the portable hi-fi Tutti Camarata gave me. Another time, while we were driving from New York to Toronto in a sleet storm, Mom sat in the backseat with Paul and me. Paul and I were kissing a little, but Mom didn't say anything. She understood how important we were to each other then.

Because of the time difference between Europe and California, Paul sometimes called in the middle of the night, and the phone ringing at 3 A.M. often roused the whole household, which my folks did not appreciate. Nor were they happy that I stayed up for hours, talking to Paul and listening to him sing me songs he'd just written, when I knew I had to be at the studio near the crack of dawn. To their credit, they tolerated these intrusions, just to make me happy. Every week or so I'd receive a beautiful gift from whatever part of the world Paul happened to be in, and that and a few special words from him would somehow make everything better.

My parents had met Paul's parents, whom they liked very much, and our romance seemed to be leading to something more serious. But as time passed, and our careers tore us from each other more often, jealousy and suspicion crept in. Naturally, the fan magazines had a field day, their headlines trumpeting, "Caught in a Teen-Age Triangle: Annette, Avalon, Fabian" or "Annette Funicello and Paul Anka Discover the Thrill of First Love," but that was just publicity. Yes, I dated, but very casually. I truly did love Paul, but I think that because I was so much less mature than he was he simply didn't believe me. This caused more than a few arguments, which often ended with me in tears. *Why doesn't he understand?* I would ask myself. *Why can't he see?*

Once when I told Paul that I really did care for him, he sarcastically retorted, "What script did you get that line from?" He quickly apologized, but I was devastated. No one I loved had ever hurt me so deeply. This was all new to me, and even though seeing me so unhappy upset my mother and father terribly, they never intervened. They trusted that I would learn these hard but inevitable lessons on my own, and they were right. Although we dated several times afterward and remained very close friends, we faced the fact that, all the love songs aside, there are some things even true love cannot overcome.

After the Caravan of Stars tour ended, I still traveled to make appearances and do Dick Clark's shows, as well as other television programs, but much of the time I was back where I always longed to be: home with my family. Shelley Fabares and I were still the best of friends, and a lot of our so-called social lives revolved around one of us visiting the other and then passing the hours sitting in a bedroom, listening to records, and talking. The festivities marking our "swinging" New Year's Eve consisted of the single glass of champagne we each sipped in my bedroom at midnight while a stack of records played on the hi-fi and my menagerie of stuffed animals looked on.

As we grew into our later teens and she started appearing on *The Donna Reed Show,* we went on countless double dates together. Lots of these were date layouts for the magazines. Other times, when we found ourselves in a situation we weren't too pleased about or were stuck with dates that were less than dreamy, we would talk to each other in our own secret language, which we called "ivy talk." It's very, very hard to actually speak in ivy talk, and even harder to describe. Basically, it's an extremely intricate, tongue-twisting form of pig latin, in which the words get so mangled no one can even begin to guess what we are talking about. Or so we hoped.

Once Shelley and I were double-dating two guys who we thought were nice enough, but after we got to a drive-in movie they broke out some bottles of beer and started drinking. I quietly whispered to Shelley in ivy talk, "I think these guys are drunk. Should I go to the snack bar and call a cab to take us home?"

Imagine my shock when my date turned and replied to me—in ivy talk!—"I am *not* drunk, and I can drive you home, and we'd better go right now!"

I apologized profusely, but it was no use, and I can't say that I blame the guy. Shelley and I were not the type of girls who would place themselves in that kind of situation. We both knew there were guys who had preconceived notions about what young actresses were like and what they would do. I always think of these as the "hey, baby" guys. But they were wrong about us. I guess you could say that we both came from sheltered backgrounds, and in our cases, being in show business just made us draw further into the safety of our homes, families, and closest friends.

Growing up is never easy, and growing up in public is especially hard sometimes. Especially after spending so much time around other young performers, I became very concerned about my shyness. Until then, I had considered it an unchangeable part of my personality—something I was born with—and I dealt with it. But I'd met young actors and singers who were so much more self-assured and independent. And I longed to be like them. One day I asked Mr. Disney if I could please be sent to a psychologist who could help me become more outgoing, more self-confident.

As always, Mr. Disney was kind but frank and to the point. "Annette," he said gently, "you have a certain charisma that people respond to. I think your being a little bit shy is part of your appeal. Going to see a psychologist would change that. Why do you want to change that?"

I had no answer, so I let it drop, although years later I have occasionally wondered how my life might have been different had I ignored his advice.

For someone as reserved as I was, it wasn't always easy to pick up a magazine and read references to my newly blossoming figure. Mr. Disney preferred that I didn't discuss my measurements, and I was happy to oblige him. It was certainly nice to be noticed for having a good figure, but sometimes the amount of attention mine received seemed—pardon me—out of proportion. Even today when people, men especially, attribute my popularity as a Mouseketeer to my developing bustline, I often feel as if I should point out that I was still fairly flat-chested then, and there were other girl Mouseketeers as "curvaceous," and I use that term loosely, as I was. But of course, I don't.

After so many years, I've learned to gracefully accept having been so many young men's "first love." Amid my fan mail I received expensive wristwatches, school rings, and engagement rings. Most of the time I'd mail them back with a friendly note thanking the boy for his gift, but explaining, nicely, that I just couldn't accept it. That was the right way to handle it, or so I thought until I started getting letters from irate mothers, informing me how hard Johnny or Timmy had worked to save the money for the gift and how dare I return it?

For the most part whatever infatuation boys had with me was perfectly innocent, even if there was an element of sex appeal involved. I still get a kick when a middle-aged woman says, "You know, Annette, you were my husband's first love."

But even back in those innocent, carefree days, there were dangerous, maladjusted people who were attracted to stars. I was still doing *The Mickey Mouse Club* the first time such a person entered my life. Although the studio people protected me and I never saw him, I did learn that security had intercepted a man with a knife outside the gates after he was heard screaming, "Annette! Annette!" Later, when I was on tour promoting a record, a young boy approached my mother in a hotel lobby, ostensibly to give me a song to record. But a boy had been writing me disturbing, obsessive letters, and when my mother spotted this young boy acting suspiciously in the hotel lobby, she instinctively knew it was him. She quietly alerted security, and he was taken out, but not before he revealed that he intended to hurt me.

Fortunately, incidents like these were rare, and with very few exceptions I always felt safe. For my parents, however, these times were frightening, and in the wake of them, the innocent pranks people played at our house—like breaking the empty milk bottles we left out for the milkman, letting the air out of all the cars' tires, or calling out my name as they drove by late at night—assumed a different cast. As I grew older, I came to feel more responsible for any hardship or trouble my career caused my family. Yet after so many years of it, we all more or less surrendered to the flow. It was part of my job. There wasn't anything we could do to stop it, and it seemed silly to waste time worrying.

I made no films in 1959, instead concentrating on my recording career. In early 1960 "First Name Initial," another of the Sherman boys' vibrant, poppy tunes, went to number twenty on the charts. Then later that spring, my second-highest charting single, "O Dio Mio," hit number ten. After a few cool months, my records seemed to be on a winning streak. Just the month before, *Annette Sings Anka,* my most popular album, was high on the charts as well.

Later that year the Sherman Brothers and Tutti Camarata started work on the first of the three "Annette" theme albums: *Hawaiiannette,* which led to *Italiannette* and *Dance Annette. Hawaiiannette,* the most successful of this conceptual trilogy, mixed traditional Hawaiian musical fare, such as "Aloha Oe" and "Song of the Islands," with the Shermans' own genre-blending compositions like "Luau Cha Cha Cha" and my last Top Twenty hit, "Pineapple Princess," my personal favorite. A rare rock 'n' roll showcase for ukulele and steel guitar, "Pineapple Princess" boasts that sweet mix of romance and whimsy that marked so many of the Shermans' songs.

I understand that today collectors are especially interested in *Hawaiiannette,* and I'm not surprised. It's truly an artifact of its time. The album cover itself is a Technicolor work of art, with me in all my lei-covered splendor against a stunning aqua background, and posing on the back, decked out in a muumuu and, in another shot, caressing a pineapple. In the wake of Hawaii's joining the Union only the year before, Americans were going crazy for all things tropical: luaus, Hawaiian print shirts, pineapple on everything. We all knew it was kind of gimmicky, and after *Italiannette* and *Dance Annette*, even the Shermans, Tutti, and I often joked, "What's coming next?"

"How about BasAnnette?"

"Or BayAnnette?"

"Or KitchAnnette?"

Despite my not working on films that year, 1960 soon would be as much a whirlwind for me and my family as 1959 had been. That spring I learned that Mom and I would be going to New York City, where Disney's film *Pollyanna*, starring the young English actress Hayley Mills, would open at Radio City Music Hall. For the first two weeks of the movie's run, Radio City presented a live stage show, which included me as well as singer Dick Roman and the Rockettes.

When I first got word that Mr. Disney wanted to send me to New York City, I was devastated, because it would mean missing my high school graduation. Having been tutored privately all those years, I hadn't actually set foot in a regular high school. Still, it would be my time to graduate, and technically I would be graduating from University High. The ceremony would be just like anyone else's, complete with speakers, caps, and gowns. It was a day I'd been dreaming of for a long time, one of the very few typical teenage rites of passage I could take part in, and I was determined not to miss it for anything.

After crying my heart out, I phoned Mr. Disney's office, something I almost never did. "Mr. Disney," I said tearfully, "I just can't go to New York City. If I do, I'll miss my high school graduation, and it means so much to me. Please don't make me go."

Mr. Disney was silent for a moment, and then in his patient yet firm voice replied, "I understand what you're saying and how you feel, Annette, but you must go. However, young lady, I promise you the greatest graduation anyone could ever have."

What could I say? I was under contract, so I was going, and that was that. And while I had no idea what he could possibly mean when he said "the greatest graduation anyone could ever have," I trusted Mr. Disney; his word was gold. I just had to wait and see.

When Mom and I left for New York City, my graduation was not the only family celebration we knew would be ruined. My littlest brother, Michael, was to be receive his first holy communion while we were away, and so my mother left Daddy and the boys in Encino reluctantly. I knew that Mom would have walked across the continent to be back with her baby for his big day, but when the time came, her ingenuity amazed even me.

As the day of Michael's first holy communion neared, Mom got sadder and sadder. A child's first holy communion is such an important day in a parent's life, and Michael was her baby. But she had a plan. My tutor at the time, Mrs. Rose Fine, agreed to cover for Mom, and the gentleman who was then head of the Disney Studio arranged for her plane tickets and a limousine to the airport. Of course, this was all going against regulations, and when she left me alone in New York I would technically be without a guardian, even though Mrs. Fine was with me. I think everyone could see how distraught Mom was, so here's what happened.

She left after my last show on Saturday evening and flew back to Los Angeles. She secretly arranged to have a friend of hers pick her up at the airport, and when she let herself into our house around midnight, Daddy, watching television in the den when he heard the door open, was beside himself with surprise and happiness. They decided not to wake Michael, but the next morning when Daddy got him up to go to church, my mother overheard him saying, "I had a dream last night that I heard Mommy talking."

They spent a wonderful day together, she got to witness Michael's communion, and then, typically, she spent her last few precious hours at home cooking, with Michael, Joey, and Daddy at her side. Around midnight, about twenty-four hours after she'd arrived, she boarded an eastbound jet and was unpacking in our hotel suite on Monday morning, before anyone even knew she was gone. For Mom the only bad part of that weekend was coming back to New York to find me sporting the new false eyelashes the Rockettes had given me. At that point I still wasn't allowed to wear much makeup, and false eyelashes, especially in those days—well, you can just imagine.

Whenever we traveled to New York City, the first thing I did on arrival was phone my friend Steve Brandt. I'd met Steve a year or so before through other friends in the music business. He was a show-business publicist, and he introduced me to many of his friends, who seemed to be everybody who was anybody. His best friend then was a young actress named Sharon Tate.

Every so often in life you meet someone with whom you just hit it off, and it was certainly that way with Steve and me. He had a wacky sense of humor and found something hilarious in just about everything. I'll never forget his telling me, "There's this great movie you absolutely have to see. But you have to go with me, nobody else. You'll love it." What was the movie? Alfred Hitchcock's *Psycho*, which is pretty tame by today's standards, but was horrifying and quite controversial at the time. From then on, that was the nickname we gave each other: Psycho.

When I was going through my scrapbooks, rekindling my memories of those long-lost days, I came across an article Steve wrote about me for one of the teen magazines. Entitled, in typical fan-magazine style, "The Annette No One Knows," it was intended as a behind-the-scenes personal look at me. But with the passage of time it's become some-

thing more like a letter from the past, from Steve. In it he re-
counts a snowball fight we once had in Central Park (my
first!), my crying after reading a lie printed about me in a
magazine article, and several practical jokes he, Shelley
Fabares, and I were all parties to. He begins by writing, "I
have never written a story about Annette before. Frankly, I
never intended to. I have always felt that friendships were
matters of the heart, not words to be printed on paper." At
one point, he wrote, "I am honored to be one of these few
whom Annie—her nickname—calls a friend."

And we were such great friends. After rehearsing with everyone at Radio City, I still felt so inadequate standing on the
stage singing "Train of Love." Not that it's not a wonderful
song, because it certainly is. But after hearing Dick Roman
perform a booming, majestic rendition of "Love Is a Many-
Splendored Thing," I felt silly singing about a train of love
while a chorus of background singers went "Wooo! Wooo!
Wooo! Wooo!" It was not the first time in my career and certainly not the last when I would ask myself, *What am I doing
here?*

I confided all my fears to Steve, and he did what any friend
would do: He got all of his friends to pack the first few rows
of Radio City Music Hall and then give me the most rousing
welcome and applause you ever heard. Whenever I needed a
little jolt of confidence, I just glanced down at the front rows
and saw Steve smiling up at me, and I was set.

Our friendship continued, which was easy since his work
often brought him to the West Coast. One time he gave me a
beautiful jewelry box. Inside he'd had it specially inscribed:
"I love you, Psycho."

Sadly, several years after the Radio City run, his mother
called me from New York to tell me that he had tried to commit suicide. Being so young, I couldn't imagine how anyone
could do such a thing, especially not Steve. He seemed so
happy and had so much to live for. I phoned him in the hospital immediately and said, "Don't you dare leave me, Steve.

You know I love you. You have to promise me you'll never try anything like that again."

"I promise, Annie," he replied quietly. And I believed him. But a few years later, his mother called again and said simply, "This time Steve did it." It was the first time in my life anyone close to me had died, and the first time anyone near my own age had passed away. Through the years I've often wondered why, but neither I nor any of his other friends seemed to ever know.

As my graduation day, or what was supposed to have been my graduation day, loomed nearer, I began worrying. Maybe someone had forgotten. Maybe I wasn't going to get to "graduate" at all. But, as always, Mr. Disney had made a promise, and he kept it in the grandest style. The scene of my graduation was the stage of Radio City Music Hall. With a full audience watching between shows, I received my diploma from an official of the New York City Board of Education while the Rockettes kicked and stepped, singing, "Happy Graduation, Annette." My dressing room overflowed with flowers from practically everyone I knew, the Rockettes made me an honorary member, and the event was front-page news in the New York papers. It turned out to be everything Mr. Disney had promised.

My mother threw me a wonderful surprise graduation party in the Warwick Hotel's ballroom, one I will never forget. Music was provided by my friend Neil Sedaka, who played the piano and sang almost all night. The rest of the guest list read like a Who's Who of early-sixties rock 'n' roll. Frankie Avalon gave me a cornucopia charm for my charm bracelet, someone representing my record label gave me a little gold record charm, and Shelley sent me a cap-and-gown charm. Dion DiMucci gave me a travel clock. Pat Boone, whose show *Coke Time* I appeared on with Paul and Frankie while in New York, also attended, as did the Rockettes.

The only sad remembrance of the day was missing Daddy and the boys. They'd wanted to be there so badly, but the boys weren't out of school yet, so Dad sent a telegram: "Dear Dolly: Congratulations on completing your high school years. Sorry that I cannot attend the event in person as I would have liked to. Will see you Sunday. Love, Dad." Knowing my father, he'd written something simple and to the point, but someone in the Western Union office must have tried to "help" by making it so formal. Still, Daddy's love came through. Later he would accompany me on the occasional trip away from home, and those were very special times.

A few months later Mom and I flew to England, where I filmed *The Horsemasters*, a movie that was released in theaters in England and Europe and shown in two parts on *Walt Disney's Wonderful World of Color*. The experience of making *The Horsemasters* was a series of "firsts" for me. It was my first costarring role, my first dramatic film, and my first time filming outside the country.

I had always loved horses; in fact, for my eighteenth birthday my parents purchased an inexpensive "claimer," a trotter we named Troy Hedgewood (don't ask why; the rules that govern the naming of racehorses are incredibly complex) and raced at Hollywood Park. Because in the film I played the daughter of an Olympic horsewoman, I had to train very hard so that I could ride in the English style and like a horsemaster, and that took some doing. Tommy Kirk and I were sent to England a couple of weeks early solely to learn to ride. Although a stunt rider sat in for me during the many dangerous jumping shots, I performed some of the jumps myself and—not counting the many times I was thrown—spent over half the film in the saddle, which is not the most comfortable way to pass three months. Thanks to the magic of film and good acting on both our parts, my character, Dinah, and her horse, Corny, appear to be best friends. In reality, however, my horse sensed my fear, and we never got along at all.

After fourteen straight days of work, I had one day off.

Mom and I took in the sights and did a bit of shopping. I loved seeing the changing of the guard at Buckingham Palace and all of the old buildings, so rich in history. We never developed a taste for English cuisine, with its boiled meats and vegetables and room-temperature beverages, but we loved the tradition of teatime and had our first truly great French meals, so the handful of times we did eat out were memorable.

It was while in England that I had my first of many experiences with a phenomenon I guess you could call "television time warp." "Pineapple Princess" had been released there, but the only picture the English kids could put to my name came from old reruns of *The Mickey Mouse Club*, which had recently gone into syndication. So there was twelve-year-old, prepubescent, mouse-eared Annette on the box, then (almost) eighteen-year-old grown-up Annette in person, which prompted not only a lot of confusion, but remarks like "How can you be Annette? You're too old to be Annette!" I've yet to figure out a good answer to that one.

I had written to Dad faithfully almost every day, and now and then Mom and I placed a transatlantic phone call home, just to hear everyone's voices. As always, we were homesick and anxious to be back in Encino. Toward the end of our time overseas, Mom got a little depressed, which may explain why it was so easy for me, with the help of Vidal Sassoon, to talk her into dyeing her hair red. I thought Mom looked great, and with a new, shorter cut, she was positively chic.

When we stepped off the plane in California, Mom walked behind me. Daddy and the boys ran to hug me and didn't even recognize Mom at all! When Daddy realized what Mom had done to her hair, he got very upset. I think this was the first—probably the only—time Daddy really got angry with Mom. He always preferred her natural black hair, but she never changed back.

Tutti and I went right to work recording *Dance Annette*. Several songs attempted to bring older, popular dances up to rock speed, so the Shermans wrote a few special songs, like "Rock-a-Cha" and "Rock-a-Polka." I loved this album, because I love any kind of dance, but also because it led to my parents' making their show-business debuts. Contrary to popular belief, music videos of a sort existed long before MTV. In the late forties and early fifties, there was a machine called the Panoram Soundie: basically a jukebox with a television screen that played short films of artists singing their records. The Soundie didn't last too long, but later in the decade came the Scopitone.

I made a number of short lip-syncing films for *Dance Annette*, but my favorite was "The Rock and Roll Waltz." The lyrics tell of a teenager who comes home late after a date and spies her parents in the living room, trying to waltz to one of her rock 'n' roll records. Someone thought it would be cute if Mom and Daddy played themselves, and since their parts called for them to dance around a living-room set and they were such great dancers, they figured, Why not? The day of the filming we were all surprised to find my mother standing in Daddy's arms stiff as a board. She was so nervous she couldn't move! We did take after take after take, until finally Daddy got her to relax enough so that she could at least follow him.

I returned to the Disney lot to film my last *Zorro* episode, "The Postponed Wedding." It was so great to be back among my friends. Here it was nearly six years since I first stepped through the gates on South Buena Vista Street and I waved hello to the same guards, workmen, gardeners, directors, and crew I'd known from the start. I suppose I especially appreciated being back after my experience on *The Horsemasters*, when some of the married cast and crew members were carrying on affairs, and in his less attractive moments my director would refer to me dismissively as "the Disney girl" and make unflattering comments about me. Of course, he was not the first and would not be the last to take a dislike to me because he felt I was Mr. Disney's "pet." I never thought of myself that way. However, if certain people in the business couldn't see Mr. Disney's interest in my career as anything deeper than favoritism, there was little I could do about it. When people have ridiculous prejudices like that, nothing you say or do will change their minds. I acted professionally and tried to ignore it, but I have to admit that at times my feelings were hurt.

I often had reason to be on the lot. For some time I'd been noticing a seemingly endless parade of blonde and red-headed young actresses coming to the lot for auditions. I wasn't sure what project they were being considered for until one day Mr. Disney and I were chatting. Finally he said, "Annette, I'd like you to go over to the hairdressing department."

"Why?" I asked.

"Let's see how you'll look as a redhead" was all the explanation he offered, and off we went. There they tinted my hair repeatedly until they got the exact warm cinnamon tone they were looking for. Then they called Mr. Disney to come over and see me. Pleased with the results, he said, "Okay, now let's take some photographs and see how Annette will look." After he saw the finished shots, that was it: I was to play Mary Mary Quite Contrary in the musical *Babes in Toyland*. Personally, I loved my new hair color, though all I could think of was poor Daddy. Now there would be two redheads in the house.

Of all my filmmaking experiences, *Babes in Toyland* is without question my favorite. It was one of those rare times when everything about making the film—from my director, my co-stars, the crew, the costumes, even the scenery—was perfect. Though some critics were less than overwhelming in their praise of the movie when it premiered around Christmas-time in 1961, it has won a place in the hearts of families and children everywhere. I'm pleased to hear from so many people that watching *Babes in Toyland* is now part of their holiday tradition, right along with trimming the tree and drinking eggnog.

Babes in Toyland was a grand fantasy wrapped around the simple love story of Mary Contrary and Tom Piper (played by Tommy Sands). The climax is their triumphant winter wedding, which occurs at the end despite the evil Barnaby (played by Ray Bolger, who was the Scarecrow in *The Wizard of Oz*), and his dim-witted henchmen's devious attempts to kill Tom so Barnaby can wed Mary.

It certainly sounds like a basic story line, but placed in a land inhabited by gypsies, a mad toymaker, Mother Goose and her talking goose, Sylvester, and a forest of walking and talking trees, *Babes in Toyland* becomes something more. In Mary's garden real cockleshells grow and pretty maids' faces beam from flowers; the children in Mary's care include Little Boy Blue (Kevin Corcoran) and Little Bo Peep (Ann Jillian in her screen debut). From the costumes, which included lemon-colored tutus for the chorus, to the lavishly constructed sets, every scene from *Babes in Toyland* resembled a beautifully illustrated page from a child's favorite book come to life. Unlike so many children's stories, *Babes in Toyland* did not trace an everyday character's journey into a land of wonder. In this film, the everyday people were the heroes and heroines of the Mother Goose tales, and their pivotal journey to Toyland simply took them from one realm of imagination to another.

It's easy to see why Mr. Disney was so enamored of this project and why so much effort and money were poured into its production. (Flawed though it may be, *Babes in Toyland* is regarded by some Disney historians as the trial balloon, so to speak, for the studio's next foray into live-action musical comedy, *Mary Poppins*.) The sets for Mother Goose Village (including the old woman's shoe), the evil Barnaby's crooked, dilapidated hilltop mansion, the talking-tree-filled Forest of No Return, and Toyland occupied four entire sound

stages. The cast, including extras in some of the musical
scenes, numbered over two hundred, and featured such
great stars as Ed Wynn as the Toymaker, Tommy Kirk as his
assistant, and Henry Calvin and Gene Sheldon (whom I'd
worked with on *Zorro*) as Gonzorgo and Roderigo, respec-
tively.

At the heart of *Babes in Toyland,* which was first produced
in 1903 for the stage, is Victor Herbert's music. We were all
very proud when the film's soundtrack was nominated for
an Academy Award that year. Although Disney songwriters
George Bruns and Mel Leven added three new songs to the
score ("The Workshop Song," "The Forest of No Return,"
and "Slowly He Sank into the Sea") and adapted the melo-
dies of others, Herbert's classic songs, including "Toyland"
and "March of the Toys," mark the film's highlights. "March
of the Toys" accompanies the toy soldiers, led by a miniatur-
ized Tom Piper, in their rescue of Mary and attack on Barnaby. Using what were then very advanced techniques, the
toys, some of which moved mechanically, seem to come to
life. To viewers of today, these sequences may appear primitive, but in the early sixties the charge of the toy soldiers represented the forefront of stop-motion animation, or "animo-
tion," as the Disney crew called it.

Over the three months of preparation, rehearsal, and
prerecording, everyone got to know one another quite well.
Naturally it was a thrill for me to meet and work with Ray
Bolger, who was such a gentleman. Probably the most memorable scene we shared was the "Castle in Spain" sequence,
where Barnaby tries to woo my reluctant Mary. Although it
had been over twenty years since he danced down the Yellow Brick Road, Ray was as limber and as deft a dancer as I'd
ever seen. Gene Sheldon taught me some amazing card
tricks, which Mr. Disney would ask us to perform whenever
he dropped by. My director, Jack Donohue, was simply wonderful. Having never done a musical comedy before and
never done the kind of singing Victor Herbert's light opera

demanded, I was more than a little nervous. Yet he managed to walk me through it all and had me laughing every step of the way. His support was especially appreciated after my experience on *The Horsemasters*.

During the time we spent working together, I grew particularly fond of Tommy Sands. Tommy had been in show business most of his life and cut his first record when he was just twelve. Managed by Elvis Presley's manager, Colonel Tom Parker, Tommy worked primarily as a country singer until he landed a role in a television drama that was originally written for Elvis. As a result of his appearance in "The Singing Idol" and the hit record the show produced, "Teen-Age Crush," Tommy briefly became something of an idol himself. He appeared in a series of films before marrying Nancy Sinatra in 1960. By the midsixties, Tommy seemed to fall out of the limelight, although he has made several successful comebacks. He was a fantastic singer and a strong comedic actor. He won the role of Tom Piper over contenders that included James Darren and Michael Callan.

Tommy was a terrific guy and very easy to work with. We recorded the music before we actually began filming. On several occasions when Tommy and I were working together in the recording studio, I noticed his wife, Nancy, staring at me. I began to feel very uncomfortable and actually worried that she might suspect something going on between Tommy and me. One day I said to Tommy, "Is something the matter? Doesn't Nancy like me?"

Surprised, he replied, "Of course, she likes you just fine. Why?"

"Well, she seems to be staring at me all the time, Tommy. I'm not sure."

He assured me there was nothing to worry about and, as I learned later, said something to Nancy about it. Now, a situation like this could go several ways. Nancy might have been offended by what I said to Tommy, or really been suspicious about it. Instead, she did something that showed me what a kind, generous person she was. She sent me a rose, a yellow one, if I recall correctly, with a letter in which she wrote that she was sorry that she had offended me and that she liked me and my work very much. She and I later became, and continue to be, friends.

As with anything worth doing, *Babes in Toyland* presented some interesting challenges. My one solo number, "I Can't Do the Sum," is a fine piece of Disney wizardry that combines state-of-the-art Chromakey techniques for the several fluorescent-hued versions of me that leap out and sing as I sit at a desk. Again, this was an effect that's become commonplace yet at the time was very unusual. The same scene also called for some special effects executed the old-fashioned way. At one point, when I wonder as I sing how much money I could save on shoes by walking on my hands, I am literally walking on my hands. Easy enough for me, except that technicians had to wire all of my clothing, down to each layer of petticoat, and I wore a wig, the strands of which were wired as well so that my hair wouldn't fall in my face while I was upside-down.

It was very hard work, especially because being eighteen years of age I could now legally work adult hours. Every day I came home exhausted. Yet every morning, when Dad would tiptoe into my bedroom with a cup of hot coffee and gently say, "Dolly, Dolly, it's time to go to work," I would wake up, ready to go.

Even my costumes, such as the now-famous ermine-trimmed red velvet cape and a stunning pearl-and-lace-covered wedding gown, were the stuff of fantasy. These weren't clothes, they were hand-embroidered silk and organza confections. In fact, I so loved the wedding dress I wore in the movie's finale that the designer, Bill Thomas, offered to create the dress for my real-life wedding day, which he did.

I suppose it's that little bit of the child in each of us that makes working on something like *Babes in Toyland* so enjoyable. It was the first, and unfortunately, I think, the last time I made a movie in which I actually danced something besides the watusi or the swim. Not to put those other films down, but I always considered myself a dancer before anything else, and through the sets of Toyland and Mother Goose Village, I danced across the screen in a way I'd always dreamed of.

One other aspect of making *Babes in Toyland* that makes the experience even more precious to me was Mr. Disney. I had spent so much of the past couple of years traveling and recording, being back again every day for six months made me realize how much I missed my "home." The cast included many children, and it warmed my heart to see Mr. Disney visit the set each day and show the same interest in them as he had shown in me and the other Mouseketeers years before. It also made me realize that, in so many ways, my days in Toyland were coming to an end.

For the rest of 1961 and through 1962, Disney's record label, Buena Vista, released a stream of singles, mostly tracks taken from the *Hawaiiannette* and *Italiannette* albums. While my records remained popular with fans and sold well, the days of big hits were over for me, and my appearances on such music-oriented programs as Dick Clark's shows tapered off. Still fan mail poured in and the phone rang constantly with requests from magazines for interviews and photo sessions.

I suppose it's safe to say that I was a teen role model, and as I grew out of my teens and into young womanhood, I took that responsibility very seriously. Now more than ever reporters fixated on my moral standards, my feelings about marriage and family, and my future plans. "I'm a Woman Now," one movie magazine headline quoted me asserting, while various articles speculated when I might marry (and I was only nineteen!); one suggested that Elvis Presley and I might make a perfect match. To glance through one of these scrapbooks, you'd think I was getting desperate to settle down, but nothing could have been further from the truth. I never worried; I knew that when the time was right, my true love would arrive.

In early 1962 Mom and I traveled to Italy. There I was to begin filming *Escapade in Florence,* another Disney film that was shown in the States only on *Walt Disney's Wonderful World of Color.* Of all the places my work had led us, Italy still stands out as our favorite. After all, we are Italian. But in addition to that, it became a wonderful trip in ways we didn't expect and a source of many beautiful memories.

Mom and I had been to Italy before. When we'd gone to England for *The Horsemasters* a year and a half earlier, we'd gone to Rome first for four days. We loved the food and the people, and found it easy to adapt to their more leisurely lifestyle. The only thing I never got used to was being pinched by men who were total strangers, but I couldn't get too upset about it, since that was their custom. We were staying in the very exclusive Excelsior Hotel, which was frequented by other show-business stars, but I spent a lot of my time flirting with an elevator operator.

We looked forward to returning to Italy, though of course—as usual—we would be on our own, leaving Dad and the boys home. This trip was in some ways perhaps the most difficult because while we were away my brother Joey developed mononucleosis. Our long-distance phone bills were astronomical, and every day Mom just cried and cried.

As usual, my mother was not one to be deterred. She concocted a brilliant scheme to reunite our family in Italy. Before we left the States, we cashed in the first-class airline tickets the studio provided, flew coach, and applied the balance to tickets for Dad, Joey, and Michael. And again we saved up our per-diem money by eating in the suite off a hotplate. About halfway through our three-month stay, we sent for them to join us. Joey was sufficiently recovered to travel, so he, Dad, and Michael were able to be with us for about two weeks. We got away for a few weekends and traveled to Naples and Venice. My parents took us to the village where some of my grandparents were born, where we had dozens of cousins. Interestingly, only the American tourists knew me; my distant cousins, like most Italians, had no idea who I was.

To see the old village my grandparents came from, where people still killed chickens in their houses and threw the heads out into the street and lived as their grandparents had, fascinated me. Someone took us to a home and showed us the very bed my grandfather was born in. To touch the bed where my great-grandmother and her baby had lain so many decades ago was a moving experience. To see how my grandparents had lived before sailing to America deepened my respect for them and what they had endured for their children and their children's children.

Even though I was nearing twenty-one, I remained happily at home. We still went on family outings together, except as I grew older some of our destinations changed. Often Mom, Dad, and I drove to Las Vegas to see some shows and gamble. When we first started going there, I was underage, a fact I tried to disguise by wearing my most sophisticated, elegant dress and a fur wrap to the crap table. I usually got to play only a short while before a security guard would say, "I'm sorry, Annette, but you have to leave."

"But I'm twenty-one!" I'd reply with what I thought was convincing indignation.

"Annette, come on. I grew up with you on *The Mickey Mouse Club*. I know how old you are. Let's go."

There were many other times, however, when I was left alone, even though they knew I was too young to be gambling. In 1963, after I turned twenty-one, my parents and I were in one of the casinos gambling when a gentleman politely tapped me on the shoulder and introduced himself.

"I'm with Elvis Presley, with his entourage," he explained, "and he would like to meet you." Cocking his head subtly, he added, "Elvis is over at the other crap table."

I glanced over and, sure enough, there was Elvis. My heart stopped, and when the gentleman asked, "May I say that you'll be over?" I just nodded numbly. Then I thought about my hands, which were getting colder by the second.

"Tell him I'll be over in a minute or so," I answered, as I planned a graceful exit.

I've met so many famous people, but the prospect of meeting Elvis was something completely different. I was such a fan and had longed to meet him for years. Yet the thought of him reaching out to touch one of my fish-cold hands just drove me crazy. (Where were those gloves when I needed them?) Worse, though, the idea of simply meeting him so frightened me I just couldn't do it.

I found my mother and said, "Mom, come to the ladies' room with me. I've got to get out of here fast!"

"What do you mean? What's wrong?"

"Elvis Presley is here!"

I don't think Mom immediately grasped what all the fuss was about, but she followed me and stayed with me as I paced the ladies' room for what seemed like hours, stalling. When I finally worked up the nerve to come out, Elvis was gone. And as often as we were in Las Vegas and despite the fact that I knew people who knew him (Shelley Fabares appeared in three of his movies), our paths never crossed again.

Now, millions of people have lived perfectly happy lives without ever meeting Elvis, so that wasn't the end of the world. But what bothered me about the incident was how I'd reacted. *Why?* I'd wonder, *Am I still so timid?* In those days it was my natural inclination to run away from anything that scared me or that I thought might make me feel the least bit uncomfortable. When presented with a chance to do or try something new, something challenging, I often said no. Looking back, especially from where I am today, I see that, as a result of my natural timidity, I let so many opportunities pass me by. My almost meeting Elvis is an amusing example of that, I suppose, but I approached other, more serious situations much the same way and would continue to do so until very recently.

In the next three years I made eight feature films, and in each I played—some might say enshrined—the red-blooded but pure-hearted girl next door. In the last two Disney feature films I made, *The Misadventures of Merlin Jones* (released in early 1964) and its sequel, *The Monkey's Uncle* (released in summer 1965), the emphasis was on pure. Once again paired with Tommy Kirk, who played Merlin Jones, a teenage genius who's regarded as a "scrambled egghead," I was his long-suffering, resourceful girlfriend Jennifer.

These films were great fun to work on. The real highlight for me was the second film's title theme, which I recorded and performed with the Beach Boys. Written by the Sherman Brothers, "The Monkey's Uncle" refers to Merlin Jones, who has undertaken the education of a chimpanzee named Stanley. (Her real name was Judy, and I befriended her with a daily banana.) Like most of the Shermans' songs for me, this one was basically a love song with some wacky lyrical twists.

The Beach Boys—brothers Carl, Brian, and Dennis Wilson, their cousin Mike Love, and friend Al Jardine—were at the start of what has proved to be a long, successful career. In less than two years, the quintet had become the dominant surf-music group, with hits like "Surfin' U.S.A.," "Fun, Fun, Fun," and "Surfer Girl." By the time *The Monkey's Uncle* was released, the Beach Boys could boast nine Top Ten hits, including two Number Ones ("I Get Around" and "Help Me Rhonda").

I never found out whose idea it was to put us together, but I think it was a stroke of brilliance. As silly as the song is in places, it really does rock, and with the Beach Boys' amazing four-part harmonies, I could sing it without echo. Working with them was really a lot of fun, too. They were all nice guys, and seemed fairly relaxed. Only later—in fact, nearly thirty years later—did I learn that they were very nervous about meeting me. I especially liked Mike and Dennis, who was both cute and outgoing. I felt a natural rapport with Dennis because he was a drummer. Whenever he was playing, he had such a look of contentment on his face. You meet so many people in this business who treat what they do as a job it's always a pleasant surprise to find people who feel passionately about what they are doing.

I didn't know that *The Monkey's Uncle* would be my last Disney feature film or that it would be the last time I would work with Tommy Kirk and my old familiar crew. Maybe it was better that way.

Both the Merlin Jones films were very popular with kids, so much so that the first film was reissued in the early seventies. Objectively speaking, these were lightweight, slightly fantastic comedies, or in a word that popped up often in Disney promotional material for them, "wacky." Merlin's amiable eccentricity, coupled with his ability to read minds, his dedication to educating Stanley the chimp, the flying machine he invents to help the college football team, drove the plots.

In a scene typical not only of *The Misadventures of Merlin Jones* but of my whole teen-queen film persona, Merlin asks Jennifer to participate in a scientific experiment to determine how kissing affects brainwaves, using a bizarre brain-scanning contraption Merlin has built on top of a football helmet. "Kiss me," Merlin implores, to which Jennifer replies indignantly, "Not here in the science building." Merlin finally wears down her defenses, and she reluctantly concedes, "If it's part of a scientific experiment, I guess it's all right." First, he tries it on himself, and while kissing Jennifer the machine practically explodes. When the helmet's on the other head—or Aqua Net-plastered bouffant, in my case— Merlin's kiss inspires no reaction but a chaste, flat line.

And there you had it. How or why the image of me presented in these films has endured to be both loved and parodied—often at the same time—is, frankly, beyond me. Body fashion changes, and what one generation finds appealing or sexy may be the absolute opposite of what their parents preferred. In twentieth-century America, however, the curvaceous female body—especially one on the more bosomy side—has never been ignored. When I made most of my films, in the fifties and sixties, Marilyn Monroe, Ann-Margret, Elizabeth Taylor, and similarly built actresses came to typify the American ideal. And you didn't have to be a rocket scientist to know that in the "language" of movies then a well-endowed woman was considered not only a sexy woman but a sexual woman.

I think that one reason the characters I played in those films became so popular is that their purity, even prudery, contradicted the message of the accepted stereotype and flew in the face of the then-burgeoning sexual revolution. To some degree most movies—except for those made by Disney—have been about sex. Maybe back in those days the dialogue was a little more subtle and the action occurred primarily in the audience's imaginations, but it was there. It's not hard to picture myself in a skin-tight dress, slit up to here and cut down to there, sashaying across the screen, leaving panting men in my wake. As a matter of fact, over the years countless directors, producers, and casting agents have offered some quite incredible propositions to see me do just that. But I always said no. Not only would such a character have been difficult for me to play but I felt that by taking such a role I would be letting down everyone at Disney, my family and friends, and my fans. Not because I think there's anything wrong with dressing in that manner. And I certainly don't have any quarrel with sex. But it wasn't me.

And this brings us to the "beach party" movies, the first of which, *Beach Party*, was filmed and released between the two Merlin Jones films. In the wake of *Beach Party*'s phenomenal success, a slew of sequels followed, all adhering to the same elementary formula. In early-sixties America the teenage vision of paradise was the beach, and not just any beach, either, but those of the California Pacific Coast. There blue-green waves made the perfect backdrop for bikini-clad blondes and their bronzed and baggied surfer boyfriends. Although people had been surfing in California for decades, the sport exploded in those years and was exported to landlocked kids across the continent via the movies and the music that celebrated a mythical endless summer.

Before there were beach movies, there was beach music, or more specifically, surf music. Whether in songs with lyrics heralding the fun-fun-fun times surfside or the dramatic guitar-led instrumentals evoking the sport's trials and triumphs (from "Wipeout" to "Pipeline"), surf music became a popular trend. Riding the crest of the surf-music wave were my friends Jan Berry and Dean Torrance, a.k.a. Jan and Dean, whose "Surf City," the first Number One surf hit, topped the chart the week before our first beach-party film premiered; the Beach Boys, whose biggest early hits, like "Surfin' U.S.A.," defined the genre; and the fabulous—and seemingly eternal—guitarist Dick Dale. I'm so happy to see that Dick is as appreciated today, nearly twenty-five years after his "Let's Go Trippin' " kicked off the surf-music craze.

I don't think you had to be a marketing genius to recognize the potential of a film that would glorify and capitalize on these teenage obsessions. And while other studios and producers made their share of beach movies, I don't think anyone approached the task with the same wry perspective and sense of fun as our producers, James Nicholson and Samuel Arkoff. They had already decided on their male lead, Frankie Avalon. Like most of the other performers who had started out as singing teen idols in the late fifties, he'd left his hit-making days behind—at least for a while. In the meantime, he'd played roles in several impressive productions, including *The Alamo,* with John Wayne; *Voyage to the Bottom of the Sea;* and *Sail a Crooked Ship,* with Ernie Kovacs.

When Mr. Nicholson, who was president of American International Pictures, first met with Mr. Disney to discuss the possibility of my costarring in the movie, he had no idea that Frankie and I even knew each other, let alone that we were good friends. This initially auspicious, almost accidental, pairing soon appeared a stroke of brilliance as "Frankie and Annette" (it's funny that people never said "Frankie and Dee Dee," which was my character's name) became the most famous young lovers since Romeo and Juliet. When offered the part, I thought, *Why not?* I knew *Beach Party* probably was not going to win anyone an armload of Oscars, but that was okay. The story was imaginative, and the cast was great. I knew it would be a lot of fun. But never in a million years did I or anyone else associated with the film dream it would evolve into such a timeless gem of pop-culture Americana.

But this is getting ahead of the story. For starters, Mr. Nicholson had no reason to think Mr. Disney would approve of the project and agree to lend me out. American International was not among the most prestigious Hollywood studios; its previous releases included *Terror from the Year 5000, Dragstrip Girl,* and *Invasion of the Saucer Men,* hardly Disney fare. Apparently, many producers had approached Mr. Disney before about me, but he always found something wrong with the films they wanted to cast me in.

Yet something about *Beach Party* appealed to him. One day as I was walking down Mickey Avenue, he approached and, script in hand, said, "Annette, can I see you for a minute?

"I've read this," he said, smiling. "It's good clean fun, and I think you'll have a wonderful time doing it. But I do have a special little request."

"Okay," I said, somewhat curious.

"Now, I see in here that all the other girls are going to be running around in bikinis, which is fine. But Annette, I want you to be different. You *are* different. I would simply like to request that you not expose your navel in the film."

"Mr. Disney, that's not a problem. Of course, I won't," I replied. And it wasn't; at least not for me. I wore a bikini around my own pool at home, but never in public. So I was happy to comply with Mr. Disney's request.

I wasn't on the set very long, however, before I found out that not everyone was thrilled by my compliance with Mr. Disney's no-navel edict. Even though everyone pretty much understood how I felt about it, as the shooting continued, invariably a producer or director would try to persuade me to wear something more revealing. Several times I was practically taunted, "So you still have to follow the boss's orders?"

I stood my ground, politely but firmly answering, "No, I do not have to follow 'boss's orders.' This is something I chose to do and will do." I was quaking inside, but I refused to let myself be bullied into doing what everyone else was doing. I think this is part of my character—both onscreen and off—that audiences sensed and responded to.

We started filming in March 1963 on a $300,000 budget that was considered skimpy even in those days. When we filmed on the beach, it was early in the morning and always shiveringly cold, especially after they'd hosed us down so we'd look like we'd just come out of the surf. Other scenes were shot on a soundstage that had been filled with tons and tons of sand. We finished all the scenes within three weeks.

Soon after its August 1963 release, *Beach Party* had recouped its costs several times over. Audiences, kids especially, loved the movie because it was simply fun. In retrospect, there are a few little risqué elements, but because of the way the story was told, it never occurred to viewers to ask where the teenagers' parents were, why none of us had jobs, why the guys and the girls slept in the same beach house with only a staircase separating the boys' sleeping quarters downstairs from the girls' slumber partying above them. In future beach-party films, a banner pointing the way upstairs may have read "Heaven's Above," but none of the boys succeeded in testing that premise, or promise.

That's not to say that they didn't try, and here is the beginning of the ongoing Frankie-and-Annette saga. In the film's opening sequence, after singing our way down a coastal highway in our hot rod stacked with beach blankets and surfboards, we arrive at what Frankie believes will be our private little lovers' nest. Of course, Dee Dee has invited the whole gang to stay with them, so there go Frankie's big plans for romance.

"You know it's more fun with the whole gang," Dee Dee explains.

"Not what I had in mind!" Frankie replies.

But Dee Dee wasn't a cold fish, either. As she confesses to Frankie, "I don't trust myself with you." And though Frankie and Dee Dee would find themselves in variations of this impasse many times in the coming films, Frankie just couldn't—or wouldn't—get Dee Dee's message: "Not without a ring, you don't!"

Of all the beach-party movies, the first was not the most commercially successful but it remains my personal favorite. The story involved Professor Sutwell, a square, timid cultural anthropologist (played by Bob Cummings), who, with his assistant (Dorothy Malone), comes to the beach to study teenage mating rituals. Like its successors, *Beach Party* revolved around Frankie and Dee Dee's breaking up. He makes her jealous by going after another girl, while she falls for the professor's softspoken charms. But they end up together again for a happy ending.

Frankie and Dee Dee provide the familiar center of a universe populated by Harvey Lembeck's Brandoesque caricature of a dim-witted, stuttering, but softhearted motorcycle gang leader and his loyal Rats and Mice (a.k.a., the "stupids"); Cappy, the philosophizing beatnik owner of the local hangout (played by Morey Amsterdam); go-go dancer Candy Johnson; and Frankie and Dee Dee's friends, played by Jody McCrea, John Ashley, and others. Swirling around the recurring characters and running gags were crazy subplots and guest and cameo roles that ran the gamut from Marta Kristen (later of TV's *Lost in Space*) as a mermaid, to comedian Paul Lynde as a pushy PR man, and Linda Evans, in her film debut, as a sexy pop singer, Sugar Cane. Established stars also joined us: Buster Keaton (who played a witch doctor in one of his two beach-party roles), Mickey Rooney, Peter Lorre, Keenan Wynne, Boris Karloff, Don Rickles, and Buddy Hackett. In the first film Vincent Price played Big Daddy, a somnolent prophet Cappy believes will issue "the word" that will give the beach kids a cause.

I made several good friends through these films, including Luree Nicholson, the producer's daughter. She worked on the set as a beach-girl extra, and within a very short time we became as close as sisters. We palled around together, and our friendship has continued through the years. In fact, my daughter's middle name is Luree, in her honor. I also became quite close to Harvey Lembeck, who, many people might be surprised to know, was an accomplished actor. Harvey was wonderful—kind and gregarious. Over the years he and his wife became personal friends of mine.

Working with so many older, established actors was always a thrill. Buster Keaton, for example, had been making films since the early twenties; Peter Lorre was a living legend. But of them all, my absolute favorites were Mickey Rooney and Don Rickles. Mickey Rooney was one of the few comedians I'd worked with who was actually as outgoing, personable, and entertaining off camera as he was on. Don Rickles, who appeared in two of our films *(Bikini Beach* and *Muscle Beach Party),* was always a lot of fun. He got his first big break in our films, and, his onscreen heckling persona aside, he proved to be a very kind, warm man. He had a wonderful ability to get people to laugh at themselves, and toward the end of a long day's shoot, that's no easy feat. Once, when he was appearing in Las Vegas, most of the cast from one of the beach-party movies traveled there to see him. We made the mistake of all sitting at the same table, and from the stage he picked on each of us mercilessly. He particularly liked my dad, and he never saw him without cracking some joke about our Italian heritage, like "Hey, Joe, I see you've got some spaghetti sauce on your tie again!" When Don was around, you were laughing constantly.

One of my best buddies from the beach-movie days was guitarist Dick Dale. No doubt our paths had crossed in the late fifties and early sixties, since we both had hit records out then, but we really got to know each other while we were making the films. Dick and his group, the Del-Tones, supplied a lot of the music, and he also appeared as an extra in some scenes.

Today Dick is enjoying a resurgence in popularity, but it seemed to me that he was always in the midst of a resurgence. Despite a lack of hit records during the sixties, seventies, and eighties, he just kept at his craft. Today he's being rediscovered and revered as a king of rock guitar. It couldn't happen to a nicer guy.

While the beach pictures were in production, I became quite good friends with Dick's sister Shirley, and Dick often stayed at my parents' home, because it was such a long drive from where he lived to where we filmed. I thought Dick was handsome and a dream come true. But we were so different from each other I knew a serious romance was out of the question. Plus he was a real surfer, and considering the bevy of long-haired blondes in bikinis who were after him, I didn't think I stood a chance.

In the time we've known each other, he's shown me much kindness. I'll never forget the time my poodle Jette was missing. We had some neighbors who didn't care for dogs and had hinted that something terrible might befall little Jette. So when she disappeared one day while we were having a barbecue, we were frantic, convinced the neighbors had stolen or hurt her. I was so upset. Jette was like my little baby. Dick immediately went out and bought me another poodle. And then, as if that wasn't sweet enough, he took the poodle back and found it a good home after Jette returned.

Then, of course, there was my good buddy Frankie, who

by then was married and had a running start on a family that would eventually include eight children. Without Frankie on the scene, the beach-party pictures would have been an entirely different experience. In fact, in *How to Stuff a Wild Bikini*, Frankie (who is somewhere in Tahiti) and I have no scenes together. Instead my would-be love interest is played by Dwayne Hickman, then best known for his title role in television's *The Many Loves of Dobie Gillis*. Dwayne had a great sense of humor, but I missed Frankie. That, and the fact that I was several months along in my first pregnancy during the filming, made this one of my least favorite beach-party films. But I'm getting ahead of myself.

The beach-party movies aren't often thought of in terms of their music, but the famous musical acts that appeared in them comprised an impressive roster. In addition to Dick Dale and the Del-Tones, we beach kids played host to the Pyramids (a bald group whose sole hit was a guitar-based instrumental called "Penetration"), the Exciters (of "Tell Him" fame), the Hondells ("Little Honda"), and the Kingsmen, who popularized the immortal "Louie Louie." In addition, Frankie and I would sing a couple of numbers, too. Perhaps the biggest star to have made a film debut in one of our films was Stevie Wonder (then thirteen-year-old Little Stevie Wonder), who performed his first Number One pop hit, "Fingertips," in *Muscle Beach Party* and then returned in *Bikini Beach*.

In just a few years the beach-party genre faded, though not for lack of imaginative plot twists; take, for example, *Pajama Party*'s Martian invaders. The scene then shifted to ski chalets, drag strips, even haunted houses, but the beach would always be the place to be. For whatever reason—blame Sunday afternoon and late-late-night TV movies—these films have found new audiences and stood the test of time in their appeal. For me their success is pretty ironic, considering I'd always hated the beach. The sea air made my hair frizzy, and as for surfing—forget it. In almost every picture, the director would call for a shot of me running down the beach, board tucked under my arm, then leaping gracefully into the surf and paddling out. But back then the boards were over six feet long and weighed upward of twenty-five pounds. I tried several times, but the most they ever got out of it was a totally winded Annette gasping in the sand, my board lying several feet behind me.

How tightly were Frankie-and-Annette woven into the American pop-culture consciousness? About as tightly as "M-I-C-K-E-Y." When my children were younger, I would take them to the beach. I'd put on a big hat, sunglasses— you'd never have known it was me, until I opened my mouth. Invariably, several nice folks would approach and ask, "Are you Annette?"

"Why, yes," I'd reply.

"So where's Frankie?"

Many times they were absolutely serious. But the confusion really hit home one day when my daughter, Gina, saw a promo for a local TV station's beach-party marathon. She pointed to Frankie (who, by the way, is her godfather) and asked, "Mommy, is that my daddy? And why does he never come home for dinner?"

Through 1964 and 1965 I also guest-starred on TV programs like *Wagon Train, The Greatest Show on Earth,* and *Burke's Law.* The latter, an early Aaron Spelling production, starred Gene Barry as the dashing Amos Burke, a millionaire playboy who works as a homicide detective for fun. In one episode, "Who Killed the Kind Doctor?," I played the mildly neurotic starlet patient of a murdered shrink. In the second, "Who Killed the Strangler?," I really played against type for the first time in my life, and it was not a pleasant experience. In this episode, which costarred Frankie as a sportswriter, I played the notorious "girl in the cage" at a famous go-go club. I didn't mind swimming and frugging up in the cage, or wearing the skimpy (for those days) white fringed two-piece minidress. But when I read in the script that I had to dance

Although my part in it was small, I found working on my first feature film, The Shaggy Dog, *very exciting. Clockwise from lower right: Shaggy the dog, Fred MacMurray, Kevin Corcoran, Roberta Shore, and me.*

Although I portrayed a champion rider in The Horsemasters, *my horse threw me countless times while we were filming in England.*

OPPOSITE TOP: *Tommy Sands and I dancing through a magical Mother Goose Village in my favorite Disney film,* Babes in Toyland.

OPPOSITE BOTTOM: Babes in Toyland's *dazzling finale: the fantasy wedding of Tom Piper (Tommy Sands) and Mary Contrary (me).*

Several years later, for my real-life wedding, designer Bill Thomas based my headpiece on the one I wore in this still from Babes in Toyland.

TOP: *A musical moment from* Escapade in Florence *with costars Nino Castelnuovo (left) and Carlo Rizzo (right).*

BOTTOM: *Tommy Kirk appeared in all but one of the feature films I made at Disney. Here we are in a typical scene from* The Misadventures of Merlin Jones.

OPPOSITE TOP: *In the course of filming my last Walt Disney Studio feature of the sixties,* The Monkey's Uncle, *I befriended my simian costar, Judy the chimp.*

OPPOSITE BOTTOM: *One of the high points of my music career was performing the title theme from* The Monkey's Uncle *with the Beach Boys. Left to right: Carl Wilson, Al Jardine, Brian Wilson, Dennis Wilson, and Mike Love.*

RIGHT: *Was that a beach party I saw on the horizon?*

The classic beach-party movie set included a coed beach house, far from parents, not a chaperon in sight, and the way to heaven clearly posted. Yet my character, Dee Dee, always made it to the end of each film with her principles intact.

RIGHT: *Everyone knows the beach-party movies helped launch a nation-wide surf craze. But think of what it did for hair spray!*

OPPOSITE TOP: *This is my favorite picture of Frankie Avalon and me from the beach-party films. We really enjoyed working together, and I think it shows.*

OPPOSITE BOTTOM: *In a two-piece suit. But faithful to my promise to Mr. Disney, I never showed my navel.*

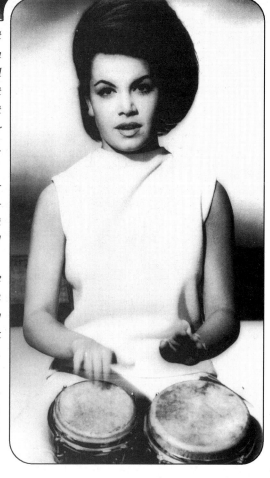

TOP: *The wedding party (left to right): Harvey Lembeck, Shirley Monsour (Dick Dale's sister), Joey Funicello, Arlene Ludwig, Frankie Avalon, Shelley Fabares, Jack, me, Marion Kruppe, Ralph Amaruso, Noreen Corcoran, Frank Alessia, Irene Rosenthal, Johnny Macchia, Luree Nicholson, Ted Witzer.*

BOTTOM: *My parents greet actress Deborah Walley, and I get a kiss from John Ashley, two beach-party costars who attended my wedding.*

I appeared as a Hollywood go-go dancer on television's Burke's Law, 1965. Regardless of what some would-be producers and directors thought, playing it hot and sexy just wasn't for me.

Of all the roles I've played, none has been as fulfilling as being a mother. In my daughter Gina's bedroom with her baby brother Jason, and Jackie, 1974.

*From all-American girl next door to
all-American mom was an easy transi-
tion for me, especially since I loved
peanut butter.*

*No matter how many years
pass, some things never
change: Frankie and I
together again.*

*One of my favorite
photographs.*

LEFT: *Working with actors in costume was nothing new to me. I made many appearances on television's* Fantasy Island.

BOTTOM: *One of the few times through the years I've visited with Paul Anka.*

OPPOSITE TOP: *With the group Fishbone I reprised my 1964 album track "Jamaica Ska" for my favorite of all the beach party films, 1987's* Back to the Beach.

OPPOSITE BOTTOM: *A family portrait from my second wedding, May 3, 1986. Left to right: Gina, my father, me, Glen, Jason , Mom, and Jackie.*

Glen and I at our wedding reception with our very special
celebrity guest. For every important occasion, it seems I
have Mickey Mouse at my side.

provocatively, then run down a staircase and passionately kiss Amos Burke on the lips, I froze. I knew I couldn't do it. Gene Barry, a consummate gentleman, walked me through the scenes over and over again, encouraging me.

It might sound like I was overly sensitive; after all, I was an actress. But little things like kissing really bothered me. In the twenty years that I was basically retired from show business, people often asked if I didn't miss the work, the excitement, the glamour. It's hard to explain to someone who thinks being a performer is the most wonderful job anyone could have why I was happy to leave it behind. So many things contributed to my decision: knowing I'd never find a work environment as safe and supportive as the one I'd known at Disney, the unfamiliarity of new sets and crews, the shocking (at least to me) lack of ethics and morals I saw. I could see from the kinds of scripts I was being offered that producers wanted to see Annette grown up in ways that were unacceptable to me. I was not a good enough actress to be something I wasn't, or to do things that I wouldn't do otherwise.

CHAPTER 7

O n Father's Day 1964, right after *The Monkey's Uncle* was finished and *Muscle Beach Party* hit the screen, my retirement plans were set when my agent, Jack Gilardi, asked my father for my hand in marriage.

I had known Jack for several years. In fact, we first met at the Hollywood Bowl, when I was introduced to Frankie Avalon. At the time, Jack was Frankie's agent, and later Fabian's as well. Around 1963, when I began working away from Disney, Jack also became my agent as well.

For many years, our relationship was strictly about business. Jack was twelve years my senior, so initially it didn't occur to me to date him. My mother and father, though, liked Jack. Whenever his parents visited from Chicago, they would go out to dinner with Mom and Dad, and we soon found that our families had a lot in common. In addition to being Italian and Catholic, Jack's family was as close-knit as mine. Though Jack had been a bachelor in Hollywood for years, we shared the same basic values and had the same ideas about married life.

We had known each other as manager and client, and as friends. One evening, I don't know what happened. He looked at me, I looked at him, and suddenly we knew we were in love.

The day he asked my dad for my hand in marriage was one of the happiest and the saddest days in my life. We were having a barbecue, and Jack and Dad were out by the pool alone. My father was initially shocked; perhaps he didn't think his little Dolly would ever get married and leave home. But he was also so happy for us he cried. Then we all toasted one another with champagne, and soon I was wearing a three-and-a-half-carat diamond engagement ring.

Because I believed I would marry only once in my life, and because Mom and Dad never got to have a formal wedding, Mom and I went all-out for mine. Our original plans for a Valentine's Day wedding had to be changed, because it fell during Lent, but except for that minor hitch, almost everything went beautifully. As promised years before, designer Bill Thomas created my wedding gown of satin covered by imported French chantilly lace, with a five-foot-long cathedral train frosted with crystal beads. The headpiece was adapted from the one I wore during the wedding scene of *Babes in Toyland.* My bridesmaids—good friends Shelley Fabares, actress Noreen Corcoran (of *Bachelor Father*), Arlene Ludwig (who was then senior publicist for the Walt Disney Studio), Irene Sloan, Shirley Monsour, and Luree (Nicholson) Holmes—wore formal gowns of lush red velvet. The ushers, who included Frankie and Harvey Lembeck, all looked handsome in their black tuxedos.

On the morning of the wedding, Mom opened the newspaper and turned to the comics. There Charles Schulz paid tribute to the day in his *Peanuts* comic strip by showing Linus reading a paper, clutching his security blanket, and crying, "I can't stand it! This is terrible! How depressing . . . ANNETTE FUNICELLO HAS GROWN UP!"

I suppose my dad felt the same way. As we walked down the aisle together, he squeezed my arm tightly, and I, his. Then I kissed him. I wanted to find the words to tell him I would always be his little Dolly, but I think he knew.

Like any bride, I was nervous on my wedding day, but unlike most, I had real cause for worry. A young man had been writing to me for some time, saying he was in love with me and so on. I'd received so many letters like that I had stopped taking them too seriously until just a few years before, when a young fan tried to commit suicide, ostensibly after I returned a gift he'd sent me. To judge by the letters this man was sending me, however, his mental state seemed to be deteriorating. His words assumed a threatening tone, and it was clear that his ideas about me and our "relationship" were the products of a delusional mind.

Disney security had been monitoring the situation for several months before my engagement was announced. Once it hit the news, however, the letters became terrifying. The man, a U.S. soldier stationed in Germany, wrote that he wanted to marry me, and warned that if he couldn't have me no one else would. What really chilled me to the bone was this threat: "If you leave your house to go to the church, I will kill you."

At that point, we all took the threats very seriously. My parents and I were terribly frightened. But by the time the worst letters began arriving, our plans were already set. We'd invited fifteen hundred guests to the wedding, and five hundred to the reception, including Jane Powell, Don Rickles, Hedda Hopper and Louella Parsons, Deborah Walley, Carroll O'Connor, Sharon Baird, Tommy Sands, and Nancy Sinatra. I felt that there was nothing I could do but go through with it. And, I suppose, in the back of my mind I really didn't believe that anything so horrible could befall me on that of all days.

So unbeknown to the public or to most of my wedding guests, Saint Cyril's Church became a guarded fortress filled with unobtrusive Disney security people in their best formal dress. I can't say that I didn't worry; I did. At the same time, though, I was determined to make my wedding day as wonderful as I'd dreamed it would be. Fortunately, the day went without incident. The security staff somehow had identified

the man who wrote the letters and contacted his command-
ing officers. Exactly what they did to him I never knew. I
never *wanted* to know. All I know is that the letters stopped.

The wedding ceremony was beautiful beyond my wildest
dreams. As one nationally syndicated columnist wrote the
next day: "Have you ever seen a dream walking? Well, I
did." Walking back down the aisle after being pronounced
man and wife, I felt sure that this was the part I'd always
wanted to play. Regardless of what I'd done or accomplished
in my past, the best part of my life lay ahead.

Our reception in the grand ballroom of the Beverly Hilton
Hotel began magically, as Jack and I walked under an arch of
violin bows held aloft by several pairs of violinists. As Tutti
Camarata had promised me years before, he provided the
musicians and the music for this special day: three bands in
all, including a rock group. Naturally before we danced together for the first time as man and wife (to "I Love You
Truly") the band first played "The Mickey Mouse Club
March."

The rest of the day was simply magical.

Unfortunately, shortly before the wedding I'd learned that
Mr. Disney would not be able to attend. Like so many others
who knew him, I had no idea that he was beginning to suffer
from excruciating pain, the early signs of the cancer that
would take his life less than two years later. Also missing
was my dear friend Jimmie Dodd, who had died in Hawaii
only two months before from a rare blood condition. I was
saddened and yet deeply touched when his wife, Ruth, who
did attend the wedding, told me that Jimmie had kept my
wedding invitation on his bedside table.

So it was a bittersweet day in some ways, yet as I looked
around the ballroom at my family and my friends, I felt every
bit the fairy-tale princess whose Prince Charming had arrived to sweep her away to the "happily ever after."

I honestly felt that I was ready for marriage, and I was very happy. Yet I had not anticipated how much I would miss my family. Our Mexican honeymoon was splendidly romantic—until my nose started to bleed from the high altitude in the middle of a candlelight dinner. To make things even worse, I reached into my pocket for a handkerchief and pulled out one that belonged to my mother. When I saw her initials embroidered on it, I started crying.

"I want to go home!" I said, sobbing.

"Well, we can't go home," Jack replied, then added, "Would you feel better if you called your parents?"

"Yes," I answered, choking back tears. We waited for the operator to place the call, but when my father answered, the sound of his voice made my eyes well up all over again. I was supposed to be having the time of my life, and yet not everything was perfect. Jack and I had a minor spat and didn't talk for two days. I suppose if I'd traveled alone more, if I'd spent some time on my own before I married, it might have been different. All I could think of was home.

By the time Jack and I arrived back in Los Angeles, we were again the happy newlyweds. My parents met us at the airport, and I was so happy to see them. Mom and Dad and I hugged, then Mom stepped back, looked me over closely, and said, "Annette, you're pregnant! You have a look in your eyes like I've never seen before."

To which my dad replied, "Virginia, get your mind out of the gutter!"

"But, Joe, they are married, after all," Mom gently reminded him.

"Mom," I said, "how can you know that?"

"I just do, honey," she assured me. And, sure enough, Mom was right. Shortly after returning home from New York, where I jumped and danced in a *Hullabaloo* segment, my doctor confirmed my mother's suspicions. Even though I'd always said that I wanted to start my family on my honeymoon, I didn't really expect it to happen. But there I was, married less than three weeks, with a baby on the way. All grown-up, indeed.

Settled into our Beverly Hills apartment, enjoying my new marriage, thinking about my new baby—I never thought I could be happier. I felt something in myself change. Most of my life I'd looked to my parents, and later to Jack, for support and encouragement. Now becoming a mother meant that for the first time in my life someone would be totally dependent on me. And while Jack and my parents would always be there for me and our new child, I knew from my own experience growing up that, in a child's eyes, no one can take the place of Mommy. I never took parenthood lightly, and I waited out the ensuing months fully aware of the awesome responsibility that would soon come.

My pregnancy started out typically enough, with morning sickness and a surge in appetite. I was ravenous all the time, and for once I didn't stop to count calories or fret about squeezing into a new dress. Instead, I did what I thought best for me and the baby: I ate to my heart's content. Of course, I endured the inevitable consequence, a quick and substantial weight gain, but I did so happily. I was eating for two, I reasoned, and before long my expanding waistline convinced me that I might even be eating for three! Twins ran in my family, and since my grandmother had given birth to two sets of twins, and twin births are said to skip a generation, I assumed it was my turn. I was a bit disappointed when the doctor reported hearing only one heartbeat, but I assumed there would be plenty of time to have many more babies.

I was still in my early months when we began shooting *How to Stuff a Wild Bikini*. With me tastefully covered in oversized sweaters for the chilly evening beach scenes and roomy tops for the others, no one would suspect that I was expecting. The producers kindly planned the schedule so I could finish my work as quickly as possible. As much as I enjoyed making the film, it was, as I said before, the first beach-party movie I'd done without Frankie. That made me a little blue, and, what with the baby coming, my thoughts were light years away to begin with. While other cast members talked about where they'd go out after we finished shooting or what their next job would be, I contentedly daydreamed of hand-knitted booties, fluffy pastel blankets, and the sweet smell of baby powder.

I was busy getting ready to be a mother, but I was also learning how to be a wife. I'd always helped Mom around the house as much as I could, but to be honest, that wasn't much. Once I was married I really appreciated how much time and effort Mom dedicated to keeping our house immaculate, taking care of us, and seeing that we had delicious home-cooked meals every day. Mom guided me through my early cooking endeavors, and eventually I got the hang of it. I was so proud of our home that it never occurred to me to hire a full-time cleaning woman; I was happy to do most of it myself.

While awaiting the baby's birth, I often thought back to the weeks a few years before when I took care of my little godson, Louie Pietroforte: how I'd placed his bassinet next to my bed and listened closely to his breathing, how I couldn't wait to be awakened by his cries and to give him his bottle. I thoroughly enjoyed changing his diapers and bathing him, even burping him. There was nothing about caring for a baby that didn't feel natural to me, that didn't bring me great pleasure.

On October 17, 1965, our first child, Gina Luree, was born at Saint Joseph's Hospital, right across the street from the Disney Studio. Mom, Dad, and Jack sat nervously in the waiting room, later to be joined by Gina's godfather, Frankie. Mom had always told me that she'd had easy labors and assured me mine would be, too, and she was right. It was fairly comfortable (perhaps because it wasn't totally natural), and I was heartened by my doctor's assurances that, physically, there was no reason why another eight or nine babies couldn't follow.

When I first came out from under the anesthesia and opened my eyes to see my baby, my heart filled with love and thanks to God for sending her to me. How can I express how I felt the first time I held her and her blue eyes gazed up into mine? How can you describe a miracle? Overwhelmed by emotion and still a little woozy from the delivery, I said to my doctor, "I love you."

Within hours of Gina's birth, my hospital room over-flowed with flowers, including a stunning bouquet of lavender roses from Jack. I relished feeling like every other mother in the world—but I wasn't. You can imagine the looks on people's faces when Mickey Mouse, Minnie, and Donald Duck came strutting down the maternity-ward corridor bearing flowers from Walt Disney. You might think this slightly surreal, but I felt perfectly natural calling out, "Hi, Mickey! Hi, Minnie! Hi, Donald!" Mr. Disney sent a beautiful arrangement in a little baby potty bowl with Gina's name on it. Enclosed with the flowers was a very moving, heartfelt note to me, which I treasured. In it he wrote, "Now the world has two dolls. Very Sincerely, Walt Disney."

A few days later, Jack, Gina, and I were at home, a little family at last. Following an old Italian tradition, Gina did not leave the house until the day she was christened in early November at the same church where, only ten months before, Jack and I were married. Not long after that we moved into our home in Encino, not far from my parents' house. I still live there today. I decorated baby Gina's nursery in yellow and white, with a crib topped by a canopy and animal figures on the walls. We had our daughter, our health, our family, the house of our dreams. What more could anyone ask for?

Except for a few guest appearances on television, I was for all intents and purposes retired. I adored Gina and poured my heart into every task. I took great pride in dressing her in the cutest outfits, always with matching shoes, stockings, and bows. Once her hair grew long enough, I spent at least half an hour each day just finger-curling her blond locks into a cascade of golden ringlets. Despite my previous accomplishments, nothing compared to being told by Gina's pediatrician that she was the cleanest, best-smelling baby he'd ever seen. Gina made being a first-time mother so easy. She was bright, calm, attentive, and hardly ever whined or cried. Of course, with her mother and father, her grandparents, her uncles, and our many friends doting on her, it would have been hard for her to be anything but a contented child.

Although I made sure I was home when each of my children was young, and that I saw their first steps and heard their first words, sometimes my career did call me back. However, I never ventured outside my front door without thoughts of my babies foremost in my mind. Like me, Gina never had a baby-sitter who wasn't family, and I was relieved to know that she was almost always in the loving care of Grandma and Grandpa Funicello.

The few times when I did choose to work, leaving Gina broke my heart. When Gina was about seventeen months old she stayed with my parents for a few days while Jack and I flew to New York City, where I appeared on *The Ed Sullivan Show*. When Mom told me that she'd held Gina up to the television screen, and that the baby had recognized me, I couldn't help crying. Shortly after that, I started shooting a movie with Frankie and Fabian called *Fireball 500*. Gina stayed with my parents from Monday through Friday, when I raced home after work to see her, then spent the weekends back home with Jack and her. I missed her so much that turning down projects got easier. I made several guest appearances on television series, and (not counting cameo appearances) I made only two more films, *Thunder Alley* (which costarred Fabian) and *Head,* with the Monkees. I always expected people to stop calling for me, for my career to simply evaporate, but that never happened.

These were golden days, but life always seems to have a way of crashing down on you when you least expect it. I suppose that because Mr. Disney had been such a constant presence in my life for so many years, I never dreamed one day he would be gone. Even though we rarely saw each other as time went on and my work took me off the Disney lot, I was always secure in the sense that I knew he was around and looking out for me.

I last saw Mr. Disney in late 1965. He appeared noticeably tired and drawn, but, I reasoned, he was in his early sixties by then and still keeping the schedule of a man half his age. He was also in the midst of executing his grand plans for his second fantasy park, Disney World, and the project nearest to his heart, EPCOT. I could see that he was walking a bit more slowly, and his hair had a touch more gray than I remembered. Yet his eyes still twinkled, and his spirit was still young. What I—and most people who worked for Mr. Disney—didn't know was that his health had been faltering, the result of old polo injuries and a heavy smoking habit. Despite that, he still tried to oversee every studio project in the works, his unerring eye for detail undimmed.

In early November 1966 he entered Saint Joseph's Hospital after suffering intense pain and shortness of breath. When tests revealed a suspicious mass in one lung, he underwent surgery to remove it. Typically, Mr. Disney told only his family and a few others close to him about his true state of health. Even after the surgeons discovered cancer and removed his left lung, very few people knew how seriously ill he was. After a brief recuperation period, he returned to work, by all accounts more driven than ever to see his last projects through and reluctant to talk about anything besides work.

Despite his protests to the contrary, Mr. Disney grew weaker by the day. After spending Thanksgiving with his wife and family at his daughter Diane's house, he returned home and soon reentered Saint Joseph's Hospital, where from his bed he could look out his window and across the street to the studio he had built over three decades before. Over the next two weeks his condition deteriorated rapidly, and after spending an evening discussing plans for Disney World and EPCOT with his brother Roy, Mr. Disney passed away the next morning.

I was cleaning the house and listening to the radio; I always had it tuned to a rock station. While polishing a table in the den, I felt myself jolted as if out of a dream when the announcer said, "Walt Disney died today. . . ." My immediate reaction was to think that someone was pulling a horrible prank, that this was some kind of sick joke, maybe a mistake. But as the hours wore on and my phone began ringing with reporters asking my reaction, I knew it had to be true. I sank down into a sofa and cried.

The day after Mr. Disney's death, his body was cremated and his remains interred at Forest Lawn Cemetery following a private funeral attended only by his family. It felt strange to have someone so close to me pass away and not be able to see him or in some way pay one last tribute. That night I watched television, listening numbly as anchormen tried to put into words all that Mr. Disney had meant to the world and how he would be missed. Yet all I could think of was that I had lost a very dear friend, a guardian angel.

I thought back to a very special evening in 1963 when I was asked to attend the Fifteenth Annual Emmy Awards ceremony at the Hollywood Palladium and to accept an award on Mr. Disney's behalf. Dressed in a light sequined dress with long evening gloves, my hair done up in a sophisticated bouffant, I bore scant resemblance to the girl in mouse ears and pleats. I accepted the award and said simply, "On behalf of my wonderful boss, Mr. Disney, and his staff, thank you so much." The next day in the press writers marveled at how grown-up I looked, how I'd matured, yet in my heart I would always be one of Mr. Disney's little Mouseketeers.

Mr. Disney was so special to me, and to the world, that it's very hard to accept that he is no longer here. Sometimes when I drop by the studio and walk down the lanes he used to walk, it seems as if nothing has changed there. Or when Mickey Mouse—who, of course, is an actor in a costume—accompanies me on a public appearance, it feels as if Mr. Disney's spirit is still here, and I suppose it is. It's only when I look across at the new buildings on the lot, or realize that except for a handful of people no one working at the studio today even met him, it dawns on me that he is really gone.

It's funny, but sometimes when I feel discouraged or have a problem I can't work out, I find myself thinking, *If only Mr. Disney were here, he would know what to do.* And I'm sure he would. He was always so far ahead of everyone else in his thinking and his vision. If Walt Disney could be among us today, I have no doubt he would fit right in effortlessly. And when you think of what he was able to create with the primitive technology available then and imagine what he might do today, you can't help but wonder. And wish a little bit, too.

My one lasting regret was that I never got to say goodbye to him, although I comfort myself with the belief that, wherever he might be, he knows what is in my heart.

In the years after I started my family the pop-music world I'd been so much a part of before was drastically redefined. The teen idols—Frankie, Paul, Fabian, Ricky Nelson—were swept away as new sounds and styles conquered the charts. For a while there it seemed that one of the few acts to weather the British Invasion was the Beach Boys. For the straight, clean-cut performers of the early sixties the hits stopped coming. Only those who changed their styles to fit the mood of the times—like Bobby Darin with "If I Were a Carpenter," or Rick Nelson, with his then new country-rock records—were still accepted, but by smaller audiences. For most of the rock artists I'd come up with, their time had come. And gone.

Long hair, bell bottoms, drugs, and free love were now the buzzwords and the legacy of a new generation, one for whom the wholesomeness of the beach-party movies seemed quaintly passé. Despite living in Hollywood, the center of this stunning cultural shift, I remained remarkably unaffected. I knew no one personally who had "dropped out," or who did drugs. Of course, years later I discovered that I had been in the company of several people who were experimenting with drugs, but at the time the closest I ever came to any mind-altering substance was a glass of wine with dinner.

One day I received a script titled, appropriately, "Untitled." As I perused the first several pages, it was clear that this script was unlike any I'd ever seen, with descriptions of brief, seemingly unrelated scenes and nonsensical dialogue that was totally incomprehensible. All I knew about it was that it had been cowritten by Bob Rafelson and Jack Nicholson for the Monkees, and that they wanted me to be in it.

Of course I knew the Monkees—Davy Jones, Mickey Dolenz, Mike Nesmith, and Peter Tork—from their hit prime-time television series and their hit records, like "Last Train to Clarksville," "I'm a Believer," and "Pleasant Valley Sunday." Many years before I'd met Mickey Dolenz when he was a young boy playing the title role in the television series *Circus Boy.* My part, which was just a cameo role, was to play Davy Jones's girlfriend, who begs him not to give up the violin to become a champion boxer. What did it mean? Don't ask me. In fact, no one working on the film, including Victor Mature (whose hair the Monkees romp through in one surrealistic scene), boxer Sonny Liston, topless dancer Carol Doda, or musician Frank Zappa, probably knew either.

Although *Head,* as the movie was subsequently titled, seemed to make a somewhat heavy, depressing point about the planned obsolescence of pop culture and its heroes and commented sharply on the Monkees' manufactured image, the guys themselves were actually quite happy and engaging on the set. I particularly liked Davy Jones because he was the shyest. Between takes, we had several heart-to-heart talks and a lot of fun. Even if only for a few weeks, the experience made me remember how much fun work could be, yet rarely was. In 1968, when I got a chance to see the finished film, I must admit that it made no more sense to me than it ever had. But it was a challenging, offbeat role, and I was happy to play it.

Jack, of course, was still my agent. As Hollywood and the rest of the country got wilder and wilder, so did some of the parts offered me. We could always count on seeing scripts that sought to present Annette the Doper, Annette the Hooker, Annette the Drunk. And it's true that performers with squeaky-clean images could get some mileage and a lot of attention out of playing so aggressively against type. Naturally I always turned those parts down. Not only would I have felt odd playing them, but frankly I didn't think I'd be believable, no matter how good my acting was.

That said, I did accept a role on the short-lived television series *Hondo*, which starred Ralph Taeger in the title role. Hondo was a cavalry scout who had lived among the Indians and then become a loner after the death of his Indian wife. Set in the old Arizona Territory, this series broke many TV western conventions, focusing on the psychological aspects of its scripts instead of the usual shoot-'em-ups. For a while there was some discussion that I might be cast in a recurring role, but the series was canceled after just a few months.

David Nelson and I played homesteading newlyweds, and Nick Adams (better known for his title role in TV's *The Rebel*) portrayed a sadistic, homicidal Indian. The key scene, in which the Indian breaks into the couple's cabin, ties up and beats the husband, and then threatens his soon-to-be widow (me), contains virtually no dialogue. For minutes the camera shifts from a knife my character could use to defend herself, to the Indian eying me lecherously, and to me standing against a wall, paralyzed with fear. At the opening of my next scene, my character is wandering around dazed, her clothes ripped and her hair mussed. That she was in some way sexually assaulted by her husband's killer is strongly suggested.

Even though I was now married and had a child, some people in the business still wouldn't give up on trying to drastically change my image. I know that a prominent men's magazine had made a handsome offer to Mr. Disney a few years before to feature me in a nude pictorial. Can you imagine the look on his face when he heard that? But of all the ludicrous propositions Jack and I ever fielded, one in particular took the cake. I might say, Picture this, but actually I'd prefer you didn't: me, onstage in Las Vegas, doing a slow, sensuous strip until there was nothing left but my Mickey Mouse ears. Really!

On February 10, 1970, Gina welcomed her new little brother, Jack Gilardi, Jr. At almost four years of age, Gina was going through that sweet maternal stage little girls do, so she was pleased to be Mommy's little helper whenever she could. And, believe me, when it came to Jackie (who, it goes without saying, I love dearly with all of my heart), I soon needed help—lots of it. I'd always wanted to have a hearty, red-blooded boy who craved adventure and knew his own mind. I just wasn't prepared to deal with these qualities in a nine-month-old.

I suppose that Gina spoiled me. Sweet, docile, as obedient as any happy, normal, curious child can be, she was a mother's dream. I never worried about her for a minute. From the moment Jackie started walking, at an amazing nine months of age, I never got another full night's sleep. Shortly after learning to walk, he executed several successful escapes from his crib. It was bad enough that I had to worry that Jackie was roaming our large ranch-style home in the dark, but he quickly learned to maneuver my kitchen stepladder into the foyer, climb it, then open the front door. On several occasions I found him wandering in the front yard, perilously close to the street. Finally, we had no choice but to install a security system, so at least when he opened the doors an alarm would sound.

Brave, precocious, headstrong, Jackie was not your typical kid. One night when he was about three, I got up and found him missing from his bed. The alarm hadn't gone off, so I knew he was in the house. I looked in every room, under every piece of furniture, behind every door. No Jackie. Then as I passed the laundry area off the kitchen I heard a faint, muffled "Mom! Mom!" Jackie had crawled into the clothes dryer and locked himself in. Another time when he was around five, I discovered him standing on the roof with one end of a rope tied to a nearby tree branch and the other fastened in a noose around his neck. And he was ready to jump.

"Jackie!" I screamed. "Take that rope from around your neck and get down! Now! What were you thinking? You'll kill yourself."

"Well, Mom," he explained, "I saw Superman do it!"

Yet another time we were getting ready to go to the airport to pick up my in-laws. Somehow in the confusion, Jackie ran across the street, climbed a neighbor's tree, then fell out, severely breaking his wrist. Then there was the day he turned blue after almost choking to death on a piece of candy. The list goes on. I've known lots of children but very few like Jackie. Kindhearted, well-meaning, but an accident waiting to happen, I always called him. In fact, his family nickname was "Perpetual Motion."

Within a year, Gina started school, beginning my life as a carpooling mother. Today, when asked what I did for those "missing" twenty years, I say "carpool," and people think I'm joking; I'm not. By the time my last baby, Jason, arrived four years after Jackie, I was practically living in the car. But I didn't mind. I really wanted to be with my kids; I enjoyed them.

Jack's flourishing career often required him to go out of town, sometimes for a few days, other times a week or more in Europe. Initially he begged me to go with him, and a few times I did. But in my eyes, the glamour and excitement of Cannes paled next to the sight of Gina, Jackie, and Jason playing together in the backyard.

When we were first married, I tried my best to accompany Jack wherever he had to go for business. With a client list that at various times included Nat "King" Cole, Carroll O'Connor, Sidney Poitier, and Cliff Robertson, among others, naturally Jack was expected to attend evening performances, dinners, and parties. In the beginning I accepted this as something that was required of me, too, but I never truly enjoyed it, even though I liked most of the people I met, and we spent wonderful times together. Inevitably the conversations always came back around to shoptalk, and the farther I moved away from my career, the less it appealed to me. And, to be fair, I'm sure that my preoccupation with diapers, birthday parties, and play dates was of interest only to other mothers.

Most important, though, was that I never truly fit in among the Hollywood glitterati. One evening we attended a very posh party. I made it a point to dress especially nicely that evening. Several people had complimented me on how beautiful I looked. A flamboyantly dressed woman I hardly knew approached me, looked me up and down disdainfully, and cracked, "Oh, what a sweet dress. Did you make it?"

"Why, no," I answered, half in shock. "I bought it."

"Oh," she replied coolly.

My first reaction was to crawl under the rug. How nasty and totally uncalled for, I thought. Then I reminded myself, *This is typical Hollywood.* This was the side of the business I could never grow a thick enough skin to ignore. From then on I always made it a point to stay near friends, the wives of other agents we knew, where we could discuss our home lives and our kids.

I'm not ashamed to say that even the small amount of entertaining I did at home was incredibly trying. Every so often we were expected to host a dinner, and each time I suffered headaches for days beforehand. I felt that nothing I could prepare would ever be good enough, and I worried incessantly over the tiny details I was sure everyone would find fault with.

For his part and to his credit as an agent, Jack loved the Hollywood life, and gradually he began going to functions alone, which meant that he spent less time at home with the children, and I spent less time with him. Slowly I became a fish out of water in his world, and he in mine. I honestly believed that having a new baby in the house would help bring us back together, but it was not to be. However, our relationship was not anything near what you would call a bad marriage. Jack was a good father, strict and conscientious, always making sure that the kids attended mass each Sunday. To everyone who knew us, we were still the ideal couple. And, in truth, our marriage was much better than most I'd seen. I resolved to stick to it and make it work.

Born in 1974, Jason, my youngest, was a very calm baby. Not that I believe all that much in astrology, but it hardly seems coincidental that he, Gina, and I were all born under the sign of Libra, the sign of balance. Every child is special, but Jason will always be a little extra special because he is the baby. And because, taking after his mother, I'm sure, he's become an excellent drummer. Like me, he started tapping incessantly when he was about kindergarten age. Of all my children, Jason bears the closest physical resemblance to me, something I'm not alone in noticing. On our refrigerator there's a magnet of me as a Mouseketeer in my T-shirt. As a joke, someone in the family wrote Jason's name on a piece of white adhesive tape and affixed it over the "Annette." And it did look like him! I have to admit that more than once I've caught a glimpse of Mouseketeer Annette on television and asked myself, "What's Jason doing on television, wearing a skirt?"

I took more pride in being a good mother than in anything else. Contrary to what a lot of parents seem to think these days, I don't believe there's any justifiable reason to lower your standards for your child's behavior, least of all because "that's what everybody else does." Sure, in today's world it's easy to throw up your hands and believe there's nothing you can do to keep your children out of trouble and focused on what's important. But giving up on them is *too* easy.

The similarities between me and my mother are so many and run so deep that it's almost uncanny, even down to the months our children were born and their birth order (we each had a daughter followed by two sons). Unlike many baby boomers growing up in the fifties and sixties, I didn't look back and critique every little mistake my parents made, nor did I make angry resolutions to "do things differently." All parents make mistakes. But the most important thing a parent can do is to show a child that he or she is loved and respected, and my parents certainly did that. Even if I got into trouble or they had cause to discipline me, I never for an instant forgot how much they loved me. My being able to depend on their love the same way I can be sure the sun rises in the east every morning laid the foundation for all that I am. By following my parents' example, I knew I would do right by my children.

You might assume that because my kids grew up in a fairly affluent, show-business-oriented community as a parent I faced special challenges, but that was not the case. For one thing, my children all attended parochial school from kindergarten through high school. Second, attending church was expected of them every Sunday. And there was never any question but that family came first.

They were involved in many extracurricular activities, but even more important, I was involved in them, too. Little League is something of a family tradition with us, so when my sons started playing, I began helping out, working in the snack bar making pizzas and keeping score. During all those years, no one ever said, "Hey, aren't you Annette Funicello?"

Instead, it was "Hey, pizza lady!" And that sounded fine to me.

I tried to attend every game, and invariably there would be several boys trying their hardest, sometimes coming up winners, sometimes not, but with no one there to root for them or comfort them. It really broke my heart. Some of the most precious memories of my life occurred around a softball diamond. To have one of my kids run up to the snack bar and say, "Hey, Mom, thanks for being here!" was the greatest feeling in the world.

My children learned very early on that, despite being strict, we didn't expect all the routine things most other parents did. For example, I never harped at them about their grades. I believe that it is better for a child to work to the best of his ability, whatever that may be, than to be cajoled and bullied into trying to do "better" and be unhappy about it. So while other mothers bragged about how their children got straight A's, I'd chuckle about Jackie's getting a detention. As much as I accepted responsibility for shaping my kids, I was also well aware that I was powerless to bend them into something they were not. In the achievement-oriented world my kids grew up in, we knew too many kids driven to despair and worse by parents determined to push them to be "the best" in everything. (As if your child isn't the best already.)

Perhaps that is one of the hardest parts of being a parent: accepting your children, faults and all. It's really not difficult to do when you stop to think how we parents are loved so unconditionally. Only a foolish mother believes that her children don't see her flaws.

So in our home there were relatively few hard-and-fast rules. Be truthful, be responsible, be willing to accept blame for your mistakes. My parents had wisely had an open-door policy; my friends were always welcome, and I did the same. I made it a point always to be home to supervise their get-togethers, and for a time my kids were very annoyed at me for being so "old-fashioned" as to phone parents at whose homes they were to be guests. "Oh, Mom," they would moan, "you're the only one who does that!"

Yet, more often than not, my phone call was the first time those parents heard of the forthcoming party. Needless to say, they had made no plans to chaperone. I think more than a few parents shared my kids' sentiments. They thought it wasn't cool for parents to butt in; they were more interested in being their kids' buddies than their parents. But, to borrow from one of my old beach-party scripts, these were my principles as a parent, and I was going to stick by them. Now that my kids are pretty much all grown-up, I think that they're glad I did.

Sure we had our fights—there were friends and love interests I didn't approve of, there were decisions they made that I vehemently opposed—but that's part of being a good parent, too. In the end, I am happy and proud to say that my children, who had no choice but to be my children, have also chosen to be my friends. For that I will always be grateful.

Today especially, as I see our culture moving farther away from the values and attitudes kids need to grow up right, it hurts me. There is nothing—no career, no amount of money in the bank, no meeting, no vacation—as important as a child. Recently I saw a bumper sticker that read, BEING A MOTHER IS A LIFE SENTENCE WITH NO PAROLE, and it made me think what a horrible attitude that expressed, even if only in jest. How can we possibly hope to teach our children to value themselves and others if they get the message that we view their existence and our parenthood as some kind of punishment? Because children don't ask to be born, I think that more people should ask themselves before they have children whether or not this is what they really want. More important, Is being a parent a responsibility I can assume with joy and thanks? Years ago, before I had my own children, I held a low opinion of anyone who said, "I don't want children; I'm too busy with my career," or "I'm happy with my dog and my cat." But today, after seeing so many people take a halfhearted swing at parenting and fail their children so miserably, my attitude has changed.

Children need parents who want to be parents. This is not to say that they have to give up everything to care for their children. But as a society we need to reprioritize our values and put our kids first.

Since through my career art has imitated life, and vice versa, destiny surely had a hand when I was asked to portray myself, a typical American mom, for a series of Skippy peanut butter commercials. I'm not exactly sure how the Skippy people found me, except that my love for peanut butter was pretty well known. Just like my character in *Back to the Beach*, I always had a jar of Skippy in the house, so it was easy for me to pitch, because I really believed in it. I was Skippy's spokesperson for a decade. In the first couple of years, Gina, Jackie, and Jason "played" my kids in the commercials. But, after finding out that viewers spent more time looking at my kids than paying attention to the spot, the Skippy people decided to use child actors instead. Gina sort of enjoyed being made up and having her hair done, and for a short while dreams of show business danced in her head, but when she saw what hard work it was, that was the end of that. Thank goodness.

Over the years, I've endorsed a number of products, including Mennen baby products, Coppertone suntan lotion, Max Factor cosmetics, Clairol hair coloring, Pepsi-Cola, and Armanino Italian foods. But I'll probably always be remembered for issuing the Skippy challenge: Which has more protein? (And bologna and tuna fish are not the correct answers.)

When you are young and healthy, it never occurs to you that in a single second your whole life could change. Certainly I had taken my good health for granted, so that when something did happen to me it came as a bolt out of the blue. Only later, when I discussed the incident with several doctors, did I learn this might have been the first warning sign of multiple sclerosis.

It was late one evening in 1976, and everyone was asleep except me. I was washing my face at the sink in the master bath when suddenly the room grew dark and started spinning and I heard bells—loud, crashing bells—that sounded so real I had to cover my ears, even though the sound was coming from within. Unfortunately, I ignored my first impulse, which was to sit down and wait it out or call for help. Instead I tried to make my way from the bathroom to the bed, to awaken Jack. After one step, I tripped on a ball one of the kids had left on the floor and went flying headfirst into a large, heavy dresser that was deeply and ornately carved with many sharp points. Everything went black.

I have no idea how long I lay on the floor half-unconscious and moaning. Thank God Jack heard me and jumped out of bed. The first thing I remember hearing was him screaming, "Your eye, Annette! Your eye is gone! What happened to your eye?"

I struggled to open my right eye, but it stayed closed. Instinctively raising my hands to my face I felt something warm and wet, flesh and blood; not my face at all. Of course, I was in shock, but I didn't know that then. "Jack, just help me walk to the bathroom. I need to brush my teeth before we go to the hospital."

Jack helped me up, and I walked to the bathroom mirror and gazed at my horribly torn face. One cut from the top of my forehead to near the bottom of my cheekbone ran so deep you could see muscle, but my eye was obscured. Another, on my chin, gashed out the cleft I was born with.

"Oh, Jack," I said in an oddly serene voice, "I'm going to be a monster. I'll never work again." Even being in shock, that struck me as such an odd thing to have come to my mind: *I'll never work again.* Jack handed me a washcloth, which I pressed to my blood-covered face. Despite seeing the ghastly wound, I felt absolutely no pain. I told Jack to call my parents, but they weren't home, so the neighbors agreed to watch the kids, and we drove to the hospital. In a rather strange coincidence, as Jack and I were driving to the hospital, we passed my parents on their way home. Jack signalled my father to follow us, and my parents—obviously not knowing what had happened to me—arrived at the hospital but weren't able to find us.

I was lying in the emergency room, and after they'd stopped the bleeding, a doctor approached and asked, "Do you know a plastic surgeon?"

"No, I've never used one," I replied, wondering what they were talking about. In the meantime, my parents found us in the hospital. I was lying on a bed, waiting for a plastic surgeon to arrive, when Mom and Dad finally entered my room.

"Dolly, let me see your face," my father said.

"No, Dad," I answered weakly, pressing a cloth against the wound. "You don't want to see it."

Before I could say another word, my dad gently lifted the cloth from my face. Even though I'd seen it myself in the mirror, it hadn't really frightened me until I saw the terror and revulsion on my father's face. He looked as if he were going to be ill. Only then did I know that whatever it was, it was bad.

When a plastic surgeon finally arrived and set to work, I lay there calmly and peacefully; it was like a dream. Maybe it was a dream. As the doctor worked slowly and meticulously, restoring tissue and glands to their correct positions, I remained in an odd state of alertness. I knew what was going on around me, but I really didn't. I just remember asking him, "Doctor, I have no eyebrows. What am I going to do?" And him replying, "Oh, here's some. I found some."

At one point during this bizarre conversation, I marveled, "I'm not even in shock! I feel so calm."

The doctor stopped for a moment and said, "But you are in shock, my dear. You are."

One hundred twenty-five stitches later, everything was back in place, but regardless of how beautifully the incisions healed, the incident troubled me for a long time to come. How could I, someone who had never experienced dizziness once in her life, suddenly be so overcome? And those bells ringing? What caused that? No one could give me an answer, and the doctors I talked with wrote it off as something that just happened; a fluke, a once-in-a-lifetime accident that would probably never occur again.

About six weeks later I felt well enough to get back into my usual routine, although I was still pretty heavily bandaged. I was driving along the freeway and getting ready to move into the right-hand lane when I looked across and saw a huge black area. I checked the rearview mirror, and again all I saw to my right was blackness. It took only a few seconds for me to realize my other eye was fine, and I calmly moved to the right and pulled onto the shoulder. Sitting there, I hit myself on the head and cried, "Come on! What is going on here?" After a few minutes, I started the car and cautiously proceeded the short distance home.

The neurologist I consulted believed that the blindness was probably attributable to the fall; that it was a palsy of the optic nerve and would probably pass, which it did. However, I've continued to have a black spot in my vision ever since. Today, after having spoken to many people with multiple sclerosis, I think it likely that the dizziness that preceded my fall and the temporary blindness may have been early manifestations of MS. But no one can ever know that for certain.

Both experiences left me more than a little shaken and unsure. I suppose for the first time in my life I felt physically vulnerable, especially since no one offered a firm explanation for what occurred or, more frighteningly, no assurance that it would never happen again.

As time passed without dizzy spells or further episodes of blindness, I gradually relaxed. But I could never completely dismiss thoughts of what could have happened and what my family would have done if I'd been seriously hurt or disabled.

Through the seventies I appeared infrequently as a guest star on such programs as *The Love Boat* and *Fantasy Island*. For *Mickey Mouse Club* fans, probably the biggest television event was *The Mouseketeers Reunion* special, commemorating the show's twenty-fifth anniversary, in 1980. I'd kept in touch with many of the Mouseketeers and looked forward to our all being together again. But no amount of anticipation could account for the almost magical feeling of standing on soundstage two with thirty-eight other original Mouseketeers.

People no doubt were wondering if after so many years the old bones could still move the way they did before. To be honest, more than a couple of us worried about that, too. But after a couple of weeks' rehearsal, I felt as if we'd just come back from hiatus. It was so much fun to sing the old songs again and perform our favorite numbers, like "Talent Roundup" and of course "Mickey Mouse March." The clips from old shows and a lengthy tribute to Jimmie Dodd brought back so many warm, wonderful memories. In some ways, it was like being granted a golden wish to return to your childhood, and not many people ever get that.

Not surprisingly, the show generated a lot of media attention, and in one interview with me and my kids, Gina revealed that I wasn't even her favorite Mouseketeer, Cheryl Holdridge was. That was okay, though. Being favorite Mommy was good enough for me.

CHAPTER 8

*F*rankie Avalon had been telling me for years that wherever he toured people asked the same question: When are you and Annette getting back together?

While younger people all seemed to have either succumbed to disco fever or started wearing safety pins through their noses, older kids (I mean, adults) were being swept along in a warm, sweet wave of nostalgia. The long-running TV series *Happy Days* resurrected the midfifties and early sixties, while the hit musical *Grease* (in which Frankie had a cameo role, singing "Beauty School Dropout") paid loving tribute to the innocent years, and several former teen idols (including Paul Anka) were suddenly hot on the charts again. Just two years earlier Frankie saw some chart action with an updated hit remake of his great "Venus."

We wondered if the time might be right for Frankie and Annette to get together again. To anyone who watched prime-time TV with any regularity, it probably seemed as if we'd never left. Or, if we had, it was never for long. Together Frankie and I had sung duets on *The Ed Sullivan Show*, *The Hollywood Palace*, and other variety programs, not to mention the countless guest spots we'd done on Dick Clark's various shows and specials. In 1976 Frankie hosted a four-week summer-replacement musical variety show on CBS called *Easy Does It . . . Starring Frankie Avalon.* As a regular cast member, I sang with Frankie, and we performed comedy skits, too. It seemed like no matter how much time had elapsed since the last time, every performance together felt like we'd never stopped. We were always so happy working together.

While I wasn't exactly sitting by the phone waiting for offers, with Jason nearing school age, I knew I would consider a project I'd enjoy, preferably something that didn't involve too much travel and would allow me to spend time with my family. When Dick Clark approached Frankie and me with an opportunity to costar in our own television series in 1978, it sounded perfect.

Frankie & Annette, The Second Time Around reunited the Frankie and Annette of the beach-party films; in fact, the show's opening was made of old film clips of us together. Now, in the late seventies, Frankie is a failed club singer, and Annette, a widowed college-dorm housemother at Thurston College overlooking—what else?—Malibu Beach. The two had lost touch when Frankie left the beach for a promising show-business career that soured. Annette, meanwhile, graduated from college and, after waiting for Frankie in vain, married a young man who was later killed in Vietnam. Of course, Annette, with her stringent moral code, is the perfect housemother, the butt of numerous jokes, and the sweetheart of an uptight, square dean. The hour-long pilot included the usual mixups and misunderstandings but centered on Frankie's attempts to win back Annette, the girl he'd always regretted leaving behind. By the end Frankie and I were strolling along a moonlit beach. When he makes a subtle proposition, I exclaim, "The same old Frankie!" to which he responds incredulously, "Same old Annette?" Obviously not, because we end up rolling in the sand, a happy ending that was to have led to a series.

I thought the show was very funny and had great potential. Among our costars were Markie Post (later of *Night*

Court and *Hearts Afire*) and Helaine Lembeck (my friend Harvey Lembeck's daughter, who appeared earlier in *Welcome Back, Kotter*). Unfortunately, the network did not commit to the series. Frankie and I were both terribly disappointed. As with most things that don't work out, I tried to be philosophical; it was just one of those things. Frankie, however, was determined to get us back together again, and in a big way. Whatever ambivalence I felt about my own career, Frankie more than made up for it with his ambition and tenacity.

It seemed to be a time when everyone was looking back to see an idealization of the past. Cable television programmed hours of the old sitcoms we'd all grown up on, while new wave and "power pop" music lovingly repackaged the sixties' sounds and styles. A renewed interest in the beach-party movies and surf music was not far behind. Some people thought the movies were kind of kitschy, and I suppose for them part of the appeal was simply laughing at us, rather than with us. But for many others, those films and songs were treasures, the happy pop relics of a simpler, innocent era.

Having been a part of that, I didn't always understand what all the fuss was about. Anytime my kids caught one of my movies on TV, they'd casually call out, "Hey, Mom, you're on again!" and then go about their business, or change the channel. But I was always grateful to the fans, who through their kind letters and words reminded me how much those films and *The Mickey Mouse Club* meant to them.

Among my fans was a young director and writer named Steve Silver, who for the previous seven years had been producing a show in San Francisco called *Beach Blanket Babylon*. As Steve told me later, when he discovered that his agent knew Jack, he invited me up to see his sharply satirical spoof revue. Jack and I flew to San Francisco, where I saw the show and fell in love with it. When he asked me to make a special appearance in his seventh-anniversary show, "Beach Blanket Babylon Goes to the Stars—and the Beach," I said yes.

Beach Blanket Babylon was not what you would call family entertainment. A sendup of practically every currently popular trend in entertainment, it was an outrageous, campy, yet affectionate tribute to show business. The audience was instructed to attend in beach attire, eleven tons of sand and several beach umbrellas covered the theater floor, and waitresses and ushers in swimsuits served drinks and took tickets.

Steve created a special production number for me, the finale to the regular show. I made my entrance, in mouse ears of course, and was hoisted by seven musclebound beach boys in orange ANNETTE tank tops. The crowd, which had already performed its own emotional rendition of "M-I-C-K-E-Y," went crazy as I sang "Pineapple Princess." To give you a better idea of the type of show I'm talking about, at my feet as I sang were men dressed in white sailor caps, yellow sunsuits, and . . . corsages! I had so much fun there, and when I heard that scalpers were getting $150 a ticket for the show, I was absolutely flattered. Perhaps one of the best parts of the experience was having made a new friend in Steve.

One day not long after, I gathered Gina, Jackie, and Jason together on my bed, and I said, "I have something to tell you. You know Daddy and I have not been getting along lately, so he is going to go away for a little while. We're going to have a trial separation and try to work things out. But I'm sure he'll be back."

Gina, in her teens then, had an idea that things were not right with Jack and me. For the boys, however, I think it came as more of a surprise. They knew we were having problems, but still it was hard for them to think of Daddy not being at home.

Jackie, who was just eleven then, said, "Don't worry, Mom, I'll be the man of the house! I'll protect you." And to this day, he still does.

That broke my heart. I assured the kids that everything would be all right. It had taken me years to finally ask Jack for a separation. Going straight from my parents' home to a husband's felt natural back in 1965. Practically everyone else I knew did it; my mother had done it. Wasn't that the way it was supposed to be? But as I matured, I began to see that marriage wasn't as easy as cutting the wedding cake. Looking back on the experience, I have to confess I didn't really know how to make it work. I didn't know how to be a real partner, or how to give and take.

Our situation was also complicated by a very basic difference in our natures. Jack would be the perfect husband for a woman who wanted to go out all the time, traveling and being seen around town. As much as I loved being home with our children, I grew to resent his frequent absences. In more emotional moments, I wondered why he couldn't be more like my dad. But that wasn't fair, either; he wasn't my dad.

I think that Jack was surprised when I told him I wanted the separation and later the divorce. There had never been a divorce in either of our families. I used to joke that the Funicellos didn't even know what the word meant. And when Jack and I married, we did state our vows fully believing that only death would part us. After years of growing apart, I had to admit that my marriage was coming to an end.

In a time when people are so blasé about divorce, about living together before marriage, about being married three, four, five times, I guess I'm still a bit old-fashioned. No matter how clearly I could see that my marriage was not working, the mere thought of divorce terrified me. Even though I could understand that our marriage was in trouble and why we had drifted apart, to me divorce meant something more complex than simply the end of a marriage. To me, divorce symbolized failure; I had failed and disappointed not only Jack but my family. I would be removing my children's father from their daily lives; I would be admitting that I had made a mistake.

It's so hard to express how heavily this weighed on me, and for years I postponed making the decision. The few people I confided in told me that I was wrong to wait until all the kids had grown up. After all, Jason wouldn't be eighteen for another dozen or so years. They argued, and I finally agreed, that the kids would suffer more by living with two parents who couldn't get along. And they were right.

I did everything I could to keep our separation and divorce out of the papers. I was determined that my children wouldn't have to suffer for our decision. I didn't tell them about our filing for divorce, and when one of Gina's classmates brought to school a copy of a tabloid with the news and taunted her about it, she was devastated. She came home from school crushed, and said, "You're getting a divorce, Mom." I've often wondered if the people who publish the tabloids really understand or care about the pain they cause.

I was not prepared to live as a single parent. The parent part I had down pretty well; it was the single business I had trouble with. When I informed Jack that I would be taking care of all the bills and running the household, rather than having our business manager do that, I had no idea what I was getting into. Although nearing forty, I had never once balanced a checkbook! I didn't understand how the mortgage worked, or how or when to pay the property taxes.

"Mom, how much money should I leave in the checking account? How much do you think I'll need for the month?" I used to ask. Between my parents and Jack, I'd never worried about money in my life. I was greatly relieved to learn some years later that there are many women from all walks of life whose experience was similar to mine. But at the time I felt absolutely helpless and inept.

Even though Jack hadn't been around the house all that much when we were together, once he was really gone I realized how much I'd depended on him. Suddenly, I was the only one waiting up for Gina and Jackie to come home, the only one making decisions, the only one doling out punishment. Before, I'd always had the option of going to Jack and getting him to talk to the kids when I felt like I wasn't getting through. Now it was just me.

Around the time Jack and I broke up, Mom warned, "Annie, you'd better change your phone number, because once it gets out that you're single again your phone is going to ring off the hook."

I wasn't ready to jump into a new relationship right away, of course, but I wasn't resigned to becoming an old maid, either. Surely, I thought, of all the people I'd met, among all the millions of little boys—now men—who'd professed their love for me, certainly a few, maybe a dozen, would call. But no one ever did. I suppose it was something of a self-defense when I did change the number. That way I could reassure myself that my phone wasn't ringing because no one knew my number. But I wasn't fooling anyone but me. I was alone. And as I watched my kids grow older, as I saw Gina through her high school prom, and Jackie nearing his high school graduation, the prospect of growing old by myself became very real. Before long I was fully convinced that I would never marry again. I threw myself into making a good home for my children and hardly went out at all, unless it was for them.

In 1981 Mickey and Minnie and I were presenters at the Thirty-third Annual Emmy Awards show. I had no one to accompany me, and ended up going with my brother. I didn't know anyone there, and my nerves were jumping until Danny DeVito, then starring in *Taxi,* told me what a fan he was and how lovely I looked. At that moment it sounded like one of the sweetest things anyone had ever said to me.

I'd made a decision that I knew was for the better, yet nothing is ever perfect. Being a single parent is no easy job, and there were times when I lost my temper. One day when

Jason was eleven or so, I asked him to do something for me.

"Why don't you ask Gina or Jackie to do it?" he replied in a smart-mouthed tone of voice I didn't like.

Maybe it was the end of a long day, or maybe I just wasn't in the mood for his freshness, but I walked up behind Jason and said, "Don't you talk to me like that! And do what I asked you to do!"

I don't know what came over me, but I went to slap him across the shoulder. In a split second, he turned his head, and I ended up landing a punch right to his nose. Blood gushed everywhere, and I started screaming. Little Jason looked up from his bloody face with tears running down his cheeks and said softly, "Please don't hit me again, Mommy." And that was it: the end of my world. Thank goodness my parents happened to be over. They grabbed him and carried him to the bathroom, where Mom stopped the nosebleed, which looked a lot worse than it was, and comforted him while I stood in his room, shaking and crying. *I'm such a bad mother,* I told myself over and over. *I'll never be forgiven for this.* But I was.

After a few years of being alone I met the man who would become my second—and last—husband, Glen Holt. Actually, I should say I "remet" him, since Glen and I had known each other casually since I was eighteen. Glen bred and raced trotters, and so he often had horses at Hollywood Park in the stables near ours. After our first horse, Troy Hedgewood, Mom, Dad, and I owned a series of others, including Virjoe, Giuseppe Joe, and Mickey Mouse. We were in the winner's circle quite a few times, and our horses always earned their keep, but we did it more for fun than anything else.

A friendly guy, Glen would always stop by our stable and ask if we needed anything, if we wanted to borrow some hay. At the time Glen was married and had four children. And since he was twelve years my senior, the romantic possibilities never entered my mind then.

Years passed, I got married and had the kids, and I went to

the track less frequently. After my divorce, Mom and I would take the kids there. They could go back by the stables and see the horses, then we'd all sit in our box and watch the races. One day we left the kids with Dad, and Mom and I were sitting in our box when Glen came up and asked if he could sit with us. We got to talking and soon learned that we were both divorced. It wasn't love at first sight or anything quite so dramatic. We went to dinner with my parents a few times, then we went out alone. We fell in love, and on Valentine's Day 1985, Glen proposed, and I accepted.

If someone had told me before that I'd one day marry a cowboy, I'd have laughed. But that's what Glen prides himself on being. An ex-policeman turned rancher, Glen is the quintessential country boy. Sometimes in the beginning Glen and I would go out to our Kern County ranch, maybe attend a rodeo or a county fair, then I'd wake up the next morning to the cocks crowing and the horses whinnying. I'd think, *What am I doing here?* Sometimes it's a little bit like *Green Acres*, except that I've grown to love the country as well.

Under the rough and tough exterior, Glen is a romantic. I often wake up to find he's cut some roses from the backyard for me or written "I Love You" on a Post-It note and stuck it to the fridge. I don't think I've ever known anyone who is so self-sufficient and independent. Glen is the kind of guy who, if the end of the world came, would be sure that we would all be taken care of. He'd go up in the hills and get us food; he'd make the pool water drinkable.

But 1985 wasn't all fun. On one occasion, what started out as a typical day turned into a nightmare. One morning I'd gone to my regular appointment with my beautician for a hair treatment I'd been receiving for years. We decided to try a new formula, and because it was supposed to be a gentler product, skipped doing a patch test. Minutes after she applied the mixture, I felt as if my head had been set on fire. The solution was quickly rinsed off, but I could feel my hair falling out in clumps. Needless to say, I was devastated. For many months afterward, I had to wear wigs while the scalp burns slowly, and painfully, healed.

I drove home in shock and pain. But the worst was yet to come. No matter how old your children get, you can never stop worrying about them. When Jackie was about fifteen, he started riding a motor scooter, which, needless to say, I was not happy about. I'd always remind him to wear his helmet. He'd say, "Sure, Mom," but I knew the minute he was out of my sight he took it off. He thought it was "sissified."

That very same day he rode his scooter through an intersection. A car ran a red light, broadsided Jackie, and sent him flying. Despite having two seriously broken legs and being in shock, he managed to make it to a nearby apartment house to call me. When I picked up the phone, all he said was "Mom, come and get me. I've been hurt." Then his legs gave out and the kind person whose phone he was using told me where he was.

I rushed out of the house and drove like a maniac to the address, but by the time I arrived an ambulance had whisked Jackie to the hospital. Out on the street was a scene from every mother's nightmare: a twisted scooter lying at the curb and a helmet in the middle of the street. Racing to the hospital, all I could do was pray that my son was going to be all right.

I thought I would die when I saw Jackie lying on a gurney, crying in pain. His legs were so badly swollen the doctors said they couldn't even begin resetting the fractures. All I could do was be there with him and squeeze his hand, but I guess that was enough. I learned that Jackie was wearing his helmet only because his friend who was riding on the back didn't want to wear it and there was no place else to put it. That little inconvenience saved Jackie's life.

Once Jackie came home, he was under strict doctor's orders not to stand or try to walk. Although both legs were fractured, the doctors worried about his left leg, since there was reason to believe that his extensive injuries threatened the bones' ability to heal and regrow. For the next eight weeks Jackie sat with both legs straight out, wrapped tightly in casts. Several times I'd be walking through the house and swear I'd caught a glimpse, in my peripheral vision or in a mirror, of Jackie hobbling. Then I'd think I was losing my mind. It couldn't be, but it was. "Jackie, aren't you afraid you're going to ruin your legs?" I'd ask in exasperation and worry.

"No, Mom," he replied confidently. "I'll be okay."

And he was.

Although I spent most of my time with Glen or the kids, I did fulfill a lifelong dream by recording a country-music album. Now, if "country" isn't the first thing you associate with me, you're not alone. Going into it I had no illusions about becoming a threat to Dolly Parton. I did it because I'd always loved country music and wanted to record at least once in Nashville. When a producer offered me the chance, I went for it.

I hadn't sung publicly in years, so I was feeling more than a little trepidation as I opened the heavy door to the Hot Licks studio. What would I sound like? What would the musicians think of me? There they were, sitting with their instruments, looking quite serious—but in mouse ears. After they broke into "Mickey Mouse March," I knew everything was going to be okay.

One day at the racetrack I'd told Glen that I wanted to write a song for my parents, a song that would tell the world what they'd done for me and my brothers and how much I loved them. I'd never written a song in my life, but slowly the lyrics started coming together, and before I knew it I had written a song called "The Promised Land." I recorded it, as well as five standards and more originals. Although one of the singles, "The Promised Land" backed with "In Between and Out of Love," got a sprinkling of airplay, I wasn't disappointed.

"The Promised Land" holds a distinct place in the Annette discography for being the only record I ever made that sparked a serious controversy. Imagine that! As I was writing the song I remembered reading somewhere that many years ago my hometown of Utica was known as Sin City. Now, Utica wasn't the only town to have earned such a reputation in its early days, and it's a fine place today, so I really didn't give it too much thought. As I played with the song's opening line, "From Sin City in the East to the City of the Angels," it sounded great. "Sin City" was a great image, and with that little bit of alliteration, even a novice songwriter like me could hear this had a nice ring to it. It was certainly more poetic than "From Utica in the East."

I never imagined that my referring to Utica as Sin City would prompt an all-out anti-Annette campaign. Utica citizens were so upset about what they viewed as my slur against their fair city that they removed my picture from all the municipal buses. One day a disc jockey from Utica called to interview me via phone about the controversy, but I was busy, so Mom decided to sit in for me. Maybe I shouldn't be telling this at this late date, but Mom and I speak very similarly, so over the years she has done a number of phone interviews for me. I listened in as Mom defended my position, but by the time we hung up I was sweating and nearly in tears. I apologized to the city of Utica, and when Frankie and I took our Back to the Beach Tour there in 1990 I had been reinstated as one of Utica's favorite daughters. By then I'd also changed the line to "From my city in the East." Being a cause célèbre once was enough for me.

My only other major project around that time was costarring with comedian Martin Mull in The Disney Channel film *Lots of Luck.* The tale of how my character's winning a lottery ruins her husband's (Martin's) and family's life, *Lots of Luck* costarred Fred Willard and Polly Holliday (Flo of *Alice*). It was nice to be working again, but even nicer to be back on the Walt Disney Studio lot for the first time since *The Mon-*

key's Uncle twenty years before. Oddly, nothing ever seems to change there, except perhaps the faces. The old buildings still stand; the commissary, the soundstages I used to wander around as a teenager hadn't changed a bit. Had it really been so many years? I didn't feel any older. If anything, I felt as if my life were beginning again.

On May 3, 1986, Glen and I married. We planned a small, intimate ceremony followed by a dinner for about fifty in a local restaurant. Gina was my maid of honor, and Jackie and Jason took part in the ceremony, as did two of Glen's four grown children. I had everything planned, but I wanted to invite one very special guest: Mickey Mouse.

I called Lorraine Santoli, Disney's manager of corporate synergy and my longtime friend, and asked if Mickey could please attend a special party I was having. I didn't tell her it was a wedding. She explained that because of a new corporate policy the characters could no longer be lent out. "Not even for my wedding?" I asked.

"I'm sorry, Annette," she replied. "Not even for your wedding. You know if it were my decision, he'd be there."

A few days later I got a call from Arlene Ludwig, my very dear friend who was Director of West Coast publicity and had been a bridesmaid at my first wedding, with good news.

"Annette, everyone here at Disney talked it over, and we believe that Walt Disney would have wanted Mickey at your wedding, so he can come!"

"He can!" I was so excited, but I made sure everyone at Disney was sworn to secrecy, and I told no one, not even my kids or my parents. This was my surprise wedding gift to Glen.

The day of the wedding was absolutely beautiful. As he had the first time, my father walked me down the aisle. He was quite emotional about it, only this time he whispered, "I don't ever want to have to do this again, Dolly."

"Don't worry, Dad," I whispered back, "you won't."

We had a simple ceremony, then it was off to the reception. Among our guests were Sharon Baird and Shelley Fabares and her husband, Mike Farrell. At one point during the reception Glen and I toasted each other. I said, "I love you, honey, and I know the second time around is always better. I just want you to know that I want to make it to the finish line with you." And I meant it.

I was having the time of my life, just marveling at how I'd almost given up on ever finding love again, and yet here was Glen. It seemed almost too good to be true. But after a couple of hours had passed, I started glancing at my watch and thinking, *Where is that mouse?*

Suddenly I heard a knock, and as nonchalantly as possible I said, "Glen, honey, why don't you see who's at the door?"

When Glen opened the door and saw Mickey—in bow tie and tux, holding a platter of cheese—his jaw dropped. Everyone in the room burst out laughing and applauding. Mickey and I danced together, and it was so lovely. Mickey is more than a mouse to me; I am honored to call him a friend.

As 1987 began, I was entering a new phase of my life. Glen and I still felt like newlyweds. (Yes, love *is* lovelier the second time around!) My children were well on their way to independence. Gina, at twenty-one, was attending college in San Diego. Jackie, then seventeen, wouldn't be home too much longer, and twelve-year-old Jason—my baby—was heading into his teens. I was proud of each of them and happy to see them grow up into such great kids.

But time was passing too quickly. The years of all-consuming momhood would be coming to a close soon, and with Glen gone a few days a week taking care of business at the ranch, I began thinking about my career again. I wasn't about to jump at anything, but if the right project came along, I was game.

Ever since our try at a television series Frankie Avalon and I had discussed reviving our swingin'-and-surfin' alter egos

Dee Dee and Frankie in an updated beach-party film. But it was a big project, and so many things needed to come together to make it happen. I wasn't holding my breath. In the meantime, we'd done a few things together, including recording a Christmas duet called "Together We Can Make a Merry Christmas." Frankie had joined Bobby Rydell and Fabian on a successful "Boys of Bandstand" tour.

When Frankie and I kissed and made up after our last on-screen spat in the sand, in 1966, girls were wearing miniskirts for the first time and boys were sporting "long" hair—to their collars. By the early eighties our images were as firmly fixed in the public's mind as a fin on a surfboard. While some viewed us as early-sixties teen equivalents of such immortal screen lovers as Fred Astaire and Ginger Rogers, or Nelson Eddy and Jeanette MacDonald, to me we were more like the Ma and Pa Kettle of the surf set. But I didn't mind.

When Frankie first approached me with the idea, I said okay, as long as we could create something we both would be proud of. As executive producers, we met with several teams of writers and posed the question, What would Frankie and Dee Dee be doing today, twenty years later? Of course they would have to be married; Dee Dee, as you well know, wouldn't have had it any other way. There would probably be a couple of kids. But what else? The possibilities were endless. What seemed like a simple premise wasn't so easy to shape into a good script after all. We felt that the characters should be funny and sympathetic. We wanted to spoof the old films, but we wanted the audience to laugh with us, not at us. It took us a while to get what we wanted, but we finally struck that fine balance.

By the time Frankie and I finished ironing out all the details in the script, we surprised everyone with our irreverent take on our pasts. Having been forced to retire from the beach after a traumatic surfing accident, Frankie (a.k.a. the Big Kahuna) had married Annette (not Dee Dee this time), and twenty years later they lived somewhere in Ohio. A highly stressed car dealer, Frankie had forgotten how to have fun, while Annette seemed oblivious of everything but shopping, her kitchen shelves a virtual wall of Campbell's soup cans and Skippy peanut-butter jars. Still balancing that bouffant, my character, whom Frankie describes as having "been in a good mood for twenty-two years," has a disposition as perky as her polka-dot wardrobe. As for our children, our son (Demian Slade) was a young teenage punk, who menaced the family poodle with a knife while lamenting the emptiness of our lives, and our fairly normal daughter (Lori Loughlin) was in college, in California, on the beach.

A big change from its low-budget predecessors, *Back to the Beach* cost $9 million. It was all shot on location (Frankie and I no longer had to take our strolls on the beach on a treadmill as surf footage rolled behind us), and we had a huge and wonderful cast, including Connie Stevens, Edd "Kookie" Byrnes, Bob Denver, Alan Hale, Jr., Barbara Billingsley, Jerry Mathers, and Tony Dow. We were in the process of casting when one day Frankie said, "Annette, come over to the Paramount commissary. There's someone I would like you to meet."

A handsome young man with longish hair and a black leather jacket approached our table. "This is Paul Reubens," Frankie said. Never in a million years would anyone have recognized him as Pee-wee Herman. We had a pleasant lunch together, and he struck me as very intelligent. When Frankie asked if I wanted him to be in the movie, I said yes.

Over the course of filming, Paul and I became good friends. Between takes, we'd sit and talk. He'd been a huge fan of *The Mickey Mouse Club*. One day he asked me to autograph a photo for him, and he got such a kick when he read what I'd written: "I wish you had been a Mouseketeer." Later Frankie and I (in a tight green sweater and red poodle skirt) made a guest appearance on his children's show *Pee-wee's Playhouse*. We were among many celebrities on Pee-wee's Christmas show, but we were the only ones he forced to make a thousand Christmas cards, "by sundown." Because Paul had to wear such heavy makeup for Pee-wee, the soundstage was kept extremely chilly, and I spent every minute between takes wrapped in a coat. But we had a wonderful time, and I've always been proud to call Paul my friend, even after his legal troubles, which I feel were really much ado about nothing. When his show was canceled, I felt that children had lost some of the most original, imaginative programming out there.

Pee-wee's big number in *Back to the Beach* was "Surfin' Bird," and Frankie and I sang as well. One of my numbers, with newcomers Fishbone, was a remake of "Jamaica Ska," which I'd originally recorded in the sixties. Director Lyndall Hobbs told me it was one of her favorite songs, and I must say that it really held up. And, of course, what would a beach-party movie be without Dick Dale? Except for his punked-up jet-black hair, Dick was as amazing as ever, especially in his sizzling guitar duel with Stevie Ray Vaughan on the instrumental surf classic "Pipeline."

Dick and I had kept in touch through the years. One day in the late seventies I was driving the kids someplace (as usual) when I heard on the news that Dick Dale had been seriously injured in an accident in his home. Dick had been cooking, and somehow a whole pot of boiling oil spilled on his arm. Doctors predicted he would never play guitar again, but Dick refused to believe them. One day I stopped by his house to visit, and he said, "Here, Annette, let me show you something." And he sat down at the piano and started playing like nothing had ever happened.

So between Dick and Frankie, it felt like old home week again, but not completely. My friend Harvey Lembeck, who played Eric Von Zipper, had passed away in 1982. And several of the other beach-party regulars had left the business. Back together again, we were reliving our youth, I suppose, but we knew that.

I never regretted having semiretired from show business,

yet it felt great to be back on a set—even though it meant a return to the sticky lacquered bouffant that made Aqua Net a household word. I loved the camaraderie between the crew and the other actors. But the person I most looked forward to seeing each day was our director Lyndall Hobbs's little baby girl, Lola. Once a mom . . .

It was while reading my script for *Back to the Beach* that I first noticed something was wrong. It seemed as if every time I started to read, the letters on the page appeared blurrier and smaller, and it took me an unusually long time to focus. Before my accident, I'd always had perfect vision, but of course I knew that everyone of a certain age experiences difficulty doing close work and reading because of physiological changes in the eye. So I just wrote off the sudden deterioration in my eyesight to old age and tried putting it out of my mind.

In a matter of weeks, however, my vision worsened so rapidly I had to consult an ophthalmologist. He prescribed reading glasses, which helped considerably, for a while. But when we began filming, I started to experience other strange things that concerned me. Every now and then I would feel a cold tingling sensation in my feet that would come and go for no apparent reason. Once we started shooting out on the beach, I found it difficult to keep my balance in the sand. Several times the simple act of getting up from a sitting position left me feeling wildly off kilter, as if I'd been spinning. It's hard to explain, but for a few seconds I would feel as if I had no sense of balance at all. Frankie, noticing something wasn't right, helped me up, then joked, "Annette, I think you've had a little too much to drink!"

I smiled. When it happened the first and second times, it was funny. But when it kept occurring over and over, I started to panic. Suddenly my own body seemed beyond my control; I was telling it to do things, and it just wasn't listening.

Typically, I kept this to myself. I didn't want to sound like a complainer. There was probably a logical explanation for it. Yes, we were getting back to the beach, but there was no fooling anybody: We weren't kids anymore. Maybe, I told myself, that's what it was all about.

My problems with balance remained pretty consistent— neither improving nor worsening—over the course of filming. But a couple of months after getting myself a stronger pair of reading glasses, the letters looked as fuzzy as ever. At the time I had no reason to put these two symptoms together or worry that they were somehow related. My eye doctor strengthened the prescription, and everything was fine for a while, but, once again, within weeks I felt as if I were trying to read through a fun-house mirror. When I went to him for the third time in less than six months, he was visibly concerned.

"Annette, I don't think this is just old age creeping up, because, first of all, you're not that old. And," he added, "it's happening too quickly."

He performed a test in which he injected some dye into my bloodstream. The dye collected in my eyes, making it easier for him to see any blockages, abnormalities, or infection. He examined me very carefully. After he finished, he said nothing about what he saw or what he suspected. But he didn't say everything was okay, either. I knew immediately from his subdued tone of voice that he'd discovered something terribly wrong.

"My testing is really not extensive," he said. "I'm going to refer you to a neurologist, a doctor who specializes in the brain."

As chance would have it, the neurologist I'd consulted when I fell and injured my eye several years earlier had an office in the same building. My ophthalmologist phoned down to his office, and an appointment was made for that same day. I met with the neurologist and explained what was happening with my eyesight and the trouble I was experiencing with my balance. Without mentioning a possible cause, he suggested I go for a diagnostic test called an MRI.

Naturally I wanted to know what he thought was wrong, but I found the opposing sides of my nature hard at work. There was the optimistic Annette, eternally looking for the bright side and reassuring myself that everything was going to be all right. And in the other corner was me the worrier. Lying in bed awake for hours at night, all I could think of was what I envisioned as "the worst": a tumor or other fatal condition that would take me away from my children, my parents, and my husband. Most of the time I found myself worrying more about them than about myself. *Maybe,* I thought, *It will be nothing.* Maybe there are logical explanations for everything that's been going on. Maybe it's just coincidental that the problems with my balance and my eyesight are occurring now. Maybe, maybe, maybe. All I could do was pray.

My answers would be found in the MRI scan. MRI stands for magnetic resonance imaging, a process that uses radio and magnetic waves to produce detailed images of internal tissues and organs. Unlike other forms of diagnostic imaging, such as x-rays or the CAT (computerized axial tomography) scan, MRI does not use radiation. Although not entirely infallible, the MRI is currently considered one of the best ways to make a definite diagnosis of multiple sclerosis.

The scanner itself is really something. It reminded me of a giant iron lung or some kind of space-age capsule. For the test I was strapped down onto the scanner bed, basically a moving table, and a device resembling a football helmet was placed on my head. After everything was in position, the "table" moved slowly into the scanner. I felt like a head of lettuce on the conveyor belt at the supermarket checkout counter. Inside the scanner I could hear nothing but an occasional *"Bang!,"* which I was told was caused by radio waves being turned on and off and nothing to worry about.

I lay there perfectly still, as I was asked to do, for the next forty-five minutes and tried to relax. After the procedure ended, none of the technicians could tell me what the scan revealed. Glen and I drove home in silence. Now all we could do was wait.

CHAPTER 9

*S*everal days later, as I sat in the neurologist's office with my mother and Glen, the doctor's words seemed to hang in the air.

"Multiple sclerosis."

"MS." I heard him speaking, but I couldn't seem to grasp what he was saying or what it meant for me. I looked at my mother, whose face registered pure shock. And then I glanced over at my husband. All I can recall feeling at that moment, oddly, was relief. *Thank you, God. I don't have a brain tumor. I'm not going to die.*

To help us to better understand the situation, the doctor then showed me the results of the MRI. There on the exposure, which is the MRI equivalent of an x-ray image, was a "picture" of my brain and spinal cord. Scattered across them were bright but shadowy spots. These, my doctor explained, were lesions, or plaques, and their presence confirmed that I had multiple sclerosis.

Gradually I began to absorb what he was saying, although I must admit that very little of it sank in that day. Multiple sclerosis is an illness of the central nervous system, the brain and the spinal cord. Both organs contain literally billions of nerve cells, thin, fragile fibers that constantly relay thou-

sands of sensations, impulses, messages, and commands between the brain and every other part of the body. Protecting
the nerve cells is a coating of white fatty substance called myelin. Like the plastic insulation on a piece of electrical wire,
the myelin forms a protective barrier around the nerve cells.
It also ensures that the messages traveling along the cells at
an amazing 225 miles per hour complete their journey
quickly and deliver their "information" accurately so that
our brains can issue the appropriate response.

Even a simple, seemingly "automatic" act that one takes
for granted, such as pulling back one's hand from a hot stove,
results from a series of nearly instantaneous exchanges between the nerve cells in the hand, the brain, and other nerve
cells in the muscles. Even when we're sleeping, the central
nervous system processes information. We often think of
those things we do consciously: seeing, hearing, touching,
smelling, tasting, walking, running, and so on. What we usually don't think about—because when our nervous system is
functioning properly we don't have to—is the subtle, "invis-
ible" role it plays, regulating heartbeat, sense of balance,
breathing, and a host of other bodily functions.

The symptoms of multiple sclerosis result from a multi-
stage process in which the myelin sheath becomes inflamed
and is damaged, followed by the body's attempts to repair
the myelin damage. This produces scar tissue, also known as
plaques or lesions. These are what appear as white spots on
the MRI scan. Over time these plaques harden—"sclerosis"
means hardening or thickening—and may disrupt or block
the nerve impulses as they course through the cells. Fortunately, myelin has the ability to repair itself. This process,
called remyelination, makes possible the sudden disappear-
ance of symptoms and the common but unpredictable remis-
sions many people with MS experience.

The myriad symptoms of MS all result directly from the
diminished ability of the nerve cells to transmit messages
quickly and accurately between the brain and spinal cord

and the rest of the body. Why one person might experience a loss of balance and another might be totally unable to walk depends on several factors, such as the size of the individual plaques, where they are located, and several plaques are present at the same time. In this, as in almost every other aspect of MS, the results are unpredictable and highly individual. No one's case is exactly like anyone else's.

As the doctor spoke, my head filled with questions: *Was there a cure? When could I start treatment? What did the future hold for me and my family? How did I get it? When would it go away?* Throughout it all, I was very calm. I didn't know what MS was, so, in an odd way, it didn't frighten me. After he explained all this, I asked, "But what does this mean?"

I soon learned what everyone who lives with MS knows all too well: There simply are no answers to these and hundreds of other questions this baffling illness raises. Instead you go from day to day collecting an infinite number of clues—from doctors, people who have MS, medical reports, newspaper and magazine articles, and sometimes from people who claim they have the cure. From these clues you try to fit pieces of a puzzle that you fear may never come together.

Over the years, I've collected and memorized all the factual minutiae of my illness. Most people who develop MS lived before their eighteenth birthdays somewhere in the temperate zone, usually no farther north than 40 degrees latitude and no farther south than 60 degrees latitude. MS is more common in cooler climates; Canada has double the rate of MS the United States has, for example. Richer countries have more MS than poorer countries. Certain African ethnic groups, as well as gypsies, Lapps, and Eskimos, never develop MS. In the United States women develop MS at approximately twice the rate men do, and no one can explain why women are affected most often from the waist down, while men's symptoms seem to disrupt most commonly from the waist up.

There are several leading theories that attempt to explain

MS, but so far none has been proven conclusively and none has been ruled out. Instead, there are dozens of observations and patterns that one day just may fit together. Like a compass in a magnetic storm, the current research seems to point in twenty different directions at once. There are cases to be made for the possibility that one might inherit a susceptibility to developing the illness though not the illness itself; that one or several slow-acting viruses may invade the body and then trigger the illness after years of latency; that MS may be a form of autoimmune disease, meaning that one's immune system mistakes the myelin for a foreign body and attacks it as it would a virus or a bacterium.

On the less conventional end of the medical spectrum, there are those who believe that MS results from exposure to the toxins in our food and environment; that electromagnetic waves and other forms of radiation trigger or exacerbate the symptoms; that high doses of herbs, vitamins, and/or enzymes can correct some internal imbalance and alleviate symptoms. Over the years, Glen and I have read literally thousands of letters and spoken to hundreds of people, all of whom—in good faith—have recommended everything from such seemingly harmless practices as acupuncture and dairy-free diets to the use of untested medical appliances and massive doses of a witch's brew of who knows what.

Believe it or not, as serious chronic illnesses go, multiple sclerosis came with some good news, relatively speaking. For starters, it is not fatal, nor is it always progressive. Contrary to popular belief, MS is not really a "degenerative" illness, like Alzheimer's disease or ALS (amyotrophic lateral sclerosis), also known as Lou Gehrig's disease. Whereas those two conditions follow a predictable course marked by continued and dramatic loss of functional ability, multiple sclerosis is distinguished by its unpredictability. Theoretically, the possibility of complete or at least long-term remission of symptoms exists for almost everyone.

No one—not even the best doctor in the world—can say with certainty that someone with MS will definitely be in worse shape one, five, or ten years from now than he or she is today. As a matter of fact, there are those, like singer Lola Falana and many others I've spoken to or corresponded with over the years, who one day awaken to find their symptoms have disappeared. Listening to people who've had such an experience, I've heard it attributed to everything from prayer to sky jumping. The only conclusion I can draw is another question: Who really knows? Looking on the bright side, there are few chronic conditions that offer this kind of hope; for those who have experienced major, long-term remission, it's nothing short of a miracle. I don't think I have to tell you how the dream of that moment keeps many of us going from day to day. It certainly helps me.

I also learned that MS is not contagious, nor is it heredi-tary. And while, yes, my symptoms could persist, increase, or otherwise cause me greater discomfort and inconve-nience, it was also true that this might be the worst it ever got. There was simply no way to know. I left the doctor's of-fice feeling both relieved and depressed. Most people with MS endure, on average, eight years of tests and treatments for a host of other conditions before they get the definitive diagnosis of MS. For them, the diagnosis is an answer. In my case, however, the moment's impact on my life would not become totally clear for some time.

Naturally, my first thought was of my family. Having MS wasn't just my problem; it was my parents', my children's, and Glen's. Sure, it was a condition in my body, but it was happening to all of us, and we were all in this together. But, like so many things about my having MS, it wasn't all that simple.

From the beginning, my mother and I decided not to tell my father. I know it might strike some people as odd that I chose not to share this devastating news with my own father.

But I think that before anyone can judge that decision they would have to know my dad.

As I'm sure I've made clear by now, he is one of the sweetest, kindest, gentlest men alive. Time has done nothing to diminish his youthful charm and quiet capacity for showing love and emotion. Even before it became fashionable, my father was a nurturing, caring man, never ashamed to cry.

As my parents grew older, I naturally began to feel more protective of them, more inclined to shield them from worry. I knew that the course of my MS was a big question mark. While it was quite possible that eventually my condition would deteriorate markedly, it was equally possible that my symptoms would stabilize. And there was always the chance that I would go into remission the next day and never experience another bout of MS again. When I weighed all these possibilities, the decision not to tell my father became clear. After all, I reasoned, why should he have to worry over something that might never happen? As it would turn out, it would be two years before I looked into my father's eyes and saw that I could fool him no longer.

Mom, of course, heard the diagnosis firsthand, yet in a strange way she decided not to believe it. She had a lot of trouble reconciling her healthy-looking daughter with someone who had just been informed she has MS. Mom told no one, not even her closest friends. Not having Dad or my brothers, who also learned a little later, to discuss it with, my diagnosis must have been a horrible burden.

My children were another matter. My relationship with Gina, Jackie, and Jason has always been based on honesty. Sure, I could have sheltered them from the truth. Most mothers' first reaction would be, "I don't want my child to worry or to be burdened by my illness." Even before our children are born, we see ourselves as their protectors. As they grow up and away from us, it's difficult to shift gears. Did it break my heart to have to tell them? Of course. Just the idea that one day I might not be physically able to do everything for them—or for my future grandchildren—is one aspect of this illness I may never totally accept. After all, I am their mother. But at the same time I firmly believe that children learn more from what you do and how you act than from what you say. I wasn't about to let my having MS change that.

Before we talked, I read a book my neurologist gave me. I wanted to be prepared to answer any of my kids' questions honestly and accurately even though my first inclination was not to read too much about MS. I felt that how I responded to having MS was going to influence how they dealt with it, and since this was going to be a part of our lives for a very long time to come, I wanted to start out right. It was crucial for all of us that I tell them the facts, being careful not to create false hope or, by the same token, unwarranted pessimism.

Still, nothing could prepare me for their hurt and confused expressions as we all sat on my bed. I explained that the doctor told me that I have MS.

"What's MS, Mom?" Gina asked.

"What have you got?" Jason added.

I explained it in a way they would understand. At the time, Jason, my youngest, was just twelve. Despite this, he and his sister seemed, at least outwardly, to accept the news as well as could be expected. I guess I would describe their reactions as stunned. Jackie, however, became very upset.

"But, why, Mom?" he asked angrily. "You never do anything to hurt anybody, and you're the kindest person I know. Why you? Why does anything have to happen to you?"

That was just one of hundreds of questions I'll never be able to answer.

From that day, though, I've felt my kids behind me all the way. Rather than shield them from the MS, I brought them into it, so to speak. For example, if we were watching television together and my foot went numb, I would say, "Okay, now my foot's asleep, and that's another sign of the MS." I tried not to make a big issue out of every little thing, but I needed for them to know what was happening and to become familiar with this uninvited guest who seemed to be here to stay.

It is well known that people who face death or serious illness go through several steps of emotional adjustment: denial, bargaining, anger, depression, and acceptance. In my case, it didn't follow that course exactly, because, although I was diagnosed as having MS, for four years I enjoyed something of a reprieve. My eyesight did not improve, and my balance was sometimes off. But other than a slight tingling or numbness in my feet, I felt fine. Once at the dinner table my fork started shaking uncontrollably until I lost my grip on it. That night my temperature shot up to 104°F, yet by morning I was normal again. It was a frightening, distressing moment, to be sure. But it happened that once and never again.

During those early years, MS was part of my life but not really part of *me*. I had MS, but I didn't consider myself an MS patient. That's probably not easy to understand, but the fact is that for the first few years MS changed nothing in my life. I could still drive, run errands, ride my horse at our ranch. Intellectually, I knew that an attack could come on at any moment, and I also knew that my new symptoms might range from a bout of tingling in my feet to blindness. Yet I managed to keep those thoughts in the background. Except for the odd incident or a new strange sensation, MS remained more an abstract concept than a hard reality.

Looking back, I can see that I went through my own stage of denial, which manifested itself in my avoiding everything and anything that had to do with MS. There was plenty of literature available from my doctor and the local MS society; there were books at the library; there were programs on television; there were peer support groups for people with MS and their families. But I just didn't want to know any more than I did. I'd always had a tendency to shrink from the unknown, and at first MS was exactly that. Unlike what you see in so many made-for-TV melodramas, learning that I had a serious illness didn't suddenly make me a different, braver person. I felt that the less I knew, the less afraid I would be. I have to say now that I think this was my biggest mistake in dealing with MS, and it's something I do not recommend to anyone.

It's human nature to want to avoid what makes us uncomfortable, anxious, or sad. But in the end I realized that in some ways I worried more by not knowing the whole story than I would have if I hadn't chosen to bury my head in the sand. Today my first advice to anyone who has MS is to learn all that you can, to read every piece of literature you can get your hands on. Talk to people who have MS or know someone who does. There is a wealth of anecdotal information— tips on how to cope with certain common situations, practical advice—out there waiting for you. Make use of it as early and as often as you can.

MS was so small a part of my life at first that I often quipped that if this was the serious illness I was meant to have, it wasn't so bad after all: "I could have done a lot worse." This is not to say that MS wasn't affecting my life, because it certainly was. But it was on such a minor scale, and the changes that were taking place in my eyesight and my equilibrium were so gradual that the differences seemed noticeable only when I looked back over a period of time. It wasn't as if I woke up one day, got out of bed, fell down, and couldn't get up.

Shortly after my diagnosis, *Back to the Beach* was released amid a flurry of publicity, all of it nostalgic and upbeat. Of course, there were a few critics who didn't warm up to the film, but overall the press and public gave us a wonderful reception. It was quite heartening to feel that fans still enjoyed watching Frankie and me, and that our chemistry still worked. By all measures, the film was a big enough success to warrant a sequel. We made no bones about it: *Back to the Beach* was something of a spoof, and we envisioned the next movie, which would take place on an African safari, as a comedy, too. We had never taken the beach-party films very seriously before, and we weren't about to now. Frankie and I, again as executive producers, had writers working on the second script, and we were both looking forward to continuing in this direction. *Back to the Beach* had been my favorite filmmaking experience since *Babes in Toyland.* I was very proud of my work in it, and I couldn't wait to start the next film.

But I had MS, and now I was faced with deciding whether or not to tell Frankie the truth, or to hem and haw around the issue. Initially I opted not to tell him, because I was feeling so well. I didn't see the point of making an issue out of something that really wasn't yet a problem. Then I realized I was being a little selfish. I saw Frankie's excitement over the new movie and his enthusiasm for its sequel. Here he had waited all those years for me to finally take off my apron and get back to work with him, and things were looking so promising. Suddenly when I spoke with Frankie, I wasn't as encouraging, and I think it probably confused him somewhat. I let him know, gently and vaguely, that I didn't really want to do the next film. I'm not even sure how I said it, but Frankie knows me so well he got the message.

We were both disappointed, and I often wondered if perhaps I'd made a mistake. Maybe I should have confided in Frankie early on. Maybe I should have continued with the sequel on the chance that my symptoms would stabilize or go into remission. Somehow, though, I knew I was gambling. Bit by bit my equilibrium and my eyesight were worsening, though not yet in a way discernible to anyone who didn't know about it. It would have been unfair of me to commit to something I feared I couldn't complete. My decision would affect not just me and Frankie but dozens of staff and crew. Finally, I made the decision that I thought best for everyone.

Hiding the truth from my father and from my dear friend Frankie marked probably the first and for quite a while the most profound way that MS changed my life. It was Sir Walter Scott who wrote, "Oh, what a tangled web we weave,/ When first we practice to deceive!" Over the next five years, as I struggled to keep my MS a secret from almost everyone I knew and the world at large, those words would haunt me. Today, over two years after having made my illness public, I must confess to being a little confused myself as to why I held so tightly to this fiction. What was I afraid of? What did I think would happen if people knew? Whatever the force that drove me to protect my secret, it was certainly very strong. Against my basic nature, against my own conscience, for the next five years I was living a lie.

Oddly enough, one of the unexpected results of having MS was also one of the more positive. Almost a year after *Back to the Beach* came out, Frankie called and asked, "So are you ready to hit the road?"

"What?" I replied. "Frankie, you know I hate to travel, and I'm scared to death to sing live."

"Yes, Annette, but I also know that Jason just turned sixteen and got his license, so your carpooling days are over. What do you say?"

"Frankie, let me think about it, okay?"

I hung up the phone and sat there asking myself, What am I so afraid of? People want to see us. What's the worst thing that could happen? We might get booed? I might hit myself in the head with a microphone again? But then something came over me. Through finally confronting my deepest fears, I also accepted that I had MS. I'd been doing so beautifully. But suddenly I caught myself thinking, *You know, I may not always be able to do this.* I could be in a wheelchair, or worse. This could be my last chance. I knew that I could either face my demons and go out there and do it, or risk the possibility that one day I'd regret not having gone.

I hate regrets, so for one of the first times in my life, I pushed the fear aside. Maybe I couldn't beat my MS, but those fears and worries I'd let hold me back all these years— I'd had enough! I think Frankie was in shock when I told him to go ahead and set the wheels in motion.

It wasn't much longer before we were in Dick Clark's office, planning an itinerary. Being with Dick again—boy, what memories that brought back! I remembered one day in 1960 or so when Dick and his film crew came to my house for an interview. The day just seemed to drag on, and by the late afternoon I was silly from exhaustion. Don't ask what got into me, but I saw Dick standing by the pool, so neatly dressed in a suit and an expensive monogrammed shirt, I couldn't resist the temptation to push him in. Before Dick saw me coming, he was treading water in the deep end and laughing. He was really a sport, waiting in my father's bathrobe while Mom dried his clothes. He must have known what a crush I had on him, because he gave me his shirt as a memento of the day. And I wouldn't have taken a million bucks for it.

In Dick's office I happened to notice that he had a beautiful framed letter that Bobby Darin, who had died in 1973, wrote to Connie Francis when they were in love. It brought me back to the Caravan of Stars tour, the Harwyn Club, all the shows we did, and those crazy days on the road. Gee, had it really been thirty years ago? Did time really pass so quickly?

I was ready to go, but with one stipulation: I wanted to work mainly weekends, and I wanted to be able to come home to rest every few dates. That seemed doable, so we were set. We started with just a few fall dates in 1989, beginning in Yakima, Washington, but the shows did so well that Frankie and I were intermittently back on the road for the next year and a half.

The rehearsals were a lot of fun. Together we sang "Beach Party," "Some Things Last Forever" (from *Back to the Beach*), "Beach Blanket Bingo," a rock 'n' roll tribute/medley of hits by artists like Ricky Nelson, Elvis, Buddy Holly, and Ritchie Valens, and a few other numbers. Then we each had our solo spots, with Frankie performing "Bobby Sox to Stockings," "California Sun," "Beauty School Dropout" (from *Grease*), and "Venus," while my set included "Pineapple Princess," "Talent Roundup," "Jamaica Ska," and "Tall Paul." Then, of course, we closed with a reprise of "Beach Party," and "Mickey Mouse March (Alma Mater Theme)."

My favorite parts of the show, however, were the between-songs patter we exchanged. In one part Frankie says of the old rock 'n' roll tunes we perform, "What words! What music!" to which I reply, "*What* words? *What* music?" We talked about our families, about old times together, and the crowds loved it. At our second show, we got two standing ovations.

I'd always hated the traveling, and we hadn't been out on the road more than a few days before I knew why. We were trying to get out of Seattle after our first show, but were fogged in. Somehow Frankie talked the pilot of a private plane into taking us, and he agreed with one stipulation: "If I can have both of your autographs and a kiss on the cheek from Annette, I'll do it for free!" And he did.

Within just the first few dates, I began to feel almost comfortable onstage. Frankie had been right all those years: People really did love us. And I suppose knowing in the back of my mind that I might not ever do this again made it even sweeter. The fear that I might lose my balance onstage never left me, though. I had lost some of my depth perception, so if I was wearing, say, black shoes and black pants, and we were working on a black stage, I felt as if I were dancing in a hole. At one point in one of our skits, Frankie bends me back and kisses me, and there were a couple of times when I wasn't sure if I was going to be able to pull myself upright. Soon, however, Frankie started holding me a little tighter. I said a silent thank you and marveled at how sensitive Frankie was.

In March 1990 *The New Mickey Mouse Club* celebrated its first anniversary with a special featuring six of us originals: Sharon Baird, Bobby Burgess, Sherry Alberoni, Don Grady, Tommy Cole, and me. Except for the logo and the new

Mouseketeers' bright-eyed enthusiasm, this show and its old namesake were quite different. I suppose what they shared was being products of their respective times, but despite that, the Mouseketeer spirit seemed the same. We taped the special at the Disney-MGM Studio's Theme Park in Orlando, where we rehearsed and filmed over three days.

Then it was right back to the road with Frankie. For the most part, I felt reasonably fine, although there were times when my equilibrium was a touch off, and sometimes at the end of the night, I had the feeling that one of my legs wasn't as strong. Some stages had steps leading up to them, so Glen was always right there to lend support. I thought no one had noticed anything, but just last year I learned from Bobby Burgess and his wife, Christie, that she suspected something was wrong when they saw our Knott's Berry Farm show in April 1990.

Although we performed in over thirty cities, from spring into fall, the most memorable show for me was the one we did in my birthplace that May. Interestingly, we performed at Utica's Stanley Performing Arts Center on the very stage where my mother had received her high school diploma fifty years earlier. Because we still had so many relatives nearby and others flew in from around the country, the show became a family reunion, so I wanted to plan something very special for my parents.

I'd been singing "The Promised Land" in concert, and it always brought down the house, especially when I introduced my parents, who by song's end would be teary-eyed. But how to make it really special for Utica? Through the tour Frankie's sons had been playing in the band, Tony on guitar, and Frank, Jr., on drums. We agreed to fly Jason secretly to Utica and made plans to keep him stashed away in a separate hotel so my parents wouldn't know he was there. Right before my solo spot, the stage went dark and, unseen by the audience, Jason took Frankie Avalon, Jr.'s place on drums.

I said, "Please bring the lights up again. I have a big surprise for everybody. My son Jason is here from California to help me with a song that I wrote for my parents." A gasp arose from the crowd; some of my relatives hadn't seen Jason in about ten years.

Singing that song alone always made me choke up, but knowing that Jason and my family were there made it almost impossible to get through it. Of course, from the stage all I could see was darkness, but I felt my parents' love, and I knew by the time the last verse came around they were sobbing.

I began with a short recitation: "I don't remember too much about the trip, my first trip to California, because I was only four. But I do know of the hard times my family had afterward. . . . It held the promise of a better life." Then I sang, "From my city in the East, to the City of the Angels . . ."

As the song came to a close, I could hear my father crying. Frankie introduced Jason on drums, and the audience went wild, especially my parents and relatives, many of whom were sobbing, too. Afterward Jason kept saying, "Thanks, Mom!" More than the highlight of the show, it was one of the highlights of my life.

When it came time to do our last show in Owensboro, Kentucky, everyone was getting choked up. But it wasn't the end. In January 1991 Frankie and I took our show to the Golden Nugget in Las Vegas. Frankie was familiar to Vegas audiences, having played that circuit for many years. But this was my first time, and it was exciting. There was some talk that Frankie and I might host a variety show that would tape in Las Vegas, which I'd have loved if for no other reason than my dear friend Sharon Baird had recently moved to Reno and I missed her so.

I'd always loved going to Vegas, and performing there with Frankie brought our touring days together to a beautiful end. Sure, there had been times when I questioned whether I'd done the right thing, such as when I felt unsteady as I reached forward from the stage to shake fans' hands or made a quick turn and saw the room spin. Yet standing on the stage, hearing the applause, and knowing that I'd done what I always told myself I couldn't do, made me feel so proud, so happy. To think that it might not have happened at all!

As we performed our last dates, I began feeling shakier on-stage. The bottoms of my feet burned and the tingling in my legs intensified. One night I said to Glen, "I can't keep this from Frankie anymore."

"Honey, don't worry," Glen replied. "You don't need to tell him."

"Yes, I do, Glen. I feel like I'm living a lie. I have to tell Frankie."

"Okay, darlin'," Glen answered, "if that's what you think is right."

The next morning Frankie and I had breakfast together in our hotel. I was very nervous, not knowing how he would respond, but I suggested, "After breakfast, let's sit down in the lounge. I have something I want to tell you."

We sat on a couch together, and I began, "You know your friend Tom Dreesan who puts on the telethon for his sister who had multiple sclerosis?"

"Sure," he answered.

"Well, every year he invites me, you know, and I always have a reason why I can't go. Do you know why?"

Frankie shook his head.

"Because, Frankie, I have what she had. I have MS."

Frankie was shocked, and a tear welled up in his eye. "Oh, Annette . . ."

"That's why I'm so glad that you've been holding me on-stage when I walk close to the edge. That's why I'm so glad that you're there."

We talked more and had a good cry together, and I felt as if someone had lifted a ton off my shoulders. About two years later I was on Vicki Lawrence's first TV talk show. I was being interviewed in my home, so I was talking into a camera lens, while Frankie sat in the studio with Vicki. When the subject of my MS arose, through my earpiece I heard Frankie say, "Annette, Vicki, I have something to tell everybody that Annette has never found out." He proceeded to recount how Glen told him about my MS *before* the tour began and asked him to watch out for me.

I was stunned, but knowing I was on camera I tried to hide my shock and, yes, I admit, my anger. I forget exactly what I said to Frankie while we were being taped, but the minute the camera went off, I was furious.

"Glen, why did you do that behind my back? You made me feel like a fool in front of everybody!"

"I was so worried about you, honey," he replied. "I know you like to go down to the edge of the stage and shake hands with people. I just had to do it."

Then I was angry at Frankie, because I felt that when I opened my heart to him he should have told me that he already knew. But after I thought it over, I realized what a delicate position everyone was in. Glen was worried about me, and he did what I know I'd have done were our roles reversed. And Frankie couldn't bear to betray Glen's trust or hurt my pride by letting me know that he'd been looking out for me all along. I know that if I'd been in Frankie's position, I'd probably have done the same thing. I knew that both Glen and Frankie had based their actions on love and concern for me, and for that I could find no fault.

What the experience made me realize was that I was mad at the illness. I was angry at it for all the energy I had to expend just to keep it hidden, all the lies I had to tell to protect my secret. After a short time, everything blew over, and today Frankie and I can joke about the incident. I often tease him by saying, "I didn't know you were such a good actor, Frankie," to which he retorts, "See, Annette, I told you I was always underrated!"

As time passed and my symptoms started becoming noticeable, it became harder to keep the secret from my family. Mom especially was under so much stress. Eventually she told my brothers, who took it badly, especially my younger brother, Michael. It broke my heart to think of the burden Mom had to bear all alone, but she agreed that it was best that Dad still not know.

Beginning around 1989 I would notice Dad looking at me oddly, especially when I tried to get up out of a chair. I'd see this look of confusion and concern in his eyes, and he would sometimes ask me if I was all right. By then I had my story down pat: I must have pulled something, it was tendinitis, it was an old dancing injury acting up. There were so many times when I'd see a hurt, quizzical look on his face, and I'd just want to run to him and say, "Oh, Daddy, there is something wrong!" and feel him hold me. But I couldn't.

Eventually, those stories started to wear pretty thin. And I began thinking about how I would feel if, God forbid, one of my children was suffering in secret and denied me the chance to help. So one day when we were alone, I said, "Dad, I have something to tell you. You know the way I have trouble walking sometimes? That's because I have multiple sclerosis."

"Do you mean the thing Jerry Lewis puts the telethon on for?" he asked.

"No, Dad, this is something else." I explained everything to him and why I'd kept it a secret from him, and he seemed to take it pretty well. I later learned that once my father got home, he dropped his facade and withdrew into a silent sadness. Like everyone else, he's since grown accustomed to seeing me when I'm not having a good day. And I know that whenever I ask for his arm to steady me he is so proud.

In April of 1991 we held a huge party to celebrate my parents' fiftieth wedding anniversary. Looking at my parents as they restated their vows, I couldn't believe they'd been married for fifty years. To see them together, you'd think they'd just fallen in love yesterday.

They'd recently moved to Palm Springs, which seemed like a good idea, especially since smog, crime, and over-crowding, in their opinion, had tarnished the Los Angeles they'd moved to over forty years before. Their moving was a heartbreaking experience for everyone, since that house had been the scene of many wonderful holidays and celebrations. It had never occurred to me to go home again to my parents, but somehow just knowing that my bedroom was still there had made me happy. Although we visit back and forth quite often, I must say that I miss not having them a few minutes away.

Regardless of what happened, I've always tried to keep things in perspective and maintain a healthy sense of humor. I've always enjoyed gambling, the occasional drink, and before my MS thing, as I call it now, I even smoked a couple of cigarettes a day. You can't imagine how many times people have seen me with a drink or a cigarette and remarked, "Why, Annette, that's so un-Disney-like!" or "Annette, I had no idea that you did *that!*"

Rather than be offended or upset, I simply respond with a smile, "Well, I have three kids, so guess what else I do!" Al-most everyone laughs, though I sometimes wonder if maybe there aren't at least a few who find that shocking. You never know.

The owner of one of my favorite restaurants got into pub-lishing and thought it would be interesting to pair celebrities who came from totally different worlds and have them inter-view each other. The magazine, which should be published in 1994, is called *Twist,* and if publisher Quay Hays was aim-ing for the ultimate in unlikely couples, he certainly suc-ceeded when he asked me to sit and talk with heavy-metal star Ozzy Osbourne.

When I first heard that Ozzy was to be my partner for the piece, I admit I was a little taken aback. Like most people, I'd heard the bad publicity about his biting the head off a dove and later (though accidentally) chewing the head off a bat (it turns out that a fan handed it to him in concert, and he thought it was a toy). And then there was that song of his, "Suicide Solution," which Jason blasted often enough for me to get the idea that I didn't particularly care for it.

When I told Jason about the offer, he was ecstatic. "Oh, please, Mom, if you really, really love me, you'll do it!"

"Well, Jason, I don't know . . ."

Then Jason cut right to the chase, and my heart: "Show me that you love me, Mom. Please say yes!"

"Well, Jason, I don't think I really want to meet him, because I don't approve of that song 'Suicide Solution.' I think it sends kids a bad message."

"No, wait, Mom, let me tell you the words, because it's not saying you should commit suicide, it's saying that you should *not*." He recited the lyrics, and I listened, and he was right. Like millions of parents, I'd jumped to the wrong conclusion. But I'd listened to my son and let him teach me something for a change.

"Okay, Jason," I said. "If it will make you happy, I'll do the interview with Ozzy. And you can stay home from school that day and come along." Needless to say, Jason was over the moon.

At the interview Jason and I met Ozzy and his little boy Jack, who was about four and so cute. I can never resist a baby. Knowing everything about Ozzy, Jason had prepped me for the interview. And of course I'd seen pictures of him, in his dark eye shadow, tattoos, and black leather. But I have to admit I was a little surprised at what a gentleman he was. Intelligent, sensitive, and obviously a very caring father, he won my heart within just a few minutes.

We spoke for quite a while, and Ozzy was very open about his newfound sobriety after years of substance abuse. Who could imagine two people with less in common? Yet we shared our thoughts about Walt Disney, raising children, Elvis Presley, stage fright, even our admiration of Connie

Francis. Like Frankie and me, he had fans who brought their kids and grandkids to his concerts. At one point toward the end, Ozzy said, "Life is forever going to change, you know. I mean, who would've thought you and I would be sitting around a table ten or twenty years ago?"

"Is this a kick?" I replied, laughing. "Whoever dreamed?" The whole time I was thinking to myself, *Life is full of surprises.*

C H A P T E R   10

*A*lthough I generally felt fine, through 1991 it was getting harder to deny that something was wrong. For a
few days I was overcome with what felt like a bad case of flu,
complete with chills and a fever so dangerously high that I
had to lie in bed on packs of ice. Because I have MS, and viral
infections are known to exacerbate symptoms, I found myself suddenly unable to walk. If Glen wasn't there to carry
me, I had to maneuver myself onto the floor and crawl to the
bathroom. It was terrifying, yet after a few days the symptoms disappeared.

Just learning that you have MS is such a devastating shock
you sometimes think nothing else could shake you like that
again. But to have any chronic illness is to experience a constant series of frightening surprises, some annoying, others
almost emotionally devastating. For me the bout of flu really
drove home what this MS thing was all about. Even though I
had occasionally needed a cane to walk, until then I still
thought nothing truly awful could ever happen to me. I
guess you could say I almost started to believe my own press.

Now I walked unsteadily with a cane or leaning on someone's arm. Each time I left the house I worried not only about
how I would keep my balance, but how I would explain what

214

was wrong. Over the past year I'd spun a dizzyingly intricate web of excuses and stories about my bad knee and my tendinitis. I even wore a knee brace and would make a point of raising my slacks to show it to any friend who inquired. But lately I found just keeping up with the winding trail of white lies getting harder. Had I told so-and-so it was tendinitis? What should I say when she asks if I ever called the orthopedist she'd recommended last time? And so on. Even I could see in some friends' faces that the story wasn't adding up.

Worst of all, though, was the stress that telling lies and keeping the stories straight brought about. Fatigue and stress often exacerbate the symptoms of MS, and so, ironically, my attempts to hide the truth actually made the problem more evident. If any neighbors and friends suspected anything, they never mentioned it to me. But before long reporters got wind that there was "something wrong" with Annette. To be honest, anyone who didn't know I had a physical problem but saw me walk or slowly rise from a chair could easily, and understandably, conclude that I was drinking.

In early 1992 I was dining in a local restaurant. One of Jackie's friends happened to be there. The next day he told my son, "I saw your mom leaving the restaurant last night, and boy, did she have one too many." I was embarrassed for my son more than anything else, but it was beginning to dawn on me that I couldn't hide forever.

Pretty soon reporters from the tabloids started hanging around my neighborhood, knocking on doors and asking my neighbors, "What's wrong with Annette?" Naturally, they would call to tell me what had happened, and I'd always say, "I think they're just trying to stir up some gossip. You know, I have this knee problem . . ." But the tabloids were not to be denied, and gradually their tactics and targets hit closer to home. One phoned Glen at the ranch, another phoned my brother Joey, who is also my agent; then relatives back in Utica began getting calls.

I was sitting at home when the phone rang.

"Hello?"

"Annette?"

"Yes?" I wondered who could be calling on my private number.

"I'm from . . ." and he named a leading supermarket tabloid. "We understand that you're ready to go public, and we're willing to pay you a handsome fee if you'll give us the exclusive."

Without admitting that anything was wrong or asking him how he got my number, I stammered, "You mean you're talking dollars and cents when it comes to my health and my private life? No thank you!" By then I was so furious and so unnerved the receiver shook in my hand.

"We knew you would react that way, Annette," he answered softly. "God bless you. We wish you the best."

And he meant it. "Thank you very much," I replied, crying.

I don't recall exactly what day it was, but I knew the supermarket tabloids would be out on Friday, and I was sure there would be some story about me, true or not. The only thing to do was to tell the story myself. I called Lorraine Santoli at Disney immediately and said, "Lorraine, this is it. I want to go public, and I want to beat the tabloids." Lorraine thought the best strategy was to make the announcement through a nationwide publication, so that it hit everybody at once. "Fine," I said, "call Tom Green, who is at *USA Today* now, and tell him I have a story for him."

I chose Tom because he'd interviewed me many times over the years, beginning when I was a Mouseketeer, and I'd always liked and trusted him. When Lorraine first called Tom and informed him I had an announcement to make, his first question was "Does Annette have AIDS?" Lorraine replied no, but said nothing else.

On Wednesday Tom came to my house, and I told him the whole story. At one point I remarked, "Haven't you always felt that I've had the perfect life?" Thursday on the front page of *USA Today*'s "Life" section ran the headline "Funicello Fighting Multiple Sclerosis." That morning I read and reread the story, feeling so exposed, yet so relieved. I could go anywhere now and never have to lie again. Nor would my kids, or Glen, or anyone else I cared for. To finally be free just to talk about it after all those years—I can't even explain what that meant.

Then the doorbell rang. Then the phone rang. And before the day was over I'd received dozens of floral arrangements and talked to people I never thought I'd hear from again. And so it continued for several weeks afterward. I received lovely flowers from Frank Sinatra, whom I'd worked with as a spokesperson for a brand of Italian foods, and his wife, Barbara, along with a beautiful note. I had a warm conversation with Paul Anka, whom I hadn't spoken to in many years. Paul Reubens wrote a touching letter. And, of course, Frankie let me know he and his wife, Kay, were there for me as well.

I was deeply touched by the thousands of cards and letters, all expressing warm wishes and many containing tips on dealing with MS. And the flowers! Some mornings I'd wake up and walk from room to room, amazed that these were all meant for me, that so many people cared so much. At the same time, though, I also felt a glimmer of panic. *What have I done now?* I thought to myself. *How can I ever thank everyone for their support?* Sometimes I'd look at the unopened envelopes that filled my kitchen table and worry about how I would ever be able to read every one, let alone answer them all. Sometimes I wondered if I hadn't made a mistake.

The first time I went out in public and no one asked me what was wrong, I knew I'd done the right thing. Going public also gave me countless opportunities to talk about MS and to heighten public awareness about this baffling illness. For me, though, the most valuable aspect of being known as a person with MS is getting to meet others who either have it or care for someone who has it. I decided then that I would use my public recognition to do something concrete in the fight against MS, so I founded the Annette Funicello Research Fund for Neurological Diseases, which will finance the search for the answers to MS as well as other illnesses, including myasthenia gravis and Lou Gehrig's disease.

Another result of my announcement was an avalanche of books, pamphlets, videocassettes, and phone calls from people claiming to have a line on an effective treatment. By the time I spoke with *USA Today*, I'd gone through a series of various treatment regimens, including rounds of acupuncture and acupressure, steroids, B-12 shots in my legs, myelin pills, and massive doses of vitamins and other nutrients. At one point I was swallowing over fifty different pills a day; needless to say, when I heard about another plan that would require me to take over 180 daily, I said no thanks.

Glen, God bless him, reads every piece of mail that comes our way. He talks to people who claim they've had success treating people with MS, and he's flown all over the country searching for my answer. But so far the trail's come up cold. That's not to say that there aren't people out there with MS who have had some relief from their symptoms, or what appears for now to be a total remission. But nearly three-quarters of all MS patients experience a spontaneous remission, making it virtually impossible for anyone to pinpoint exactly the cause or evaluate the effectiveness of any given treatment.

Of course, I am speaking only for myself when I say that I'm a little leery of anyone who claims to have all the answers. Glen and I have met earnest physicians and researchers who've impressed us with their understanding and their dedication. We've also met our share of zealots whose insistence on secrecy scared us away. Anyone who has suffered or witnessed a loved one's suffering knows how desperate you can get. Most of us naturally think that we would go anywhere, do anything, pay any amount to anyone who held out even the tiniest branch of hope. But in reality it's never that simple. No matter how good, safe, or promising something sounds, you can't jump headfirst before you know every requirement, every risk, every side effect. Most honest people will concede that they have no idea whether or not whatever they're proposing will work for me. After so many disappointments, I'm a lot more skeptical and cautious than before.

But I'm not just sitting around waiting for a cure. I follow the low-fat diet recommended for people with MS, I quit smoking, I exercise, I rest, and I try to lead as stress-free a life as possible. Beyond that, there's very little I can do except become a subject in someone's research program. That is not something I'm willing to do right now, although I understand that there are many people with MS who would volunteer gladly for any number of clinical trials and unproven therapies. With MS, as with everything else in life, you must find and follow the course that feels right to you.

Over the past seven years I believe that I've come to terms with MS. It's a part of my life that I could certainly do without, that I would give up joyously if I had the chance. Have I accepted it? Well, it depends on what you mean. Am I happy I have it? Of course not; no one is. But the difference between my attitude now as compared to several years ago is that while I fight the illness every way I can, I no longer fight the realization that I have it. This is not to say that I've given up hope, which I certainly have not and never will. But I've stopped expending valuable energy on the why of it all—I'll never know why—and instead focus on what's good about each day, whether it be something as simple as a hug from one of my kids or as grand as a public award. Or, as I used to sing about fifty years ago, I ac-cent-tchu-ate the positive. It works.

In the meantime there is the practical, day-to-day challenge MS presents, and in that I've had my disappointments.

Until last year I did very well walking with a cane. I've collected quite a number of them, including one of clear Lucite that the Disney artists decorated with characters. But last spring I noticed it was getting harder to find my balance. One day I started to fall and missed toppling face first into a glass tabletop by mere inches. I started using a walker on those more difficult days, and that summer, after trying hard to avoid it, I allowed myself to be seen in public in a wheelchair. Glen and I were at the airport, and our gate was the farthest from the main terminal. I knew I wasn't going to make it. Yet it was hard to ask for it. For me, as for many people, the wheelchair symbolizes disability in a way a cane does not. It marks another step in the progression of the illness, something no one likes to think about.

But as Glen pushed the chair through the terminal, people stopped, grabbed my hand, kissed me, and pinched my cheeks. "God bless you, Annette."

"I grew up with you, Annette, and I'm praying for you."

"You'll get better; I know it."

By the time we reached our gate, I was crying, partially from joy, seeing how deeply people cared, and partially from the frightening realization that one day I may be in a wheelchair more often than I'd like.

Through it all the one constant in my life has been faith. My faith in God is such that I believe that my illness has a purpose and a meaning, although I would never presume to imagine what that might be. Yet, as I build my research foundation, as I travel across the country speaking about MS and my experience, perhaps I can offer others comfort and hope. Perhaps for now that is enough.

The Lord has been good to me throughout my life; He's never let me down. Perhaps this is His test for me. Perhaps it is His way to teach me something I might not have otherwise learned. Whatever it is, I feel the Lord at my side, and with Him I know that all good things are possible.

On Easter Sunday 1993 I believe I felt Him especially close to me. My whole family had gathered for the weekend, and that morning I woke up and walked as easily as ever. It was as if the MS had suddenly vanished. My legs felt light, and my balance was perfect. For that whole day I never needed my cane, I never teetered for a second. It seemed like a miracle. And yet the next day the symptoms returned. Now I pray that one day like that will come again, and then another and another.

I have a recurring dream that one day I rise from a chair and start walking. I can hear my kids saying, "Mom, look at you! You don't even have your cane!" And then I stop and realize that I really am walking again.

"You're right!" I say in the dream. "I *am* walking!" And someday that dream, that wish, may come true.

In an odd way MS has given me the impetus to do many things I would have otherwise avoided; the "Back to the Beach" tour with Frankie is one example. In 1991 I started the Annette Funicello Bear Company, through which I help design and market a line of limited-edition collectible stuffed toy bears. Working with a team of famous bear designers, I consult and help dress each bear in his (or her) special outfit. Each bear's name and costume has a special meaning. Shorty is named for my father; Brownie, after the little stuffed bear I carried with me to California as a child; Jessica for one niece and Tammy for another; Annette Beach Bear celebrates the beach-party films; and Ballerina Bear, Annette Mousekebear, Round-Up Bear, and Let It Snow Bear all commemorate special numbers I did on *The Mickey Mouse Club*.

As I've said, perfume has always been my passion. My father once said, "Annette would put on perfume even to take out the garbage," and he's probably right. My second business venture was my signature fragrance line, Cello, by Annette, which was publicly introduced in 1993 at Mlle.

Antoinette's Parfumerie in New Orleans Square at Disneyland. We started working on developing Cello in 1992. It took a long time and a lot of hard work getting all the details right, but I so enjoyed taking part in every aspect of production—from choosing the formula that captured the spirit I had in mind to perfecting the packaging, down to the bottle and the label.

We hit some bumps along the way. For example, the box's graphic design featured part of a cello's neck and what they call the belly, or the rounded top, of the instrument body. Everyone involved agreed on one particular design, which we believed fit perfectly until test-marketing focus groups who saw it told us that it reminded them of a woman's breast in profile. None of us ever saw it that way, but after we heard that, it was all we noticed, so we went back to the drawing board. Eventually all the pieces fell into place, and I'm proud to say that Cello and the Annette Funicello Bears have both enjoyed great success.

My past two birthdays have been the occasions of the most wonderful celebrations of my life. In 1992, on Jason's birthday, the day before my own fiftieth birthday, I was honored to receive the Disney Legends Award in recognition of my contribution to the Disney legacy. The ceremony, held in front of the Walt Disney Theater on the lot where Mom used to wait for me to finish work every day, honored seven others, among them Jimmie Dodd and Roy Williams.

As my balance has worsened, I've found it more difficult to walk on hard surfaces, so at one point during the ceremony, I had to slip out of my shoes. Glen helped me to kneel down in front of the theater steps, and there I placed my handprints and wrote "Annette" in wet concrete. In the same concrete block were set metal medallions honoring Jimmie Dodd and Roy Williams. Roy's wife was there to receive Roy's award; he had passed away in 1976. Jimmie's award was accepted by Ruthie Dodd's second husband, Harold

Braun. Ruthie, sadly, had passed away from cancer. As always, Mickey and Minnie were there, as were Roy E. Disney, Walt's nephew, and Disney Chairman Michael Eisner.

And in 1993 my birthday present was a star on Hollywood's Walk of Fame. My children had wanted me to have a star for a long time, but I always dissuaded them from pursuing it. When Gina told me that they planned to unveil my star in front of the El Capitan Theatre on my birthday, she was so afraid I would say no that she had a friend there. I'd been so adamant about the kids' not going to any trouble getting me the star that she was afraid that, if we were there alone, I'd say no.

But as I listened to my daughter explain to her mother why Annette Funicello deserved that honor, I started to cry. I think it was more out of thanks to God for giving me such loving, caring kids than anything else. Just a few months before, all three had taken part in the Super Cities Walk to raise money to fight MS; between the three of them they raised several thousand dollars.

The fall of 1993 found me busier than I'd been in years. Not only was I to receive my star, but Walt Disney Records was releasing a double-CD retrospective called *Annette: A Musical Reunion with the Girl Next Door.* Months before the release, a Disney camera crew filmed as I sat in my home with Tutti Camarata and the Sherman Brothers, reminiscing. At one point someone from the Walt Disney Archives brought out several mementos of my Mouseketeer days, including the Mouseketeer T-shirt with my name on it. It looked so dainty and small, and when I held it up to my chest, the memories just came crashing in. It was like holding my childhood next to my heart.

When we finished taping I asked if I could possibly borrow the shirt and keep it in my home for a while, but, unfortunately, they said no. It seems that this is the only shirt with my name on it in existence, and everyone felt it was safer kept in the Disney Archives. Of course, they were right. Still, just touching that cream-colored shirt made me feel the passage of time sharply.

While the engineers and producers were putting the final touches on the CDs, Lorraine Santoli stopped by the house with a special tape she wanted me to hear. I sat back in my chair as the familiar first notes of Jimmie Dodd singing "Annette" filled the room. The recording had been so beautifully preserved that it seemed as if he were right there with me. After each verse was a spoken tribute that had been recorded and added especially for the CD version. It was such a wonderful surprise to hear my friends Frankie, Paul Anka, Shelley Fabares, and Tommy Sands speak so fondly of our past. At the very end came Mickey's voice, chirping, "Love ya!" What more could anyone ask?

In October I unveiled my star on the Walk of Fame. It was a lovely day, and as we rode in the limousine to the El Capitan Theatre, I got excited. By the time I stepped out of the car to the applause and well-wishes of the guests and fans gathered on Hollywood Boulevard, I felt like I was floating on air. All I really remember was hearing Frankie's voice rise above the rest of the crowd's: "You look beautiful! Congratulations!" Then I glanced over to Mom and Dad, who were crying.

With Mickey Mouse on my right and Glen on my left I made my way to a director's chair with my name on it and then listened to the moving tributes from friends like Frankie Avalon and Shelley Fabares. At one point my son Jackie placed a large bouquet of lavender and purple flowers in my lap, and I was so nervous I was sure everyone would see the blossoms bounce up and down. Standing to my left were my parents, my children, my brother Mike, with his wife Cyndee and daughter Tammy, my brother Joey, with his wife Jo Ann and daughter Jessica, Sharon Baird, Shelley and Frankie, Arlene Ludwig, and Lorraine Santoli—everyone dear to me. After I thanked them all, I pulled the ropes to reveal my star.

The first thing I said was "They were even able to fit my whole last name!" Envisioning the day, I'd just assumed the star would read "Annette." I was so pleased to see Funicello there as well—the name Mr. Disney promised me no one would ever forget.

We returned to the house to relax and have a catered brunch, but the emotions of the day were overwhelming. One of the ironies of MS is that the more excited I feel the less cooperative my legs are. That evening we all attended a party to launch the CD set, and it was a night of surprises. I spent a lot of the time being interviewed for various television programs and publications but found time to reminisce with many old friends. Bobby Burgess, Sharon Baird, Shelley and her husband Mike, Morey Amsterdam, Fabian, Tommy Sands, Robert and Richard Sherman were there, as were newer friends, like Rodney Bingenheimer, a Los Angeles DJ who'd been playing my old records for several years.

At the end, several guests went onstage and spoke about me. Time and again, I wiped tears from my eyes. To have known and worked with so many wonderful people—I know I was truly blessed. There were also a few surprises. Mike Love of the Beach Boys showed up and told the story of being scared to death of me (me?) before we worked on *The Monkey's Uncle,* and *Night Court*'s Richard Moll simply kept repeating, "I love you! I love you!" Richard and Robert Sherman presented their musical tribute to me, complete with funny patter, and the evening ended with everyone joining in to sing "Mickey Mouse March (Alma Mater Theme)": "Now it's time to say goodbye . . ."

The day had been such a blur of joy that I'd missed a few things. Fortunately, someone at Disney had taped both events. As I watched the videotape a few days later I saw my mother being interviewed. When she was asked to say a few words, she paused for a few seconds, then answered, "Today my daughter got a star on Hollywood Boulevard. She has been a star in my life ever since the day she was born. I'm so happy." What greater tribute could anyone ask for?

Between the big events and all the interviews, every day seemed like nostalgia day. Yet, despite being called upon to answer the same questions a hundred times, I never tire of it. The things people ask about—like *The Mickey Mouse Club* or the beach-party movies—are still dear to them, and I feel fortunate to have played a part in such fond memories. For me, however, I think the most emotional event came at the close of the Second Annual Disneyana Convention, an annual gathering of Disney fans and collectors, later that week.

The convention's climax was a spectacular show, at which I gave the tribute to Walt Disney that I had written with Glen years before. The room was dark as a tape recording of me speaking played. Because these words best express my feelings about Mr. Disney, I would like to share them here:

"Ever since the discovery of our great land we've had many heroes, from George Washington to our present president; many war heroes, such as Sergeant York, the most honored soldier in World War I, and Audie Murphy, the most decorated soldier in World War II; many pioneers, from Davy Crockett to John Glenn, our first orbiting astronaut; and many other brave men and women who fought and died to keep our country free and strong. A lot of our heroes have emerged from the big silver screen, such men as Roy Rogers, Hopalong Cassidy, Gene Autry, and many more who make films that teach our children that honesty is always the winner. And, of course, the Duke, John Wayne, who displayed strength and leadership portraying many of our heroes who made this land what it is today.

"But I want to tell you of a man I knew who was just as great a hero in my life. He never won any battles in war, but he won the love and respect of children and adults alike. In his films and his magical theme parks, he taught children how to love and appreciate nature. I'm sure he put more smiles on their faces than all the comedians ever could. His dedication was not just making people smile; he taught, in his special way, respect for life and land the world over, making people realize that if you wish upon a star, dreams really can come true. Many times I visited his Magic Kingdoms, and believe me when I say my dream came true.

"I always found Mr. Disney to be somewhat of a shy person, a kid at heart. I guess that's why he always requested we all call him Uncle Walt. But that was a name I just couldn't bring myself to say, since he seemed more like a second father to me. Just to know him was to love him, and I'll never forget all the kindness he showed me.

"I can't say enough good things about this man who was loved so much by so many. Where does one begin? His dedication and accomplishments were second to none, and to think that it all began with a little mouse. That's why, when I think of heroes, I always think of him. God bless that man.

"In 1966 the world was saddened to hear of his death, but it's such a comfort to know that his soul lives on together with his dreams. His memory will live forever in my heart."

And then curtains parted, a light shone on me standing alone on the stage, and, live, I spoke the last line, "So now, to fulfill your long request, Mr. Disney, I'll say, Goodnight, Uncle Walt."

I was on the verge of tears myself, and I could see people in the audience dabbing their eyes. As everyone rose to a standing ovation, I was joined onstage by Lonnie Burr, Tommy Cole, Bobby Burgess, Sharon Baird, Sherry Alberoni, and Karen Pendleton. Together we all sang "Mickey Mouse March" and then closed the show with "Mickey Mouse March (Alma Mater) Theme."

Over the previous days I'd gotten to spend time with the other Mouseketeers. My legs were feeling weak, so I decided to use a wheelchair around the hotel. In an odd twist of fate, Karen, who has been partially paralyzed as the result of a car accident ten years ago, also uses a chair, so there we were together, going out and having a great time. I remember thinking, *What are the odds that two of us would be in chairs at this point in our lives?* But what was more important and more amazing, I suppose, was that after all these years we were still good friends. That's what really matters. In everything. It's probably hard to imagine that one day how you get around becomes as small a detail in your day as what color shoes you wear, but it does. Life truly does go on.

In November 1993 I was honored to receive the Helen Hayes Award from the Saint Clare's Hospital and Health Center in New York City. I was chosen to receive the award in recognition of both my professional accomplishments and my work in raising public awareness about MS. Although I never had the honor of meeting Miss Hayes, I knew her son, actor James MacArthur, from our days together at the Disney Studio, which he alluded to when he presented the lovely silver rose to me. Later that evening Bobby Rydell performed, and at one point came down to my table to sing "One Girl" to the tune of "One Boy" from *Bye Bye Birdie.* It was an evening of special moments. I thought back to my seventeenth birthday, when Bobby had serenaded me during a Caravan of Stars show. Of course, those memories are precious to me, but I also treasure today. With Glen at my side and close friends all around, even sitting in my wheelchair, I felt fortunate and thankful. Life does not have to be "perfect" to be wonderful.

How pleased I would be if I could end my story here by saying that my MS had gone into remission or been cured. Unfortunately, I can't, but that doesn't mean that this book can't have a happy ending. As I have had so many opportunities to do over the past year, I simply stop and reflect on the many blessings that have been showered upon me. I draw strength from my belief that the Lord stands beside me, along with my parents, my children, my husband, my friends, and, of course, my fans. And Uncle Walt and Mickey Mouse. I have found peace knowing that wherever I go, however I may get there, they will be with me. In that way, whatever dreams I have wished have come true.

APPENDIX

Domestically Released Feature Films

The Shaggy Dog (1959), Disney.
Babes in Toyland (1961), Disney.
Beach Party (1963), American International.
The Misadventures of Merlin Jones (1964), Disney.
Muscle Beach Party (1964), American International.
Bikini Beach (1964), American International.
Pajama Party (1964), American International.
Beach Blanket Bingo (1965), American International.
The Monkey's Uncle (1965), Disney.
Ski Party (1965), American International.
How to Stuff a Wild Bikini (1965), American International.
Dr. Goldfoot and the Bikini Machine (1965), American International.
Fireball 500 (1966), American International.
Thunder Alley (1967), American International.
Head (1968), Columbia.
Back to the Beach (1987).
Troop Beverly Hills (1989).

The Television Series and Guest Appearances

The Mickey Mouse Club (1955 through 1959), ABC, which included
   the serials *Adventure in Dairyland* (1956), *The Further Adventures*

of Spin and Marty (1956), *The New Adventures of Spin and Marty*
(1957), and *Annette* (1958).
Elfego Baca (1959), part of *Walt Disney Presents*, ABC, in the
episodes "Attorney at Law" and "The Griswold Murder."
These episodes were later combined with others in the *Elfego
Baca* series and released as a feature film in England entitled *Six
Gun Law* in 1962.
Zorro (1959), ABC, in the episodes "Please Believe Me," "The
Brooch," and "The Missing Father."
Make Room for Daddy (1959), CBS, in episodes including "Gina for
President," "Gina's First Date," "Frankie Laine Sings for Gina,"
"The Latin Lover."
Zorro (1961), shown on *Walt Disney Presents*, ABC, in the episode
"The Postponed Wedding."
The Horsemasters (1961), shown in two parts on *Walt Disney's
Wonderful World of Color*, NBC. Released theatrically in Europe.
Escapade in Florence (1962), shown in two parts on *Walt Disney's
Wonderful World of Color*, NBC. Released theatrically in Europe.
Disneyland After Dark (1962), shown on *Walt Disney's Wonderful
World of Color*, NBC. Released theatrically in Europe.
The Golden Horseshoe Revue (1962), shown on *Walt Disney's
Wonderful World of Color*, NBC. Released theatrically in Europe.
Wagon Train (1963), ABC, in the episode "The Sam Pulaski Story."
Burke's Law (1963), ABC, in the episode "Who Killed the Kind
Doctor?"
The Greatest Show on Earth (1964), ABC, in the episode "Rosetta."
Burke's Law (1965), ABC, in the episode "Who Killed the
Strangler?"
Hondo (1967), ABC, in the episode "The Apache Trail."
Love, American Style (1971), ABC, in the episode "Love and the
Tuba."
The John Byner Comedy Hour (1972), CBS.
The Mouse Factory (1973), Walt Disney Studio, syndicated, in the
episode "A Salute to Mickey Mouse Cartoons."
The Mouse Factory (1974), Walt Disney Studio, syndicated, in the
episode "Pablo, the Cold-Blooded Penguin."
The New Mickey Mouse Club (1977), syndicated.
The Love Boat (1978), ABC, in the episode "Never Fall in Love
Again."
Frankie and Annette, The Second Time Around (pilot) (1978), NBC.
Fantasy Island (1979), ABC, in the episode "The Strangler."
"The Mickey Mouse Club Reunion" (1980), shown on *Disney's
Wonderful World*, NBC.

Fantasy Island (1980), ABC, in the episode "Mary Ann and Miss Sophisticate."
Fantasy Island (1981), ABC, in the episode "The Unkillable."
The Love Boat (1982), ABC, in the episode "N.Y.A.C."
Lots of Luck (1985), The Disney Channel.
Growing Pains (1986), ABC, in the episode "The Chaperones."

DISCOGRAPHY

This does not include Annette's numerous appearances on *Mickey Mouse Club* singles and albums, nor on movie soundtrack albums.

"How Will I Know My Love?" b/w "Don't Jump to Conclusions" (Disneyland), 1958.
"Crazy Place from Outer Space" b/w "Gold Doubloons and Pieces of Eight" (Disneyland), 1958.
"Tall Paul" b/w "Ma, He's Making Eyes at Me" (Disneyland), 1958.
"Jo-Jo, the Dog-Faced Boy" b/w "Love Me Forever" (Buena Vista), 1959.
"Jo-Jo, the Dog-Faced Boy" b/w "Lonely Guitar" (Buena Vista), 1959.
"Wild Willie" b/w "Lonely Guitar" (Buena Vista), 1959.
"My Heart Became of Age" b/w "Especially for You" (Buena Vista), 1959.
"First Name Initial" b/w "My Heart Became of Age" (Buena Vista), 1959.
"O Dio Mio" b/w "It Took Dreams" (Buena Vista), 1960.
"Train of Love" b/w "Tell Me Who's the Girl" (Buena Vista), 1960.
"Pineapple Princess" b/w "Luau Cha Cha Cha" (Buena Vista), 1960.
"Talk to Me Baby" b/w "I Love You Baby" (Buena Vista), 1960.
"Dream Boy" b/w "Please, Please Signore" (Buena Vista), 1961.
"Indian Giver" b/w "Mama Rosa (Where's the Spumoni)" (Buena Vista), 1961.
"The Parent Trap" b/w "Let's Get Together" (Buena Vista), 1961.
"Hawaiian Love Talk" b/w "Blue Muu Muu" (Buena Vista), 1961.
"Dreamin' About You" b/w "Strummin' Song" (Buena Vista), 1961.

"Crazy Place from Outer Space" b/w "Seven Moons" [not by Annette] (Buena Vista), 1962.

"The Truth About Youth" b/w "I Can't Do the Sum" (Buena Vista), 1962.

"My Little Grass Shack" b/w "Hukilau Song" (Buena Vista), 1962.

"He's My Ideal" b/w "Mr. Piano Man" (Buena Vista), 1962.

"Bella Bella Florence" b/w "Canzone D'Amore" (with Marzocchi) (Buena Vista), 1962.

"Teenage Wedding" b/w "Walking and Talking" (Buena Vista), 1963.

"Treat Him Nicely" b/w "Promise Me Anything" (Buena Vista), 1963.

"Merlin Jones" b/w "The Scrambled Egghead" (Buena Vista), 1964.

"Custom City" b/w "Rebel Rider" (Buena Vista), 1964.

"Muscle Beach Party" b/w "I Dream About Frankie" (Buena Vista), 1964.

"Bikini Beach Party" b/w "The Clyde" (Buena Vista), 1964.

"The Wah Watusi" b/w "The Clyde" (Buena Vista), 1964.

"Something Borrowed, Something Blue" b/w "How Will I Know My Love?" (Buena Vista), 1965.

"The Monkey's Uncle" (with the Beach Boys) b/w "How Will I Know My Love?" (Buena Vista), 1965.

"Boy to Love" b/w "No One Could Be Prouder" (Buena Vista), 1965.

"Baby Needs Me Now" b/w "Moment of Silence" (with Cecil Null) (Epic), 1965.

"No Way to Go but Up" b/w "Crystal Ball" (Buena Vista), 1966.

"Merlin Jones" b/w "The Computer Wore Tennis Shoes" (Buena Vista), 1966.

"What's a Girl to Do" b/w "When You Get What You Want" (Tower), 1967.

"Together We Can Make a Merry Christmas" b/w "The Night Before Christmas" (with Frankie Avalon) (Pacific Star).

SELECTED SOLO ALBUMS

Annette (Buena Vista), 1959.

Annette Sings Anka (Buena Vista), 1960

Hawaiiannette (Annette Sings Songs of Hawaii) (Buena Vista), 1960

Italiannette (Annette Sings Songs with an Italian Flavor) (Buena Vista), 1960

Dance Annette (Buena Vista), 1961

Annette Funicello (Buena Vista), 1962

Annette—The Story of My Teens . . . and Sixteen Songs That Tell It
 (Buena Vista), 1962.

Teen Street (Buena Vista), 1962.

Annette, Muscle Beach Party (Buena Vista), 1964.

Annette's Beach Party (Buena Vista), 1963.

Annette on Campus (Buena Vista), 1963.

Annette at Bikini Beach (Buena Vista), 1964.

Annette in Pajama Party (Buena Vista), 1964.

Annette Sings Golden Surfin' Hits (Buena Vista), 1965.

Something Borrowed, Something Blue (Buena Vista), 1964.

The Annette Funicello Country Album (Starview), 1984.

Annette: A Musical Reunion with America's Girl Next Door (Walt
 Disney Records), 1993.